A Special Issue of
Memory

Levels of Processing 30 years on

Edited by

Martin A. Conway
University of Durham, UK

Ψ Psychology Press
Taylor & Francis Group

HOVE AND NEW YORK

Published in 2002 by Psychology Press Ltd
27 Church Road, Hove, East Sussex, BN3 2FA
www.psypress.co.uk

Simultaneously published in the USA and Canada
by Taylor and Francis Inc.
29 West 35th Street, New York, NY 10001, USA
Psychology Press is part of the Taylor and Francis Group
© 2002 by Psychology Press Ltd

British Library Cataloguing in Publication Data
A catalogue record for this book is available from the British Library

ISBN 1-84169-934-9 (hbk)
ISSN 0965-8211

Cover design by Jim Wilkie
Typeset in the UK by DP Photosetting, Aylesbury, UK
Printed in the UK by Henry Ling Limited, at the Dorset Press,
Dorchester, DT1 1HD
Bound in the UK by TJ International, Padstow, Cornwall, UK

Contents*

Levels of processing: Past, present... and future?
Fergus I.M. Craik
305

Processing approaches to cognition
Henry L. Roediger, III, David A. Gallo and Lisa Geraci
319

Organisation: What levels of processing are levels of
George Mandler
333

Limits and province of levels of processing: Considerations of a construct
Michael J. Watkins
339

Levels of processing: A view from functional brain imaging
Lars Nyberg
345

Level of processing and the process-dissociation procedure: Elusiveness
of null effects on estimates of automatic retrieval
Alan Richardson-Klavehn, John M. Gardiner and Cristina Ramponi
349

On the perceptual specificity of memory representations
Eyal M. Reingold
365

Directed remembering: Subliminal cues alter nonconscious memory
strategies
*Jason P. Mitchell, C. Neil Macrae, Jonathan W. Schooler, Angela C. Rowe
and Alan B. Milne*
381

The myth of the encoding–retrieval match
James S. Nairne
389

Levels of processing, transfer-appropriate processing, and the concept of
robust encoding
Robert S. Lockhart
397

Heterarchy of cognition: The depths and the highs of a framework for
memory research
Boris M. Velichkovsky
405

*This book is also a special issue of the journal *Memory*, and forms issues 5 & 6 of
Volume 10 (2002). The page numbers are taken from the journal and so begin
with p.305.

MEMORY, 2002, 10 (5/6), 305–318

Levels of processing: Past, present ... and future?

Fergus I.M. Craik

Rotman Research Institute of Baycrest Centre, Toronto, Canada

In this article I first briefly survey some enduring legacies of the Craik and Lockhart (1972) article on levels of processing (LOP) and address some common criticisms. In the next section I discuss whether memory can be regarded as "pure processing", the role of short-term memory in an LOP framework, measurement of "depth" in LOP, encoding–retrieval interactions, the concept of consolidation, and the reality of "levels" of processing. In the final section I offer some speculations on future directions, discussing the notion of levels of representation and a possible continuing role for LOP in memory research.

To start with some personal history, I spent a stimulating and productive year (1968–69) in the Psychology Department at the University of Toronto, imbibing the wisdom dispensed by Ben Murdock and Endel Tulving, and interacting with a lively group of graduate students and post-docs. The focus of my research was short-term memory, and this broadened out during the year to a consideration of encoding and retrieval processes in long-term or secondary memory. When I returned to Birkbeck College in London, I was intrigued and influenced by the work on selective attention being carried out by Donald Broadbent, Anne Treisman, and Neville Moray. In particular, Treisman's (1964) theory of selective attention combined aspects of previous knowledge with perception and attention; it was an exciting possibility that memory encoding and retrieval processes could also be brought into the mix, in the spirit of Neisser's (1967) call for an integrated theory of cognitive functions.

Treisman (1964, 1979) proposed that perceptual processing could be envisaged as a hierarchy of "levels of analysis" running from early sensory analyses to later analyses concerned with object properties and identification of words, pictures, and objects. In this scheme, identification and meaning may be regarded as occurring later (and thus in some sense "deeper") in the sequence of analyses than the analysis of sensory and surface features. From contemporary work on dichotic listening it also seemed that such deeper analysis of meaning required more attention than did the analysis of sensory features. Subjects were able to identify a speaker's voice as male or female on the unattended channel, but were unable to understand the meaning of the utterance. It also seemed reasonable to assume that analysis of a particular feature corresponded to conscious awareness of that feature.

In order to account for the phenomena of selective attention, Treisman also proposed that incoming information is subjected to a series of "tests" at each level of analysis, and only those dimensions of the incoming signal passing each test proceed to the next level of analysis. The tests are thought of as signal-detection problems, with signal strength a function of such data-driven variables as loudness and brightness, and criterion placement a function of such top-down variables as meaningfulness, contextual relevance, and recent experience. Early sensory analyses are carried out on virtually all incoming signals, but later analyses are progressively more

Requests for reprints should be sent to Fergus I.M. Craik, Rotman Research Institute, Baycrest Centre, 3560 Bathurst Street, Toronto, ON, Canada M6A 2E1. Email: craik@psych.utoronto.ca

Preparation of this article was supported by a grant from the Natural Sciences and Engineering Research Council of Canada. I am grateful to Ellen Bialystok and Morris Moscovitch for insightful comments on an earlier draft of the article.

DOI:10.1080/09658210244000135

selective so that we are consciously aware of the physical features of unattended signals (e.g., a woman's voice) but generally unaware of their meaning. It seemed possible that the strength and longevity of the memory of the signal, as well as its qualitative nature, depended on its depth of processing in this hierarchy of analyses. One striking observation in favour of this speculation was Treisman's (1964) experiment in which identical speech messages were played to the two ears in a dichotic listening paradigm, but with the messages staggered in time. The question was: How close in time must the messages be brought for the listener to realise that they are the same? The answer depended on whether the attended ear message preceded or followed the unattended ear. In the first case subjects recognised the identity at an interval of 5 seconds, but in the second case the messages had to be as close as $1\frac{1}{2}$ seconds in time before subjects realised they were the same. That is, identification of the sounds as particular words roughly tripled their survival time in memory.

I returned to Toronto in 1971 with plans to test the idea that memory is a function of the degree to which a stimulus is analysed; more specifically that "deeper" semantic analysis is associated with higher levels of retention and longer-lasting traces. I was delighted to find that my friend Bob Lockhart had been thinking along very similar lines, so we decided to join forces to write a theoretical article invited by Endel Tulving, who was the editor of the *Journal of Verbal Learning and Verbal Behavior* at that time. Tulving alternately praised, criticized, encouraged, and berated us, effortlessly combining the roles of the 'guard with the club' and the 'guard with the cigarette' in one person, until we finished the piece in the summer of 1972. The Craik and Lockhart article appeared in the December 1972 issue of *JVLVB*. Actually, it is very pleasant to put on record our gratitude to Endel Tulving who made many constructive suggestions, and whose skilful editing improved the final version immensely.

As I see it now, one of the main contributions of the levels-of-processing (LOP) article was to reinforce the idea of *remembering* as processing, as an activity of mind, as opposed to structural ideas of memory traces as entities that must be searched for, "found", and reactivated. In particular, we suggested that memory-encoding operations should be conceptualised as the *processes* underlying perception and comprehension, and that retrieval was the corollary of encoding. In

the same vein, we argued against the notion of structural memory stores, although not against the distinction between primary and secondary memory in some form (see later). We also suggested of course that remembering reflected the qualitative types of analysis that had been performed during initial encoding processes of perception and comprehension, and that deeper processing was associated with higher levels of subsequent remembering.

These rather general ideas were backed up by the results of a series of experiments reported by Craik and Tulving (1975). Words were presented, preceded by orienting questions (e.g., "Does the word rhyme with train?", "Is the word a type of flower?") that were intended to control the depth to which the word was processed. Later unexpected memory tests showed that the level of recollection varied substantially (e.g., between 0.14 and 0.96; Craik & Tulving, 1975, Exp. 1) simply as a function of the type of question asked. At first I took the idea of "levels" rather literally, thinking that the processing was actually halted at different levels of perceptual–conceptual analysis; for that reason each word was exposed tachistoscopically for 200 ms and participants were not informed of the later memory test. Endel was sceptical of this line of thinking, however, and carried out a version of the experiment in which participants were told that there would be a later memory test, and each word was exposed for 1 second followed by a 5-second interword interval. Despite these radical changes the results were essentially the same as before; recognition varied between 0.23 and 0.81. I have a flashbulb memory of Endel phoning me from his bridge club one evening with these findings!

One unexpected result was that words that were congruent with their orienting question (e.g., "Rhymes with Spain?" TRAIN; "A type of flower?" DAISY) were better encoded and recognised than words that were not congruent (e.g., "Rhymes with Spain?" TIGER; "A type of flower?" CHAIR). Our suggestion was that congruent question–word combinations yielded an encoding that was richer and more elaborate, and that this enriched encoding in turn supported higher levels of recollection. Why should greater trace elaboration support good retention? Two possibilities are, first that a richly elaborate trace will be more differentiated from other episodic records—this greater *distinctiveness* in turn will support more effective recollection in an analogous way to distinctive objects being more discriminable in the visual field. A second (complementary) possibility is that elaborate traces are more integrated with organised knowledge structures which, in turn, serve as effective frameworks for reconstructive retrieval processes (Moscovitch & Craik, 1976). A number of theorists have emphasised the importance of differentiation or trace distinctiveness in memory (Hunt & Einstein, 1981; Klein & Saltz, 1976; Murdock, 1960; Nairne, 2002; Nelson, 1979; Stein, 1978) and I share their view. But I do not believe that the concept of distinctiveness eliminates the need for the concepts of depth and elaboration of processing. From my perspective, depth refers to the qualitative type of processing carried out on the stimulus, and elaboration refers to the degree to which each type of processing has been enriched during encoding. These two aspects of processing, along with the congruity of the stimulus to its context of presentation, combine to yield an encoded record of the event that is more or less distinctive from other encoded records. That is, depth, elaboration, and congruity describe aspects of the encoding process, whereas distinctiveness describes the eventual product of these processes (Craik, 1977).

In the Craik and Lockhart paper we made no attempt to provide an account of retrieval processes. Morris Moscovitch and I conducted some experiments a few years later to fill this gap, and demonstrated the importance of a unique linkage between the retrieval cue and the memory trace. The initial encoding operations determined the *potential* for later retrieval, and factors such as similarity of cue and trace information, and the specificity of the cue–trace linkage determined the degree to which that potential was realised (Moscovitch & Craik, 1976). In later papers (e.g., Craik, 1983) I stressed the notion that retrieval processes were similar to encoding processes (see also Kolers, 1973, 1979), essentially serving to recapitulate the original experience as closely as possible.

ISSUES: PAST AND PRESENT

In this section I will touch on some issues that have been the subject of comment and criticism over the past 30 years. Fuller comments and some answers to our critics are provided elsewhere (Craik, 1979; Lockhart & Craik, 1990).

Memory as "pure processing"

Is it reasonable to characterise remembering as involving only processes or activities of mind? Surely there must be some record of the initial event that is compared with present processing to yield a match that underlies the experience of remembering? My view is that certainly something must change in the brain as a result of the initial experience, and this change must persist until remembering occurs. But the change in question is not simply a snapshot of the original event; it may rather be a modification of the cognitive system so that when the event recurs, the consequent processing operations are interpreted both in terms of the current event and in terms of the brain changes caused by its original occurrence. Just as perceptual learning changes the perceptual system so that subsequent stimulus patterns are processed and experienced differently, so memory encoding changes the cognitive system in such a way as to change the interpretation of a repeated event. Just as the neural correlate of perceiving is the pattern of cortical activity that occurs while we are perceiving, so the correlate of remembering is the pattern of neural activity that accompanies the experience of remembering. By this view, cognitive neuroscientists should be attempting to map patterns of neural activity to recollective experience rather than be searching for "engrams" defined as stored records of experienced events.

The STM/LTM distinction

The Craik and Lockhart article is often regarded as the paper that attacked the distinction between short-term memory (STM) and long-term memory (LTM), but this is an overstatement. We criticised the notion of memory stores, including the concept of a separate capacity-limited STM in which incoming information was held before being "transferred" to LTM (Atkinson & Shiffrin, 1968, 1971). But we retained the STM/LTM distinction, recasting the concept of STM as a temporary activation of processes representing perceptual and conceptual aspects of incoming (or recently retrieved) stimuli. So in a sense STM was thought of as a temporary activation of parts of LTM (see also Cowan, 1999; Engle, Kane, & Tuholski, 1999; Shiffrin, 1975), but the short-term activity presumably also involves perceptual aspects of the input. Lockhart and I preferred the

Jamesian term "primary memory" (PM) to capture this account of STM phenomena.

By this view, PM is not a store in any sense, and is not located in one fixed place in either the cognitive system or the brain. Rather, PM involves activation of representations that correlate with present experience—the contents of conscious-ness—and thus PM activity can be located in many different brain locations depending on the type of information "held in mind". An alternative description is that "maintaining an item in PM" is equivalent to "continuing to pay attention to the item" (Cowan, 1988; Craik, 1971). This account of STM solves the riddle of how one memory store could hold a variety of different types of infor-mation—visual, auditory, articulatory, semantic—although other solutions have also been proposed (Baddeley & Hitch, 1974). Many experiments are conducted using verbal materials, and perhaps the greatest use of STM in real life is to hear and rehearse names, numbers, and other verbal materials. In such cases the contents of mind will reflect activations of cortical areas concerned with phonological and articulatory processing, and lesions of such areas will produce patients with "STM deficits" (e.g., Warrington & Shallice, 1969). Such clinical findings fit perfectly well with the present account of PM/STM; my only com-ment is that additional cortical areas may also be involved in short-term retention and rehearsal—if we maintain an image in mind, for example, think of a face, or rehearse a melody. As one final speculation, some phenomena of short-term retention may reflect recent activation of LTM structures rather than necessarily reflecting current "in mind" activations. Thus names, directions, and solutions to problems may be particularly accessible if we have recently thought of them. It seems possible that Baddeley's recent description (2000) of an "episodic buffer" may reflect this type of "primed" LTM activation, although Baddeley himself considers and rejects this view.

The elusive index of depth

One major criticism of the LOP framework is the absence of an objective index of depth of proces-sing. Lacking such an index, it is all too easy to claim that any well-remembered event must therefore have been deeply processed (Baddeley, 1978). The concept of depth of processing is not hard to grasp—"deeper" refers to the analysis of meaning, inference, and implication, in contrast to "shallow" analyses such as surface form, colour, loudness, and brightness. It also turns out that experimental participants agree well about the relative depth of encoding operations, and these ratings predict later memory performance (Sea-mon & Virostek, 1978). Nevertheless it would be much more satisfactory to have an objective index, preferably one with a decent scale of measurement.

Our first attempt was to measure the time it took to decide whether a word was or was not congruent with the orienting question (e.g., "Rhymes with Spain?" TRAIN "yes"; TIGER "no"). In the second experiment reported by Craik and Tulving (1975), yes and no decisions took about the same time as each other at each level of analysis (case, rhyme, and sentence pro-cessing), yet words associated with positive rhyme and sentence decisions were better recognised than words associated with negative decisions. It seemed therefore that processing time by itself was insufficient. When decision times were plot-ted against later recognition levels a strikingly regular pattern emerged (Figure 1). The finding that yes and no initial decision times lie on dif-ferent functions relating decision time to later recognition may mean that both depth (the qua-litative type of information processed) and ela-boration (the degree to which this type of information is enriched) must be considered before memory can be predicted. That is, for congruous ("yes") decisions, the extra time nee-ded for deeper processing operations buys better recognition performance. Unfortunately this

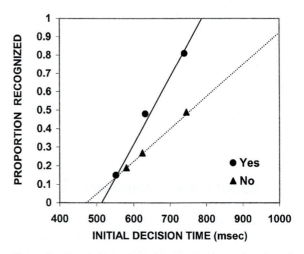

Figure 1. Proportions of words recognised as a function of initial decision time and compatibility with the encoding question (Craik & Tulving, 1975, p. 275).

account suggests the necessity for *two* different indices of processing—depth and elaboration.

A further problem for time as an index is that access time is also a function of practice and expertise. Highly familiar, well-practised stimuli (e.g., pictures) are identified and interpreted very rapidly, yet are also very well recognised in a subsequent test (Paivio, 1971). The same is likely true of specific domains of individual expertise; an expert can rapidly form a highly meaningful and elaborate encoding of a stimulus in his or her field of expertise, yet again this rapidly processed information will be well remembered (Bransford, Franks, Morris, & Stein, 1979). Clearly time cannot serve as an absolute index of depth across different types of material, although it seems possible that for a given individual and a given type of material, deeper processing will take longer to accomplish. Thus, processing time may serve as in index of depth if defined *relatively* with respect to a specific set of circumstances. The same arguments apply to the amount of attention ("processing resources") required to carry out a processing task. That is, deeper analyses generally require more attention (Craik & Byrd, 1982; Treisman, 1964) and diversion of attention to a secondary task results in shallower encoding of events processed in the primary task (Naveh-Benjamin, Craik, Gavrilescu, & Anderson, 2000), but again these relationships will be modulated by the meaningfulness of stimuli and the expertise of the person doing the processing.

Any valid index of depth must therefore measure the meaningfulness and elaboration of the final encoded representation, and not simply the ease or difficulty of achieving that representation. Unfortunately there does not appear to be a relevant psycholinguistic theory of meaning that we can buy into, so at the psychological level we are stuck for the moment with such unsatisfactory methods as agreement among judges. There are some other possibilities at the physiological and neurological levels, however. Evoked potentials signal the type of processing that is being carried out (Sanquist, Rohrbaugh, Syndulko, & Lindsley, 1980) and it seems possible that recent developments in ERP analysis can provide information both about the brain regions involved in various types of encoding processes and about the time course of the spread of activation between regions (Mangels, Picton, & Craik, 2001). Other promising leads include work on eye movements discussed in the articles by Velichkovsky (2002) and Reingold (2002), and the finding that heart-rate variability is reduced when deeply encoded words are retrieved (Vincent, Craik, & Furedy, 1996). Finally, the functional neuroimaging data provided by PET, fMRI, and MEG may help to solve the problem, although again ways must be found to distinguish differences in access time and effort on the one hand from differences in the meaningfulness and elaboration of the encoded representation on the other (see Treisman, 1979, for a useful discussion).

Encoding-retrieval interactions

As mentioned earlier, the Craik and Lockhart (1972) article dealt with problems of encoding rather than retrieval, although later publications discussed retrieval in an LOP framework (Craik, 1983; Lockhart & Craik, 1990; Moscovitch & Craik, 1976). The major idea in this area is the notion of encoding specificity (Tulving & Thomson, 1973) or transfer-appropriate processing (TAP) (Morris, Bransford, & Franks, 1977; Roediger, Weldon, & Challis, 1989). To me, the concepts of LOP and TAP have always seemed complementary rather than antagonistic; initial processing determines the qualitative nature of the encoded trace, deeper encodings are associated with a greater potential for retrieval, and this potential is realised by the provision of a retrieval environment (which may include a specific retrieval cue), compatible qualitatively with the trace information. The influential paper by Morris et al. (1977) made a stronger claim, however. They demonstrated that rhyme-related encoding was superior to semantic encoding when the retrieval test was one of rhyme recognition, and concluded that "deep" semantic processing was therefore not necessarily the most beneficial for later memory. It all depends on the retrieval test, they argued, and semantic encoding is typically very effective simply because the usual retrieval processes of recall and recognition also involve semantic processing. It is an ingenious argument and a compelling case! On the other hand, the Morris et al. data showed that the combination of semantic encoding and semantic retrieval yielded a substantially higher level of recognition than the rhyme–rhyme combination (0.68 vs 0.40 averaged over Experiments 1 and 2). My conclusion is therefore that any final theory must involve some account of encoding processes and the representations they create, as well as some factor capturing the relations between encoding and retrieval. That is, deeper encoding processes result in encoded traces that are *potentially* very memorable, provided that an appropriate cue is available at the time of retrieval. The article by Lockhart (2002) provides further useful discussion of this point.

Is consolidation necessary?

In the Craik and Lockhart (1972) paper, we suggested that the encoded version of an event—the memory trace—was simply the record of those processing operations that had been carried out essentially for the purposes of perception and comprehension. That is, there were no special memory encoding operations as such, and the memory trace could therefore be regarded as an automatic byproduct of initial processing. The evidence for these statements came from the results of studies in which encoding was "incidental" in the sense that participants were unaware of the subsequent memory test. Using orienting tasks that induced the participants to process words in a deep semantic fashion, it was easy to demonstrate that incidental encoding can yield levels of memory performance that are at least as good as those obtained after intentional learning (Challis, Velichkovsky, & Craik, 1996; Craik, 1977). Efficient rehearsal techniques and good intentional learning were assumed to represent self-initiated processes that consciously involved elaborate semantic processing.

From this perspective, impaired memory performance was seen as reflecting impoverished encoding operations, in the case of normal ageing, for example (Craik, 1983; Craik & Simon, 1980). My party line was that various conditions and situations were associated with a reduction in processing resources, and that this in turn resulted in a failure to carry out deep elaborate processing. As well as ageing, I argued that this pattern described divided attention (Craik, 1983; Craik, Govoni, Naveh-Benjamin, & Anderson, 1996) and perhaps also fatigue and sleep deprivation. One condition that is clearly *not* well described by this account is that of organic amnesia (Cermak, 1979). Amnesic patients perceive and understand communications and other events perfectly well, but do not remember them. It therefore seemed necessary to concede that some further step is necessary—beyond perception and comprehension—for events to be encoded in a way that would support retrieval minutes, days, and years later. At first I

was reluctant to acknowledge the necessity of this extra step ("consolidation"?) in conditions such as normal ageing and divided attention (Craik, 1983), but more recently I have bowed to the superior wisdom of colleagues (e.g., Tulving, 2001) and agreed that "deep processing is necessary but not sufficient for later episodic memory" (Craik, 1999, p. 102). Two pieces of evidence have pushed me in this direction; the first is some experiments from my lab that showed a decrement in memory following division of attention during encoding even when depth and elaboration were apparently equated between full and divided attention (Craik & Kester, 1999). Division of attention may well attenuate deeper levels of processing, but it also appears to affect some later processes in such a way that limits or even eliminates the formation of a permanent record. The second piece of evidence is more subjective and personal. In my middle sixties I do not feel that my intellectual processes are *too* depleted (although how could I tell if they were?!), but my memory abilities are certainly poorer than they were. Speculatively, normal ageing appears to attenuate the consolidation of cognitive operations, so that the relations between depth of processing and later memory are modulated by the effects of ageing.

The animal and neuropsychological literatures are replete with experiments and theories of consolidation which I will not comment on here, apart from saying that consolidation does not appear to have any experiential or "psychological" correlates. That is, it appears to comprise a set of neurological processes that run off outside awareness and outwith cognitive control. The processes are obviously no less interesting and important for that difference from other memory processes, but the absence of cognitive correlates (if that proves to be the case) provides an interesting challenge to studying the effects of ageing, division of attention, and other variables on the factors governing the effectiveness of consolidation.

The reality of "levels"

In the Craik and Lockhart (1972) article our notion of "levels" followed rather directly from Anne Treisman's (1964, 1979) work on selective attention. Some forms of representation, namely those concerned with meaning and implication, seemed to require more attention than those reflecting sensory and surface aspects of objects and events. We also assumed that perception proceeded from early analysis of sensory features to later analysis of conceptual features, and that changes associated with these later, deeper analyses formed the basis for good subsequent memory. This set of ideas suggested a fixed set of stages of analysis, with the output from one stage acting as the input for the next. However, in later papers, we acknowledged that a fixed progression from shallow to deep was unlikely, and that a more plausible scenario was one in which processing unfolded in an interactive manner involving both stimulus-driven bottom-up processing and conceptually driven top-down processing (Craik & Tulving, 1975). Nonetheless, performance still reflected the final depth and elaboration achieved.

The term "levels of processing" does suggest a continuum of processing, however, despite the fact that the qualitative nature of the processing operations clearly changes from early sensory analyses to later conceptual analyses. Deeper processing is not simply an extension or prolongation of shallow processing. For these reasons, Lockhart, Craik, and Jacoby (1976) suggested the notion of "domains of processing" to capture the idea that visual word processing, for example, proceeds through stages of visual and print analysis before undergoing analyses at articulatory, phonological, lexical, and conceptual stages. But are these qualitatively different types of analysis at least always carried out in the same sequence? Even this would seem doubtful. Beginning readers sound out letters, from which they assemble words and finally the meaning of a sentence; but fluent readers appear to bypass the phonological stage, and processing now moves directly from print to meaning (Coltheart, 1985). Similarly, Velichkovsky (2002) acknowledges that the sequence of events in his six-stage version of Bernstein's (1947) model of skilled action may not always run from 1 to 6. The order of processing, and the interactions between levels, will depend on the task at hand. Thus Velichkovsky concludes that he is describing a *heterarchy* of processing (Turvey, Shaw, & Mace, 1978) rather than a true hierarchy, although he also argues that there is a natural progression (reflecting both evolutionary and developmental trends) from stages concerned with muscle tone and sensory integration to stages concerned with the purposes and implications of actions.

In her excellent review of hierarchical models in cognition, Cohen (2000) distinguishes truly hierarchical models in which one level controls processing operations in the level below, from forms in which "there is simply a transfer of information from one stage to another" (Cohen, 2000, p.2). In this view she follows Broadbent's (1977) analysis of control processes in action and decision making in which control necessarily reflects top-down processing. However, during encoding, data-driven bottom-up processes also determine the nature of the representation at the next stage—visual analysis of a printed word determines which lexical representation is activated, for example, and this activation in turn determines the concept that is brought to mind. The processing modules at various levels of analysis are necessarily sequential in nature, although the specific sequence may be altered from time to time depending on the task, the subject's purposes, and his or her level of practice. Processing in this sequence of levels can also operate in a top-down fashion, reflecting expectations, context, and set, and also reflecting the likelihood that partial analysis at a higher (or deeper) level can affect attention and thus further processing at lower levels. Treisman's (1964, 1969) model of selective attention incorporates both sets of influences. In summary, it seems to me that the "levels of processing" discussed by Craik and Lockhart *do* constitute a somewhat flexible hierarchy of processing, and are not simply a set of independent modules. It is also true, however, that the present levels of encoding are not the same as the levels of control described by Broadbent (1977) and Cohen (2000).

As a final question, what about levels *within* qualitatively coherent domains of processing? Experiments by Craik and Tulving (1975) and by Johnson-Laird, Gibbs, and de Mowbray (1978) showed that recollection improves as further meaningful processing is performed at the time of encoding. In similar demonstrations Bransford and his colleagues showed convincingly that greater degrees of semantic elaboration, greater precision and specificity of encoding, and a better fit with subjects' expertise all led to improved memory performance (Bransford et al., 1979). All of these demonstrations seem better described as greater degrees of elaboration and enrichment of the encoded representation than as "levels" in any sense. It is worth remembering, however, that to be effective for later memory, further processing must enrich the representation "meaningfully" in the broadest sense. Further processing at shallow levels of analysis does not lead to better memory

(Craik & Watkins, 1973). Similarly, "distinctiveness" by itself is not sufficient. Goldstein and Chance (1971) showed subjects snowflake patterns; later recognition performance was poor despite the fact that each pattern was "unique". Performance was poor because the subjects lacked the rich semantic knowledge to classify and differentiate the stimuli in a meaningful way. Presumably a specialist in crystallography with an interest in snowflake formation *could* differentiate and categorise the stimuli, and would perform well on a later memory test. In line with Bransford's analysis, I would therefore say that good memory performance depends on the person possessing expert knowledge of the stimuli in question, and processing the stimuli in a differentiated meaningful way in relation to this knowledge. Finally, the processing necessary to achieve this detailed semantic representation typically involves a set of hierarchically ordered levels of analysis.

FUTURE DIRECTIONS

The Craik and Lockhart article was written 30 years ago, so it would be curious indeed if many researchers (including Craik and Lockhart!) still held exactly the same views expressed at the time, or regarded the article as a blueprint for future research plans in 2002. Nevertheless, there may be some ideas and points of view that are still valid and that can be used to guide future endeavours. Some of the ideas we proposed or endorsed are very much alive in current cognitive psychology. The close interactions among attention, perception, and memory have been stressed by some theorists (e.g., Cowan, 1988). The notion that primary memory or working memory reflects the temporary activation of relatively permanent long-term memory structures is also endorsed by some current theorists (e.g., Cowan, 1999; Engle et al., 1999) as it was by Craik and Lockhart (1972) and Shiffrin (1975) among others. The proposition that good explicit memory performance is related to deep semantic processing is undeniable, although hardly original with the LOP framework (see, for example, Bartlett, 1932; James, 1890; and Smirnov, 1973). Smirnov's book, published in Russian in 1966, is quite explicit in linking comprehension and understanding to good levels of retention. Craik and Lockhart's (1972) identification of remembering as processing (as opposed to thinking of memory as a structure) was

emphasised strongly by Kolers (1973; Kolers & Roediger, 1984), and is discussed persuasively by Rosenfield (1988). Finally, the central notion of "levels" as a hierarchy of processing activities still seems viable in some form, bearing in mind the qualifications raised in the preceding section. A somewhat different type of hierarchy is discussed next.

Levels of representation: General to specific

Older adults typically experience two main types of difficulty with their memory; the first is memory for names, and the second is memory for details of occurrences. The difficulty with names sometimes generalises to infrequently used words and to names of objects, but is most evident in names of people. The second difficulty shows itself in forgetting where a possession was left, in the source of newly acquired information, and in "telling the same tale (at least!) twice" (Koriat, Ben-Zur, & Sheffer, 1988). Do these difficulties reflect some common failure? The second set are clearly problems of episodic memory—the individual forgets details of specific past episodes. But forgetting names, often of people we have known for many years, is a failure of retrieval from semantic memory in memory systems terms (Tulving & Schacter, 1990). Despite their different origins, the commonality may arise because both types of information are quite *specific*, and refer either to unique persons in the case of names, or unique events in the case of forgetting source or context.

Knowledge may be represented as a hierarchy of levels of representation, in which higher levels represent greater degrees of generality and abstraction, and the lowest levels represent labels for specific people or objects, or represent specific details of an experienced event (Cohen, 2000; Conway, 1992). In a recent chapter (Craik, 2002) I suggested that older adults may experience difficulty in accessing and retrieving information from these lowest levels, almost as if they lacked the necessary "resolving power" to discriminate such specific details, although higher levels of generality *are* still easily accessed and retrieved. The suggestion is supported by similar reports from researchers studying retrieval failures in depression (Williams, 1996) and in semantic dementia (Hodges, 2000) as well as in normal ageing (Burke, MacKay, Worthley, & Wade, 1991; Holland & Rabbitt, 1990; Levine, Svoboda, Moscovitch, & Hay, in press). A useful review of hierarchical models in cognition with supporting evidence is provided by Cohen (2000).

My version of the concept is illustrated in Figure 2. With regard to autobiographical memory, the idea is that commonalities among individual instances are represented as higher-order nodes, so that there is essentially a continuum between the "episodic memory" of specific occasions and the "semantic memory" of knowledge abstracted from such specific experiences. The distinction between "remember" and "know" judgements (e.g., Gardiner & Richardson-Klavehn, 2000) may be conceptualised as reflecting access to different levels of this hierarchy. Why should it be more difficult to access lower levels? One possibility is that representations at higher levels are more interconnected and networked, thereby providing more access routes for retrieval processes; another is that the general knowledge represented by higher levels is used to interpret new events or plan new actions, and is therefore accessed more frequently than is specific event information represented by lower levels.

Future research from this perspective could profitably explore the degree to which the relative difficulty of retrieving specific types of information (both "episodic" and "semantic") holds across a wide variety of conditions associated with memory impairment. Does the generality hold for all types of organically based memory deficits for example (e.g., traumatic brain injury,

lesions in frontal, temporal, and subcortical regions), and does it hold for more "functionally based" decrements such as those associated with divided attention, fatigue, and sleep deprivation? A second set of questions concerns the neurological reality of these various hypothesised hierarchies of representation. Are different levels of representation detectable and discriminable by neuroimaging techniques for instance? One intriguing question in this regard is whether higher levels of abstraction are represented as such (as suggested in Figure 2) or are computed online from representations of individual instances, which are the only forms of experience actually represented neurologically (Logan, 1988). Optimistically, if neuroimaging methods permit a distinction between the retrieval of individual episodes and semantic abstractions (as preliminary work suggests they can) are the regions associated with episodes also involved in the activation of relevant abstractions from these episodes? It seems that they should be from the perspective of instance theory. Finally is it possible to improve access to specific representations? If successful retrieval of episodes is associated with higher levels of arousal (Williams, 1996) and adequate availability of processing resources (Craik & Byrd, 1982) is it possible to boost retrieval success by temporarily and selectively boosting attention and arousal? And given the involvement of the prefrontal cortex in retrieval processes (Tulving, Kapur, Craik, Moscovitch, &

Hierarchical Model

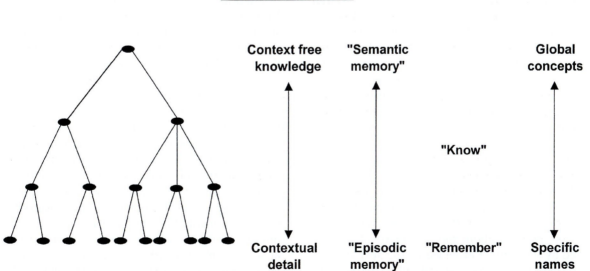

Figure 2.   A hierarchical view of cognitive representations.

Houle, 1994; Wheeler, Stuss, & Tulving, 1997) and in "resolving power" (Fuster, 2002), is it possible to increase the efficiency of frontal functioning and thereby enhance the ability to retrieve specific types of information?

How does the notion of levels of representation fit with the original LOP ideas? Craik and Lockhart's (1972) position suggested that good memory performance reflected *deeper* processing in the sense of more abstract semantic analysis, so what are the conditions for excellent encoding and recollection of specific detailed information in this framework? The answer may be that deep semantic analysis is necessary to provide a rich, organised schematic framework within which specific "surface" details are given meaning and significance. So it is not really the case that specific details are "processed deeply", but rather that deep processing provides the schematic context within which episodic details are related to each other and to more abstract representations of significance and purpose.

Levels of processing revisited

Although it now seems highly unlikely that ongoing cognitive activity proceeds in a fixed series of stages, we nevertheless must still understand the sequence of events that transpire between reception of a stimulus and the experience of perceiving, and between the activation of the memory trace (whatever that turns out to mean) and the experience of remembering. Central to this understanding are the concepts of regulation and control—how are incoming stimuli and activated memory traces guided towards interpretation, decision, and action? The linked notions of working memory and central executive (e.g., Baddeley, 2000) are invoked by many theorists at present, but what is the nature of this reclusive autocrat (lurking in the capacious folds of the prefrontal cortex perhaps?) who controls our destinies?

Bressler and Kelso (2001) suggest that control is not exerted top-down by some neural homunculus, but should be thought of, rather, as an emergent property of interacting subsystems (see also Barnard, 1985; Teasdale & Barnard, 1993). Bressler and Kelso further propose that coordination, interpretation, and control are also mediated by the context provided by the next level up in a hierarchy of processing levels. That is, components at one level combine to represent higher-order units, but the interpretation and significance of the higher unit will depend on the prevailing context at that higher level; that context, in turn, is often imposed by top-down influences from pre-existing stable networks representing schematic knowledge. They propose, for example, that "coordination in any complex system is an emergent property of groups of components" and that coordinates at lower levels are set in the context of adjustments of the overall system: "In walking, for example, not only the muscles of the legs, but also muscle groups throughout the entire body, must be coordinated" (Bressler & Kelso, 2001, p.30).

In the case of lexical processing, local cortical areas may represent specific features which then combine in a way that satisfies mutual constraints, with "comprehension" represented by a coordinated cortical network "in which each system provides constraints that jointly determine lexical meaning by causing convergence to a single interpretation" (Bressler & Kelso, 2001, p.34). Thus local cortical networks come to represent lower-order features though learning, and these combine in an interactive way in response to a specific input to form a higher-order coordinated network. Other networks at this higher level (some activated by the current input and some representing previous learning at that higher level) then combine interactively in turn to form dynamic representations at the new level. Speculatively, this process continues until interpretation is represented by a very widespread pattern of activation throughout many cortical areas. It seems to me that this set of suggestions is quite compatible with Treisman's (1964, 1969) account of attention and perceptual processing, although Bressler and Kelso are understandably more specific about possible underlying mechanisms.

Another interesting parallel is with current theories of genetics (see Keller, 2000, for an excellent overview). According to Keller, the idea of a linear fixed series of stages from gene to protein to structure and function has been abandoned in favour of a hierarchy of stages in which "control" is again a function of interactions among local representations and computations. The regulatory circuitry governing gene expression is dynamic rather than static, and this set of dynamic processes itself changes over the course of development. She writes, "I argue that an understanding of its dynamics needs to be sought at least as much in the interactions of its many components as in the structure or behavior of the components themselves" (Keller, 2000, p.100).

In the case of gene expression, one major top-down influence is provided by the external environment, thereby providing a mechanism for adaptation. In the case of memory retrieval, we may perhaps think of the neural changes corresponding to the memory trace as being analogous to the gene and that "memory expression" will therefore again depend on interactions at local levels forming higher-order dynamic networks whose interpretation is modulated by top-down influences including that of the external environment. That is, the current environmental context (including "retrieval cues") will shape the neuro-cognitive contexts at various levels in a top-down manner, thereby helping to construct the interpretation of the dynamic set of activities corresponding to retrieval of the encoded trace. To the extent that the current environment corresponds to the environment that existed during encoding, retrieval processes will yield the same conscious percept experienced on the initial occasion. Obviously this account describes the pattern of results known variously as encoding specificity, transfer-appropriate processing, or repetition of operations.

FINAL QUESTIONS AND CONCLUSIONS

One major change in my own viewpoint since 1972 concerns the necessity for consolidation as an encoding step *beyond* the "psychological" levels of perception and comprehension. Further research should explore such issues as whether consolidation *does* after all have psychological correlates or is cognitively silent, and whether the same variables that enhance memory performance at the cognitive level also affect consolidation. That is, are there variables that affect consolidation differently *after* given levels of depth and elaboration have been achieved, or do consolidation processes simply accept and consolidate the representations encoded at the cognitive level (Moscovitch, 1992)? In the latter case, do such variables as depth and elaboration affect the rate or effectiveness of consolidation?

With respect to encoding processes, the concept of depth clearly requires much greater specification. Experimental subjects agree on the relative depth of orienting tasks, and these tasks do result in levels of memory performance that reflect subjectively judged depth (Seamon & Virostek, 1978), but a more objective, and *mea-surable*, index is required. The notion of relative *distinctiveness* of encodings (Nairne, 2002) may provide a way forward. With respect to retrieval processes, models of the type proposed by Bressler and Kelso (2001) may provide some guidelines for new research; can retrieval be usefully conceptualised as a set of interactions (taking place at different levels of representation) between bottom-up processes stemming from the retrieval environment, modulated by expectations, context, and prior knowledge?

A final set of questions concerns the relations between encoding and retrieval processes. One attractive notion is that retrieval essentially recapitulates encoding (Kolers, 1973, 1979) so that the same percept or thought is experienced on the two occasions, and this equivalence is reflected in the activation of the same processing operations. Two problems with this view are, first, at the neurological level, substantially *different* areas of the prefrontal cortex are activated at encoding and retrieval (Tulving et al., 1994); second, at the psychological level, if retrieval processes are simply a repetition of encoding processes, what is it about retrieval processing that yields the experience of *remembering* as opposed to perceiving or thinking? A tentative answer to the second question is that retrieval processing activates representations that go beyond the current context and evoke details of the previous event, via pattern completion mechanisms. If we are set to remember (in "retrieval mode", Tulving, 1983) we focus on and amplify these aspects, as opposed to the operations that represent the current environment. With regard to the neurological problem, it is possible that the different prefrontal areas activated during encoding and retrieval respectively are activated by *control* processes (such as effort after meaning and comprehension during encoding, and efforts to recollect during retrieval) rather than by representational processes as such. The activations associated with the representations themselves may be located in more posterior areas of the cortex (Kapur et al., 1995). The challenge now (as in 1972) is to refine and specify such concepts as depth, elaboration, and distinctiveness.

In conclusion, I am suggesting that the idea of "levels of processing" still provides a useful framework in which to develop specific models of memory and cognition. Perhaps the most enduring legacy of the Craik and Lockhart (1972) paper is the greater emphasis on memory as processing in current theories. The similarity (at least) between encoding processes and the processes involved in the normal course of perceiving, attending, and thinking, is still valid today. We know more about the component processes of perception than we did 30 years ago, but I have seen no evidence against the propositions that the memory trace reflects those processes carried out primarily for the purposes of perception and comprehension, and that more meaningful processing is usually associated with higher levels of recollection. My optimistic hope is that findings and ideas from cognitive neuroscience may combine with findings and ideas from experimental cognitive psychology over the course of the *next* 30 years to provide us with a deeper understanding of what memory is, and how it works.

REFERENCES

Atkinson, R.C., & Shiffrin, R.M. (1968). Human memory: A proposed system and its control processes. In K.W. Spence & J.T. Spence (Eds.), *The psychology of learning and motivation: Advances in research and theory, Vol II* (pp. 89–195). New York: Academic Press.

Atkinson, R.C., & Shiffrin, R.M. (1971). The control of short-term memory. *Scientific American, 225,* 82–90.

Baddeley, A.D. (1978). The trouble with levels: A reexamination of Craik and Lockhart's framework for memory research. *Psychological Review, 85,* 139–152.

Baddeley, A.D. (2000). The episodic buffer: A new component of working memory? *Trends in Cognitive Science, 4,* 417–423.

Baddeley, A.D., & Hitch, G.J. (1974). Working memory. In G.H. Bower (Ed.), *The psychology of learning and motivation (Vol. 8)* (pp. 47–89). New York: Academic Press.

Barnard, P. (1985). Interactive cognitive subsystems: A psycholinguistic approach to short-term memory. In A. Ellis (Ed.), *Progress in the psychology of language, Vol 2* (pp. 197–258). Hove, UK: Lawrence Erlbaum Associates Ltd.

Bartlett, F.C. (1932). *Remembering: A study in experimental and social psychology.* New York: MacMillan.

Bernstein, N.A. (1947). *On the construction of movements.* Moscow: Medgiz [in Russian].

Bransford, J.D., Franks, J.J., Morris, C.D., & Stein, B.S. (1979). Some general constraints on learning and memory research. In L.S. Cermak & F.I.M. Craik (Eds.), *Levels of processing in human memory* (pp. 331–354). Hillsdale, NJ: Lawrence Erlbaum Associates Inc.

Bressler, S.L., & Kelso, J.A.S. (2001). Cortical coordination dynamics and cognition. *Trends in Cognitive Sciences, 5,* 26–36.

Broadbent, D.E. (1977). Levels, hierarchies, and the locus of control. *Quarterly Journal of Experimental Psychology, 29,* 181–201.

Burke, D.M., MacKay, D.G., Worthley, J.S., & Wade, E. (1991). On the tip of the tongue: What causes word finding failures in young and older adults? *Journal of Memory and Language, 30,* 542–579.

Cermak, L.S. (1979). Amnesic patients' level of processing. In L.S. Cermak & F.I.M. Craik (Eds.), *Levels of processing in human memory* (pp. 119–139). Hillsdale, NJ: Lawrence Erlbaum Associates Inc.

Challis, B.H., Velichkovsky, B.M., & Craik, F.I.M. (1996). Levels-of-processing effects on a variety of memory tasks: New findings and theoretical implications. *Consciousness and Cognition, 5,* 142–164.

Cohen, G. (2000). Hierarchical models in cognition: Do they have psychological reality? *European Journal of Cognitive Psychology, 12,* 1–36.

Coltheart, M. (1985). Cognitive neuropsychology and the study of reading. In M.J. Posner & O.S.M. Marin (Eds.), *Attention and performance XI* (pp. 3–37). Hillsdale, NJ: Lawrence Erlbaum Associates Inc.

Conway, M.A. (1992). A structural model of autobiographical memory. In M.A. Conway, D.C. Rubin, H. Spinnler, & W.A. Wagenaar (Eds.), *Theoretical perspectives on autobiographical memory* (pp. 167–193). Dordrecht: Kluwer Academic.

Cowan, N. (1988). Evolving conceptions of memory storage, selective attention and their mutual constraints within the human information-processing system. *Psychological Bulletin, 104,* 163–191.

Cowan, N. (1999). An embedded-process model of working memory. In A. Miyake & P. Shah (Eds.), *Models of working memory* (pp. 62–101). Cambridge, UK: Cambridge University Press

Craik, F.I.M. (1971). Primary memory. *British Medical Bulletin, 27,* 232–236.

Craik, F.I.M. (1977). Depth of processing in recall and recognition. In S. Dornic (Ed.), *Attention and Performance VI.* Hillsdale, NJ: Lawrence Erlbaum Associates Inc.

Craik, F.I.M. (1979). Levels of processing: Overview and closing comments. In L.S. Cermak & F.I.M. Craik (Eds.), *Levels of processing in human memory* (pp. 447–461). Hillsdale, NJ: Lawrence Erlbaum Associates Inc.

Craik, F.I.M. (1983). On the transfer of information from temporary to permanent memory. *Philosophical Transactions of the Royal Society, Series B302,* 341–359.

Craik, F.I.M. (1999). Levels of encoding and retrieval. In B.H. Challis & B.H. Velichkovsky (Eds.), *Stratification in cognition and consciousness* (pp. 97–104). Amsterdam : John Benjamins.

Craik, F.I.M. (2002). Human memory and aging. In L. Bäckman & C. von Hofsten (Eds.), *Psychology at the turn of the Millennium* (pp. 261–280). Hove, UK: Psychology Press.

Craik, F.I.M., & Byrd, M. (1982). Aging and cognitive deficits: The role of attentional resources. In F.I.M. Craik & S. Trehub (Eds.), *Aging and cognitive processes* (pp. 191–211). New York: Plenum Publishing Corporation.

Craik, F.I.M., Govoni, R., Naveh-Benjamin, M., & Anderson, N.D. (1996). The effects of divided attention on encoding and retrieval processes in human memory. *Journal of Experimental Psychology: General, 125,* 159–180.

Craik, F.I.M., & Kester, J.D. (1999). Divided attention and memory: Impairment of processing or consolidation? In E. Tulving (Ed.), *Memory, consciousness, and the brain: The Tallinn Conference* (pp. 38–51). Philadelphia, PA: Psychology Press.

Craik, F.I.M., & Lockhart, R.S. (1972). Levels of processing: A framework for memory research. *Journal of Verbal Learning and Verbal Behavior, 11,* 671–684.

Craik, F.I.M., & Simon, E. (1980). Age differences in memory: The roles of attention and depth of processing. In L. Poon., J.L. Fozard, L.S. Cermak, D. Arenberg, & L.W. Thompson (Eds.), *New directions in memory and aging* (pp. 95–112). Hillsdale, NJ: Lawrence Erlbaum Associates Inc.

Craik, F.I.M., & Tulving, E. (1975). Depth of processing and the retention of words in episodic memory. *Journal of Experimental Psychology: General, 104,* 268–294.

Craik, F.I.M., & Watkins, M.J. (1973). The role of rehearsal in short-term memory. *Journal of Verbal Learning and Verbal Behavior, 12,* 599–607.

Engle, R.W., Kane, M.J., & Tuholski, S.W. (1999). Individual differences in working memory capacity and what they tell us about controlled attention, general fluid intelligence, and functions of the prefrontal cortex. In A. Miyake & P. Shah (Eds.), *Models of working memory* (pp. 102–134). Cambridge, UK: Cambridge University Press.

Fuster, J.M. (2002). Physiology of executive functions: The perception-action cycle. In D.T. Stuss & R.T. Knight (Eds.), *Principles of frontal lobe function* (pp. 96–108). New York: Oxford University Press.

Gardiner, J.M., & Richardson-Klavehn, A. (2000). Remembering and knowing. In E.Tulving & F.I.M. Craik (Eds.), *The Oxford handbook of memory* (pp. 229–244). New York: Oxford University Press.

Goldstein, A.G., & Chance, J.E. (1971). Visual recognition memory for complex configurations. *Perception & Psychophysics, 9,* 237–241.

Hodges, J.R. (2000). Memory in the dementias. In E. Tulving & F.I.M. Craik (Eds.), *The Oxford handbook of memory* (pp. 441–459). New York: Oxford University Press.

Holland, C.A., & Rabbitt, P.M. (1990). Autobiographical and text recall in the elderly: An investigation of a processing resource deficit. *Quarterly Journal of Experimental Psychology: Human Experimental Psychology, 42,* 441–470.

Hunt, R.R., & Einstein, G.O. (1981). Relational and item-specific information in memory. *Journal of Verbal Learning and Verbal Behavior, 20,* 497–514.

James, W. (1890). *The principles of psychology.* New York: Henry Holt.

Johnson-Laird, P.N., Gibbs, G., & de Mowbray, J. (1978). Meaning, amount of processing, and memory for words. *Memory & Cognition, 6,* 372–375.

Kapur, S., Craik, F.I.M., Jones, C., Brown, G.M., Houle, S., & Tulving, E. (1995). Functional role of the prefrontal cortex in retrieval of memories: A PET study, *Neuroreport, 2,* 1880–1884.

Keller, E.F. (2000). *The century of the gene.* Cambridge, MA: Harvard University Press.

Klein, K., & Saltz, E. (1976). Specifying the mechanisms in a levels-of-processing approach to memory. *Journal of Experimental Psychology: Human Learning and Memory, 2,* 671–679.

Kolers, P.A. (1973). Remembering operations. *Memory & Cognition, 1,* 347–355.

Kolers, P.A. (1979). A pattern-analyzing basis of recognition, In L.S. Cermak & F.I.M. Craik (Eds.), *Levels of processing in human memory* (pp. 363–384). Hillsdale, NJ: Lawrence Erlbaum Associates Inc.

Kolers, P.A., & Roediger, H.L. (1984). Procedures of mind. *Journal of Verbal Learning and Verbal Behavior, 23,* 425–449.

Koriat, A., Ben-Zur, H., & Sheffer, D. (1988). Telling the same story twice: Output monitoring and age. *Journal of Memory and Language, 27,* 23–39.

Levine, B., Svoboda, E., Moscovitch, M., & Hay, J.F. (in press). Autobiographical memory in younger and older adults. *Psychology and Aging.*

Lockhart, R.S. (2002). Levels of processing, transfer-appropriate processing, and the concept of robust encoding. *Memory, 10,* 397–403.

Lockhart, R.S., & Craik, F.I.M. (1990). Levels of processing: A retrospective commentary on a framework for memory research. *Canadian Journal of Psychology, 44,* 87–112.

Lockhart, R.S., Craik, F.I.M., & Jacoby, L.L. (1976). Depth of processing, recognition and recall. In J. Brown (Ed.), *Recall and recognition* (pp. 75–102). New York: Wiley.

Logan, G.D. (1988). Toward an instance theory of automatization. *Psychological Review, 95,* 492–527.

Mangels, J.A., Picton, T.W., & Craik, F.I.M. (2001). Attention and successful episodic encoding: An event-related potential study. *Cognitive Brain Research, 11,* 77–95.

Morris, C., Bransford, J.D., & Franks, J.J. (1977). Levels of processing versus transfer appropriate processing. *Journal of Verbal Learning and Verbal Behavior, 16,* 519–533.

Moscovitch, M. (1992). Memory and working-with-memory: A component process model based on models and central systems. *Journal of Cognitive Neuroscience, 4,* 257–267.

Moscovitch, M., & Craik, F.I.M. (1976). Depth of processing, retrieval cues, and uniqueness of encoding as factors in recall. *Journal of Verbal Learning and Verbal Behavior, 15,* 447–458.

Murdock, B.B.Jr. (1960). The distinctiveness of stimuli. *Psychological Review, 67,* 16–31.

Nairne, J.S. (2002). The myth of the encoding—retrieval match. *Memory, 10,* 389–395.

Neisser, U. (1967). *Cognitive psychology.* New York: Appleton-Century-Crofts.

Naveh-Benjamin, M., Craik, F.I.M., Gavrilescu, D., & Anderson, N.D. (2000). Asymmetry between encoding and retrieval processes: Evidence from a divided attention paradigm and a calibration analysis. *Memory & Cognition, 28,* 965–976.

Nelson, D.L. (1979). Remembering pictures and words: Appearance, significance and name. In L.S. Cermak

& F.I.M. Craik (Eds.), *Levels of processing in human memory* (pp. 45–76). Hillsdale, NJ: Lawrence Erlbaum Associates Inc.

Paivio, A. (1971). *Imagery and verbal processes*. New York: Holt, Rinehart & Winton.

Reingold, E. (2002). On the perceptual specificity of memory representations. *Memory, 10*, 365–379.

Roediger, H.L.III., Weldon, M.S., & Challis, B.H. (1989). Explaining dissociations between implicit and explicit measures of retention: A processing account. In H.L. Roediger & F.I.M. Craik (Eds.), *Varieties of memory and consciousness: Essays in honour of Endel Tulving* (pp. 3–41). Hillsdale, NJ: Lawrence Erlbaum Associates Inc.

Rosenfield, I. (1988). *The invention of memory: A new view of the brain*. New York: Basic Books.

Sanquist, T.F., Rohrbaugh, J.W., Syndulko, K., & Lindsley, D.B. (1980). Electrocortical signs of levels of processing: Perceptual analysis and recognition memory. *Psychophysiology, 17*, 568–576.

Seamon, J.J., & Virostek, S. (1978). Memory performance and subject-defined depth of processing. *Memory & Cognition, 6*, 283–287.

Shiffrin, R.M. (1975). Short-term store: The basis for a memory system. In F. Restle, R.M. Shiffrin, N.J. Castellan, H. Lindman, & D.B. Pisoni (Eds.), *Cognitive theory, Vol. 1* (pp. 193–218). Hillsdale, NJ: Lawrence Erlbaum Associates Inc.

Smirnov, A.A. (1973). *Problems of the psychology of memory*. New York: Plenum.

Stein, B. (1978). Depth of processing reexamined: The effects of the precision of encoding and test appropriateness. *Journal of Verbal Learning and Verbal Behavior, 17*, 165–174.

Teasdale, J.D., & Barnard, P.J. (1993). *Affect, cognition, and change: Re-modelling depressive thought*. Hillsdale, NJ: Lawrence Erlbaum Associates Inc.

Treisman, A.M. (1964). Selective attention in man. *British Medical Bulletin, 20*, 12–16.

Treisman, A.M. (1969). Strategies and models of selective attention. *Psychological Review, 76*, 282–299.

Treisman, A.M. (1979). The psychological reality of levels of processing. In L.S. Cermak & F.I.M. Craik (Eds.), *Levels of processing in human memory* (pp. 301–330). Hillsdale, NJ: Lawrence Erlbaum Associates Inc.

Tulving, E. (1983). *Elements of episodic memory*. New York: Oxford University Press.

Tulving, E. (2001). Does memory encoding exist? In M. Naveh-Benjamin, M. Moscovitch, & H.L. Roediger III (Eds.), *Perspectives on human memory and cognitive aging* (pp. 6–27). New York: Psychology Press.

Tulving, E., Kapur, S., Craik, F.I.M., Moscovitch, M., & Houle, S. (1994). Hemispheric encoding/retrieval asymmetry in episodic memory: Positron emission tomography findings. *Proceedings of the National Academy of Sciences, USA, 91*, 2016–2020.

Tulving, E., & Schacter, D.L. (1990). Priming and human memory systems. *Science, 247*, 301–306.

Tulving, E., & Thomson, D.M. (1973). Encoding specificity and retrieval processes in episodic memory. *Psychological Review, 80*, 352–373.

Turvey, M.T., Shaw, R.E., & Mace, W. (1978). Issues in the theory of action: Degrees of freedom, coordinative structures and coalitions. In J. Requin (Ed.), *Attention and performance VII*. Hillsdale, NJ: Lawrence Erlbaum Associates Inc.

Velichkovsky, B.M. (2002). Heterarchy of cognition: The depths and the highs of a framework for memory search. *Memory, 10*, 405–419.

Vincent, A., Craik, F.I.M., & Furedy, J.J. (1996). Relations among memory performance, mental workload and cardiovascular responses. *International Journal of Psychophysiology, 23*, 181–198.

Warrington, E.K., & Shallice, T. (1969). The selective impairment of auditory verbal short-term memory. *Brain, 92*, 885–896.

Wheeler, M.A., Stuss, D.T., & Tulving, E. (1997). Toward a theory of episodic memory: The frontal lobes and autonoetic consciousness. *Psychological Bulletin, 121*, 331–354.

Williams, J.M.G. (1996). Depression and the specificity of autobiographical memory. In D. Rubin (Ed.), *Remembering our past: Studies in autobiographical memory*. Cambridge, UK: Cambridge University Press.

MEMORY, 2002, *10* (5/6), 319–332

Processing approaches to cognition: The impetus from the levels-of-processing framework

Henry L. Roediger III, David A. Gallo, and Lisa Geraci

Washington University in St. Louis, USA

Processing approaches to cognition have a long history, from act psychology to the present, but perhaps their greatest boost was given by the success and dominance of the levels-of-processing framework. We review the history of processing approaches, and explore the influence of the levels-of-processing approach, the procedural approach advocated by Paul Kolers, and the transfer-appropriate processing framework. Processing approaches emphasise the procedures of mind and the idea that memory storage can be usefully conceptualised as residing in the same neural units that originally processed information at the time of encoding. Processing approaches emphasise the unity and interrelatedness of cognitive processes and maintain that they can be dissected into separate faculties only by neglecting the richness of mental life. We end by pointing to future directions for processing approaches.

The levels-of-processing framework has guided research in cognitive psychology and related fields since publication of the seminal paper by Craik and Lockhart (1972) that proposed the theory and the multi-experiment paper by Craik and Tulving (1975) that developed the methods of study. Both papers built on earlier work (e.g., Treisman, 1964, for levels in the cognitive system and Hyde & Jenkins, 1969, for methods), but they stand out as unique contributions, as evidenced by their overwhelming impact on the field. According to the *Web of Science* citation counts, by May, 2002 (30 years after the original "levels" paper) the 1972 paper had been cited approximately 2700 times and the 1975 paper had been cited approximately 1300 times. We can find no other paper (or chapter or book) published in cognitive psychology during this era that is as highly cited as Craik and Lockhart's 1972 paper. Its impact has been enormous.

The levels-of-processing account generally proposed that the level at which an event is coded in the cognitive system determines later recall and recognition for that event. Although the framework and method gained immediate popularity, the framework also attracted numerous critics (e.g., many chapters in the Cermak and Craik, 1979, edited volume are devoted to this endeavour). Many of these criticisms were directed at the ideas that (1) there are strict "levels" of the cognitive system through which information flows, and (2) information processing can be arrested at a particular level. Roediger and Gallo (2002) recently reviewed several theoretical and empirical challenges to the levels-of-processing explanation of how orienting tasks influence retention. They pointed out that Craik and Tulving's (1975) original experiments, and subsequent experiments by Craik (1977) and others, raised several fundamental questions that remain unanswered. Roediger and Gallo (2002) concluded that, 30 years later, the levels-of-processing theory, in its original form, cannot explain what has come to be called the levels-of-processing effect—the powerful effect of orienting tasks on recall and recognition. They argued that we still have no satisfactory theory of the effect of orienting tasks on retention, despite the wide popularity of the method over the past 30 years.

Requests for reprints should be sent to Henry L. Roediger III, Department of Psychology, Box 1125, Washington University, One Bookings Drive, St. Louis, MO 63105, USA. Email: roediger@artsci.wustl.edu

© 2002 Psychology Press Ltd

http://www.tandf.co.uk/journals/pp/09658211.html   DOI:10.1080/09658210224000144

In this paper we do not want to deal with the mixed success of the concept of "levels of the cognitive system" and how orienting tasks determine retention. Rather, we focus on the other half of the title of the original paper—processing. More precisely, we consider processing approaches to cognition, and argue that Craik and Lockhart's (1972) paper propelled processing approaches to cognition to the forefront of the field. We consider the history of processing approaches to cognition, and suggest that the levels-of-processing approach helped to change the zeitgeist in the 1970s and succeeding decades. We then point to the need for further development of the processing approach.

PRECURSORS TO MODERN PROCESSING APPROACHES TO COGNITION

The history of psychology is replete with examples of the tension between structural and more action-oriented approaches to the study of the mind (Boring, 1950). For instance, phrenologists and faculty psychologists proposed that the mind is composed of separate and distinct faculties. Although their specific endeavour did not succeed, their spirit lives on in the work of those who seek the specific function of brain structures to provide localisationist accounts of the mind. Using different methods, Wundt, Titchener, and others of their school also attempted to discern the structure of mental life. However, they approached structure through analytic introspective techniques that eventually foundered due to unreliability of results across laboratories. Whereas these structuralists were interested in determining the structure of perceptual experience, other early researchers were interested in determining the neural structures that support memory. The first half of the 20th century was devoted to the search for the engram, or memory trace, using ablation experiments in animals, but Lashley (1950) famously pronounced the search a failure. Later cognitive models followed in the structural tradition and proposed that mental life could be captured by information flow charts using box-and-arrow diagrams. Support for the structural account also came from neuropsychological studies of patients such as H.M. whose damage to the hippocampus and surrounding areas provided fresh insight into neural structures responsible for memory functioning. All these approaches examined, in one way or the other, the structure of the mind/brain system.

On the other hand, for nearly every one of these structural approaches there was a counter "activity-based" or processing approach. For example, the act psychologists of the Würzburg school in Germany, following the lead of the philosopher Brentano, argued that the appropriate approach to mental life should focus on activity, or mental acts. According to these psychologists, all mental phenomena are inherently composed of acts and intentions—the stimulus cannot be considered in the absence of the goal or the processing of the stimulus. They contrasted their approach to the static content-based approach of Wundt's structuralists and argued that the mind/brain system cannot be usefully explained by static structures in the mind. However, the act psychologists never provided an experimental programme to study activities of mind and so the act school never developed very fully.

At various points in his writings, William James (1890) argued for a more action-oriented approach. Rather than believing that consciousness could be broken down into static structures, as the introspectionists' methods assumed, he argued in a famous quote for a "stream of consciousness" that was ever changing and flowing. In remembering, too, he noted that activity was critical. For instance, James (1890, p. 686) anticipated both the generation effect (Jacoby, 1978; Slamecka & Graf, 1978) and the testing effect (e.g., Wheeler & Roediger, 1992), when he noted that:

> A curious peculiarity of our memory is that things are impressed better by active than by passive repetition. I mean that in learning by heart (for example), when we almost know the piece, it pays better to wait and recollect by an effort from within, than to look at the book again. If we recover the words in the former way, we shall probably know them the next time; if in the latter way, shall very likely need the book once more.

An activity-based approach to cognition was also developed in Russia by Zinchenko, Vygotsky, and Leont'ev (see Wertsch, 1979). This approach was different in that it pervaded all of Russian psychology, not just the study of cognition or memory. However, in his introduction to his book, Wertsch notes parallels to the levels-of-processing tradition of memory research. For example, he describes Zinchenko's work on what he called "involuntary memory", which was essentially about the effect of various activities performed under incidental learning conditions on later retention. As in the levels-of-processing framework, the activities performed in engaging material in the environment were said to determine retention, not intent to learn the material *per se*. According to Leont'ev (1959, 1975, as cited in Wertsch, 1979) this activity can be examined at both a global level regarding the goals of an activity and a local level regarding the particular operations carried out in the service of the overarching goal. For example, if one is trying to remember a list of words and, in doing so, forms images of the words, the goal can be described as better retention of the words and the local operation as forming images in service of this goal (Wertsch, 1979, p. 19). The Russian approach to cognition can be seen as more encompassing than most western approaches in that goals and motives were an integral part of the account (and are often neglected or assumed in memory theories in the West). The work of Zinchenko (1962; translated in Wertsch, 1979) is most relevant to issues of memory and the brief summary here does not do it justice. Suffice it to say, Zinchenko's work (following on the work of Leont'ev and Vygotsky) provides another example of an action-oriented cognitive approach to explaining human memory.

Craik and Lockhart's (1972) contribution again placed emphasis on processing, or the activities of mind. They saw their approach as running counter to the "boxes in the head" information-processing approaches of the 1960s (although to be fair, the Atkinson and Shiffrin, 1968, theory, at least, emphasised processing operations as well as structures). Nonetheless, Craik and Lockhart's heavy emphasis on processing activities as important determinants of retention played a central role in the approach, and provided a new perspective in cognitive psychology. In discussing the powerful role that encoding tasks had on retention across some ten experiments, Craik and Tulving (1975, p. 290) concluded that:

> It is abundantly clear that what determines the level of recall or recognition of a word event is not intention to learn, the amount of effort involved, the difficulty of the orienting task, the amount of time spent making judgments about the items, or even the amount of rehearsal the items receive …: rather it is the qualitative nature of the task, the kind of operations carried out on the items, that determines retention".

Further, "subjects remember not what was 'out there' but what they *did* during encoding" (p.292). Craik and Tulving argued that "The problem now is to develop an adequate theoretical formulation which can take us beyond such vague statements as 'meaningful things are well remembered'" (p. 290).

The levels-of-processing account was an attempt to bring focus on the processes, or the procedures used in perception and comprehension of the world and how they affected memory. Retention was seen as a relatively automatic byproduct of the activities of mind during perception and comprehension, and "encoding" as a special process had no distinct status (but see Tulving, 2002). Crowder (1993) argued that "Modern memory theory has more or less embraced proceduralism during the last 20 years", and that "One measure of this has been the wide acceptance of the levels-of-processing framework for memory" (p. 139). While heartened by Crowder's conclusion, we think it may be somewhat premature. Although some developments in the field are coloured by processing approaches, we suggest that the field in general has not yet been able to develop an adequate characterisation of procedures that account for memory phenomena despite efforts in this direction (e.g., Kolers & Roediger, 1984).

In the remainder of this paper, we attempt to develop more fully the proceduralist account by reviewing the memory research of Paul Kolers and by using examples from research contrasting explicit and implicit memory processes. In doing so, we illustrate the tension between the procedural and structural approaches that occur even in current memory theorising. We are optimistic, though, that researchers are increasingly coming to realise that these approaches are not mutually exclusive, but rather are complementary (e.g., Roediger, Buckner, & McDermott, 1999; Schacter, 1990; Tulving, 1999).

KOLERS' PROCEDURAL APPROACH

Paul Kolers was perhaps the foremost champion of a procedural approach to the mind during the 1970s and early 1980s, before his untimely death in 1986. Kolers (1973, 1975a,b, 1976, 1979; Kolers & Ostry, 1974) provided a programme of research that embodied a more action-oriented approach to cognitive processing. He was originally interested in the study of reading, which is quite skilled in adults. In an effort to understand this skill and study how it developed, he took adult readers (college students) and challenged them by providing text for them to read that was misoriented in various ways. He discovered that, with many days of practice, students could come to read text presented (for example) upside down nearly as fast as they could read text presented in its normal orientation. In some experiments Kolers had people reread passages of text at various delays after the original reading (e.g., Kolers & Ostry, 1974) and measured the savings in reading speed. This savings measure, like Ebbinghaus's (1885/1964) original savings method, provided an indirect measure of retention. In Kolers' work the savings reflected savings of the pattern-analysing operations used in rereading the passage. In some studies, the savings in rereading were uncorrelated with subjects' conscious recognition of the content of the passages (Kolers, 1976), representing a dissociation between two measures of retention. This finding can be seen as one of the first experimental demonstrations of a dissociation between a conscious (or direct or explicit) measure of retention and an unconscious (or indirect or implicit) measure of knowledge (for related work see Masson, 1984). Other examples of such dissociations came from work conducted in both neuropsychological and experimental traditions.

In neuropsychology, Warrington and Weiskrantz (1968, 1970) compared performance of brain-damaged subjects to healthy controls on a variety of memory tests. They showed powerful dissociations between measures of conscious recollection (free recall, recognition) and measures of priming on tasks such as naming fragmented words and pictures (tasks that would later be classified as implicit memory tests; Graf & Schacter, 1985). Although Warrington and Weiskrantz did not originally conceptualise their results in this way, this interpretation is now accepted from later work in which the early findings were confirmed and extended using a variety of patient groups and measurement operations (e.g., Graf, Shimamura, & Squire, 1985; for a review see Moscovitch, Vriezen, & Goshen-Gottstein, 1993). Within experimental psychology, the search for dissociations between measures of retention also became a holy grail of sorts, with many researchers in the 1980s reporting such findings (Jacoby, 1983; Jacoby & Dallas, 1981; Roediger & Blaxton, 1987a; Tulving, Schacter, &

Stark, 1982, Weldon & Roediger, 1987, to mention just a few). Dissociations both in neuropsychological research and experiments with college student populations were the primary evidence for the postulation of multiple memory systems in the 1980s (e.g., Squire, 1987; Tulving, 1983). In virtually all of the relevant experiments of that era, two measures of memory were contrasted. One measure (usually recognition or free recall) was thought to tap a conscious, recollective form of memory and the other measure assessed priming or savings on some transfer test that did not depend on conscious recollection. The two classes of test were variously called direct and indirect (e.g., Richardson-Klavehn & Bjork, 1988) or explicit and implicit (Graf & Schacter, 1985) and different memory systems were invoked to explain these tests differences (episodic and semantic, Tulving, 1983; declarative and procedural, Squire, 1987).

As long as the experimental comparison was between two tests as a function of independent and subject variables, much evidence could be obtained to support the notion of a relatively small number of memory systems as proposed, for example, by Tulving (1983). Roediger (1984) argued that, at a minimum, studies claiming dissociations between memory systems should employ at least two separate measures of the construct of interest, not just one. So, for example, one should employ two or more measures of episodic memory and two or more measures of priming on a semantic memory task, to be sure that dissociations did not occur between tests that allegedly measured the same system. Few researchers have employed this strategy, but the work done by Kolers in his rather different tradition in the 1970s had already shown that dissociations could be quite commonplace even between highly similar measures of retention.

A good example comes from Kolers and Perkins (1975). They had seven groups of students read 24 pages in one of seven types of transformed text. The transformations are shown here in Table 1 by providing a sample sentence. After this extensive practice in reading one transformation, the students next read two pages of text in each of the seven transformations, in an appropriately counterbalanced order. Of interest was how the practice at reading one transformation would transfer to the other six. The answer is provided in Table 2, where the measure is percentage of transfer. The measure of reading the trained transformation during the test was set to equal

TABLE 1
Examples of transformed texts used in Kolers and Perkins (1975). Asterisks show where to begin reading each example.

N
*Expectations can also mislead us; the unexpected is always hard to perceive clearly. Sometimes we fail to recognize an object because we

R
*Emerson once said that every man is as lazy as he dares to be. It was the kind of mistake a New England Puritan might be expected to make. It is

I
*These are but a few of the reasons for believing that a person cannot be conscious of all his mental processes. Many other reasons can be

M
*Several years ago a professor who teaches psychology at a large university had to ask his assistant, a young man of great intelligence

r N
*On his first day in lower-school he was thoroughly disoriented. His test were above his head; dad to dash for horses ment when eh

r R
*A very young child seems as if as evyued of smees dlihc gnuoy yrev A, visual image that ensure and leaves the field of view abruptly,

r I
*Psychology became a mathematical science during the decades of the nineteenth century, at a time when european thought was determined by

r M
*Imagine two different pictures. One shows a bright red circle on a pale yellow background, the other a bright green circle on a gray background.

TABLE 2
Percentage transfer from training to test

Training	Test							Average
	M	R	rR	rN	rl	I	rM	
I	95	118	97	80	84	100	52	89
rl	92	112	90	82	100	78	72	89
rR	81	84	100	68	56	79	56	74
rM	88	67	70	57	37	44	100	66
R	87	100	70	37	58	44	41	62
M	100	69	71	72	38	28	52	61
rN	82	3	57	100	36	34	20	47
Average	89	79	79	71	58	58	56	70

100%—how well reading one type of text transferred to reading those last two pages of text in that transformation. Reading the other transformations usually (but not always) produced less transfer, so that most of the values in Table 2 are less than 100. However, in some interesting cases, reading one transformation (e.g., reading Inverted text, or I) transferred better to reading another transformation (e.g., Rotated, or R) than did reading the original transformation itself (118% transfer in this case). On the other hand, reading transformation rN hardly transferred at all to reading rotated text (3%).

Reading the final two pages of text can be considered an indirect measure of retention or transfer. Starting at Table 2, and examining many possible 2 × 2 combinations of study and test conditions, leads inexorably to the conclusion that even the highly similar tasks of reading various orientations of text can lead to numerous dissociations among memory measures. Dissociations among memory measures, even relatively similar ones, can be seen as a perfectly natural state of affairs from a procedural approach (Kolers & Roediger, 1984). The difficulty is in specifying the procedural approach and distinguishing various types of procedures.

TRANSFER-APPROPRIATE PROCESSING

During the same period that Kolers was developing his ideas about procedures of mind, Morris, Bransford, and Franks (1977) and Bransford, Franks, Morris, and Stein (1979) provided a useful parallel development by proposing the notion of transfer-appropriate processing. Briefly, they endorsed the idea that a proper account of mind and memory should emphasise mental procedures, but they criticised the levels-of-processing approach as focusing only on processing during encoding of events as determining later retention. Rather, they pointed out that retention was determined by how well the processing requirements of the test matched those used originally to encode information.

In the Morris et al. (1977) experiments, subjects encoded words phonemically or semantically. On a standard recognition test, semantic encoding led to greater recognition than phonemic encoding, the standard finding in the levels-of-processing paradigm (Craik & Tulving, 1975). However, on a novel rhyme recognition test—does this word rhyme with a word seen during encoding?—the standard levels-of-processing effect was eliminated or, in some conditions, even reversed, such that phonemic processing during encoding led to greater recognition than did semantic processing. Other researchers reported similar results from slightly different paradigms (Fisher & Craik, 1977; Hunt & Elliott, 1980; Jacoby, 1975; McDaniel, Friedman, & Bourne, 1978). Types of processing during encoding therefore cannot be said to be inherently deep or shallow (or good or bad) for later retention; rather, it depends on the demands of the situation in which knowledge is assessed (see Kolers & Roediger, 1984, for further discussion).

Roediger and Blaxton (1987b) and Roediger, Weldon, and Challis (1989b) developed the transfer-appropriate processing framework to help account for the burgeoning literature showing dissociations between explicit and implicit memory tests. The hope was that a relatively small set of principles would account for the welter of dissociations being discovered and predict new dissociations. Roediger et al. (1989b) made four assumptions. The first assumption followed directly the principles of transfer-appropriate processing or encoding specificity (Tulving & Thomson, 1973) and stated that memory tests benefit to the extent that the operations they require overlap or recapture the operations used during encoding. The second assumption is that most (but not all) explicit and implicit memory tests rely on different types of processing. The third assumption is that most standard explicit memory tests (free recall, cued recall, recognition) depend primarily on meaningful (conceptual, semantic) information for their successful performance. The fourth assumption is that most implicit memory tests in standard use rely on perceptual information, or are data-driven. For these tests, the match in perceptual processes between study and test matters much more than the match in meaning-based processing. These last two assumptions were drawn from provocative experimental work of Jacoby (1983).

The distinction between perceptual and conceptual forms of test advanced by Roediger et al. (1989b; see also Roediger, 1990) attempted to provide some further specification to the processing approach, at least in terms of two broad types of processing. The framework was successful because it permitted the prediction of many dissociations between tests. Just as Morris et al. (1977) obtained interactions or dissociations between two types of explicit recognition tests, so experiments done within the transfer-appropriate processing framework revealed dissociations between implicit memory tests. For example, Blaxton (1989) and Srinivas and Roediger (1990) showed dissociations in priming on implicit tests such that a variable could have one effect on a perceptual implicit test and the opposite effect on a conceptual implicit test. Weldon and Roediger (1987, Experiment 4) showed that two perceptual implicit memory tests could themselves be dissociated if the operations required between study and test matched or mismatched, as discussed in more detail later. Dissociations among memory measures—explicit or implicit—can be easily achieved, even when the memory tasks involved are thought to be undergirded by the same memory system (see Roediger, Srinivas, & Weldon, 1989a, for a review).

Although generally successful in explaining dissociations between tests, Roediger et al.'s (1989b) transfer-appropriate processing approach attracted critics due to both conceptual and empirical problems. A first problem is that a strict procedural approach does not concede a sharp contrast between perceptual levels of analysis (specific, data-driven) and a conceptual level of analysis (abstract, semantic) (Kolers, 1978). Rather, perceptual experience gives rise to meaning and even perceptual recognition depends on classifying objects into abstract categories (horse, tree). Roediger et al. (1989a) attempted to finesse this point by referring to perceptual and conceptual continua of experience such that a picture or word could be treated more as a perceptual object or more as an abstract entity; the two dimensions need not trade off against one another (see also Weldon, 1991).

In addition to this conceptual problem, problematic data also appeared, showing dissociations among perceptual and conceptual tests (e.g., Cabeza, 1994; Hunt & Toth, 1990; McDermott & Roediger, 1996; Tenpenny & Shoben, 1992; Vaidya et al., 1997; Weldon & Coyote, 1996). For example, McDermott and Roediger (1996) and Weldon and Coyote (1996) showed that pictures and words produced equivalent levels of priming on two conceptual implicit memory tests, rather than pictures producing greater priming, as predicted by Roediger et al.'s (1989a) theory. In contrast, Cabeza (1994) showed an unexpected dissociation in priming between two conceptual implicit memory tests. Thus, although the distinction between perceptual and conceptual pro-

cesses helps to capture a large-grained distinction of importance, clearly the theory must be developed much further to capture the more fine-grained aspects of retention on the many different types of memory test (see Roediger & McDermott, 1993). We note, though, that many of the dissociations among conceptual or perceptual tests can be accommodated within a proceduralist approach to memory if the exact type of conceptual or perceptual processing is considered (see Geraci & Rajaram, in press; Geraci & Rajaram, 2002). Therefore, we argue that performance on both explicit and implicit memory tests—and therefore, we would argue, on all memory tests—hinges on highly specific aspects of encoding/retrieval interactions, a point to which we turn next.

SPECIFICITY OF PROCESSING

One central tenet of the procedural approach is that performance depends on the *specific* match of encoding and retrieval (a point emphasised in this issue by Reingold, 2002). This claim is in contrast to abstractionist theories such as those of Anderson (1990, p. 122) that claim that:

> Representations that do not preserve the exact perceptual structures of the events remembered are the mainstay of long-term memory. It is important to appreciate that these meaning representations are neither linguistic nor pictorial. Rather they encode the meaning of pictures and linguistic information.

The proceduralist programme of research has shown, to the contrary, that recapitulating specific encoding and retrieval operations enhances performance.

Let us consider one example of such processing specificity involving pictures and words. Weldon and Roediger (1987) had students study pictures and words and then different groups were given either an explicit free recall test or an implicit word fragment completion test. As is often found, pictures were better remembered than words in free recall (the picture superiority effect). However, words produced much more priming than did pictures on the implicit word fragment completion test. In a later experiment, the one of more interest for present purposes, Weldon and Roediger again presented pictures and words during study but now participants received an implicit test of either word fragment completion or picture fragment naming. Now, as expected, the experience of studying pictures and words transferred differentially to tests: pictures showed more priming on picture fragment completion, whereas words showed more priming on word fragment completion.

McDermott and Roediger (1994, Experiment 4) replicated this pattern under somewhat stricter test conditions and their data are shown in Figure 1. Again, on the verbal implicit test, words produced more priming than pictures; on the pictorial test, pictures produced more priming than words. The amount of cross-form priming was quite low and not significant, showing the highly specific nature of the encoding/retrieval match necessary for priming. For example, seeing a picture of an elephant produced essentially no priming on completing a word fragment of e_e_h_n_. Interestingly, if subjects were given a picture during study and asked to imagine the written name of the concept, then a small amount of cross-form priming did occur (and conversely when words were studied with the imagine-a-picture instruction on the picture fragment naming test). So, cross-form priming was obtained when subjects had imagined words at study (when given pictures) or imagined pictures at study (when given words). McDermott and Roediger (1994) pro-

posed that instructing subjects to form relevant images engaged top-down imaginal processes that could transfer to the test situation, albeit at an attenuated level relative to actual perception (see Pilotti, Gallo, & Roediger, 2000, for relevant findings with auditory materials). These dissociations between priming tasks demonstrate similar processing specificity as shown in Table 2 from Kolers and Perkins' (1975) work. Roediger and Srinivas (1993) and Reingold (2002) review many examples of specificity in implicit memory tests, but of course the same kinds of encoding/retrieval interactions can be obtained in explicit tests, too (e.g., Balota & Neely, 1980; Morris et al., 1977). The concepts of encoding specificity and transfer-appropriate processing were, after all, first developed to explain such effects on explicit tests (cued recall and recognition).

The transfer-appropriate processing framework was originally intended as an alternative to memory systems interpretations of these data. However, accumulating evidence over the years has made it clear that the original framing of the question in terms of "systems and processes" was too simplified. Performance on tests designed to measure the "same" system can be dissociated, which poses a problem for the idea that only a few memory systems underlie all performance. For

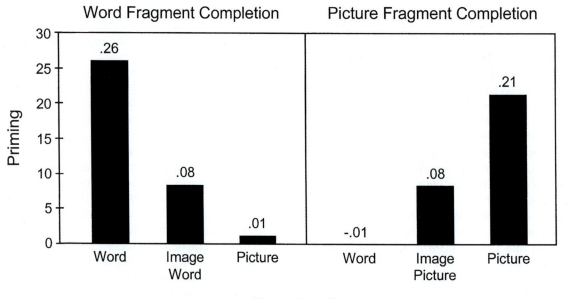

Figure 1. Demonstration of processing specificty between encoding and retrieval (McDermott & Roediger, 1994, Experiment 4). Subjects studied words or pictures, and were asked either to make pleasantness ratings of the presented stimulus or to form a mental image in the opposite format (and to rate its vividness). Implicit memory was tested using either a word fragment completion test or a picture fragment naming test.

example, when Blaxton (1989) showed dissociations between tasks that should, according to Tulving's (1972, 1983) theories, reflect semantic memory, Tulving and Schacter (1990) proposed that some tasks (including the ones used by Blaxton) were underlain by a perceptual representation system. Therefore, dissociations between tasks could be explained by appeal to differences between perceptual representations (essentially data-driven or perceptual processing in Roediger et al., 1989b) and other systems.

This idea is fine as far as it goes, but within perceptual or data-driven tests it is perfectly possible to dissociate verbal from pictorial tests (McDermott & Roediger, 1994; Weldon & Roediger, 1987), auditory from visual tests (Habib & Nyberg, 1997), and visual from tactile tests (Srinivas, Greene, & Easton, 1997). In short, "the" perceptual representation system really refers to the fact that priming can occur in various modalities that transfer imperfectly from one to another. Even for visually presented words there can be different levels of priming depending on the match or mismatch in perceptual features between study and test (Graf & Ryan, 1990; Roediger & Blaxton, 1987b), and similarly for auditorily presented words (Church & Schacter, 1994; Pilotti, Bergman, Gallo, Sommers, & Roediger, 2000). Hayman and Tulving (1989) argued that perceptual systems exhibit "hyperspecific" priming effects. Kolers' work from the 1970s had demonstrated the same point (Kolers, 1975b; Kolers & Perkins, 1975). We assume no one would propose that a different memory system underlies reading of each type of transformation of text shown in Table 1 that produces the dissociations seen in Table 2. Rather, an appropriate account should appeal to the perceptual/cognitive procedures used in developing skill in reading various kinds of transformed text.

Of course, neurocognitive systems underlie all cognitive performance, so there is no gainsaying the need to refer to these systems. The point to emerge from the procedural framework is that neurocognitive systems are complex and interactive, not encapsulated. Moscovitch (1992, 1994) and Roediger et al. (1999) have championed a components-of-processing approach in which any task can be seen as a more or less complex concatenation of component processes that are underpinned by local neurocognitive systems. Changing task requirements can easily add or subtract one or more components that can produce dissociations. The upshot is that to dissociate

any two tasks one only need change one component (see also Hintzman, 1990; Tenpenney & Shoben, 1992). Roediger et al. (1999) proposed that future memory systems theories may appear more like the wiring diagrams discovered from animal work for the visual system (Van Essen, Anderson, & Felleman, 1992), with complex interactive patterns of connection. The neurocognitive systems that underlie retention will involve components from many brain regions in complex networks. As Crowder (1993, p. 145) noted, "The resolution of the systems argument is obvious from a proceduralist point of view. Of course there are different systems of memory, but systems as defined by different ensembles of information processing units—different codes— not different organizational or operational rules." For example, a principle such as transfer-appropriate processing or encoding specificity may apply to retention in all systems. To continue with Crowder's point, "In general the number of different memory systems is a count of the number of different information processing ensembles that can be recruited to do the cognitive work required for a task" (Crowder, 1993, p. 145).

FUTURE DIRECTIONS

"Proceduralism, in memory theory, is the idea that memory storage for an experience resides in the same neural units that processed that experience when it happened in the first place" (Crowder, 1993, p. 139), as opposed to some special store or system in which information resides after it has been processed. Modern neuroimaging experiments are showing the truth of this central tenet of proceduralism that could not have been imagined when the 1972 levels-of-processing paper was originally published. This work shows that brain activation patterns at test mimic the processing from study. For example, Wheeler, Petersen, and Buckner (2000) had people study pictures and sounds that corresponded to a descriptive label (e.g., the word "dog" was accompanied either by a picture of a dog or the sound of a dog barking). At test, subjects were given the same descriptive label and asked to mentally recall the corresponding referent (i.e., the picture or the sound). Using event-related fMRI methods, Wheeler et al. (2000) showed that successful picture recall was associated more with visual cortex activation, and successful sound recall was associated more with auditory cortex activation. Importantly, these regions were a subset of those regions that were activated during a perception task, in which subjects saw the same descriptive labels paired with their actual percept (the picture or the sound). Similar findings have been reported by Nyberg, Habib, McIntosh, and Tulving (2000), who showed that some of the same auditory regions that were active during the encoding of sounds were reactivated during the recall of those sounds. Collectively, these studies suggest that similar neural structures support perception, encoding, and retrieval, which is consistent with the proceduralist point of view.

McDermott and Watson (2002) provided further support for the idea that retrieval relies on brain regions that were involved in encoding. Participants read lists of words related in terms of either phonology (*beep, weep, peep, sheep ...*) or in terms of meaning (*bed, rest, awake, dream ...*) while neural activity was assessed with fMRI. During encoding, some regions (e.g., within left anterior ventral inferior frontal cortex and left middle/superior temporal cortex) were more active for the meaningfully associated lists, whereas other regions (e.g., within left posterior dorsal inferior frontal cortex and bilateral/inferior/superior parietal cortices) demonstrated more activation for lists of rhyming words. Using a free choice recognition test, patterns of reactivation were obtained; that is, some regions showing preferential activation for semantics during encoding also showed greater activation for hits studied in the context of semantic associates (e.g., *rest*) than for hits studied in the context of rhymes (e.g., *peep*). Conversely, some regions showing preferential activation for phonology during encoding also showed greater activation for hits to words studied in the context of phonological associates than for hits studied in the context of semantic associates.

The design of McDermott and Watson's study permitted a novel comparison that was not possible in the other studies cited earlier. Their materials were designed to elicit false recollection of a nonpresented word (*sleep* for the materials just described). After reading the list of phonemically or semantically similar words, false recognition of a related word such as *sleep* occurs very frequently (Roediger & McDermott, 1995; Sommers & Lewis, 1999). Interestingly, when subjects falsely recognised the related word in McDermott and Watson's study, the patterns of activation were similar to those obtained for the studied words. That is, when falsely recognising *sleep* after the

relevant phonemic list, the phonological regions were preferentially active, whereas when falsely recognising *sleep* after the semantic list, the semantic regions were preferentially active. This pattern is even more striking, because the actual test item (e.g., *sleep*) was the same in the two cases. McDermott and Watson's experiment shows that the type of processing during test recruits the same brain regions as engaged during study even with the test item held constant.

Neuroimaging studies of memory retrieval have generally shown that retrieval processes require a complex interaction of cooperating systems. Many of the brain regions identified through neuroimaging studies are ones that had not been identified from patient or animal studies as important to learning and memory. Just as visual perception involves the complex interaction of neural systems, so recent results suggest that similar complex systems underlie language processing (Dronkers, Redfern, & Knight, 2000) and memory processing (Roediger et al., 1999; Nyberg, Forkstam, Petersson, Cabeza, & Ingvar, 2002).

The procedural approach argues that encoding is not the passive laying down of traces, but a constructive activity. Another discovery from recent neuroscientific approaches that is consistent with this aspect of the procedural approach is that of mirror neurons in premotor cortex. The majority of work in this area has involved single-unit recordings in monkeys, but a few neuroimaging studies have extended the basic findings to humans (see Rizzolatti, Fogassi, & Gallese, 2000, for a review). The basic finding is that populations of mirror neurons selectively respond to specific types of motor actions both when an action is performed (i.e., an object is grasped) and when the identical action is only observed (i.e., another monkey grasps an object). Further, more than half of these neurons are very specific, in that they will only respond when a very specific type of action is performed or observed (e.g., grasping vs placing). These findings suggest that the same neural assemblies that are active during the perception of a behaviour (which ostensibly involves identification from long-term memory and encoding into episodic memory) are also involved in the actual performance of that behavior. Further, Nilsson et al. (2000) have shown that when people perform action events during encoding and recall them later, motor cortex is reactivated during their retrieval (relevant to an appropriate control). These findings fit well with an action-oriented approach to cognition as embodied in the procedural approach.

CONCLUSION

The procedural approach to understanding the mind/brain system in general and human memory in particular has proven quite fruitful. The levels-of-processing framework helped to develop the approach in the 1970s, along with the developments of Kolers' procedural viewpoint and transfer-appropriate processing theory. Although there are a variety of approaches to studying memory, the processing or procedural approach surely has and will continue to have a central role in furthering our understanding.

REFERENCES

Anderson, J.R. (1990). *Cognitive psychology and its implications* (3rd Edn.). New York: Freeman.

Atkinson, R.C., & Shiffrin, R.M. (1968). Human memory: A proposed system and its control processes. In K.W. Spence & J.T. Spence (Eds.), *The psychology of learning and motivation: Advances in research and theory, Vol. II*, (pp. 89–195). New York: Academic Press.

Balota, D.A., & Neely, J.H. (1980). Test-expectancy and word-frequency effects in recall and recognition. *Journal of Experimental Psychology: Human Learning & Memory*, 6, 576–587.

Blaxton, T.A. (1989). Investigating dissociations among memory measures: Support for a transfer-appropriate processing framework. *Journal of Experimental Psychology: Learning, Memory, & Cognition*, 15, 657–668.

Boring, E.G. (1950). *A history of experimental psychology*. New York: Appleton-Century-Crofts.

Bransford, J.D., Franks, J.J., Morris, C.D., & Stein, B.S. (1979). Some general constraints on learning and memory research. In L.S. Cermak & F.I.M. Craik (Eds.), *Levels of processing in human memory* (pp. 331–354). Hillsdale, NJ: Lawrence Erlbaum Associates Inc.

Cabeza, R. (1994). A dissociation between two implicit conceptual tests supports the distinction between types of conceptual processing. *Psychonomic Bulletin & Review*, 1, 505–508.

Cermak, L.S., & Craik, F.I.M. (Eds.). (1979). *Levels of processing in human memory*. Potomac, MD: Lawrence Erlbaum Associates Inc.

Church, B.A. & Schacter, D.L. (1994). Perceptual specificity of auditory priming: Implicit memory for voice intonation and fundamental frequency. *Journal of Experimental Psychology: Learning, Memory, & Cognition*, 20, 521–533.

Craik, F.I.M. (1977). Depth of processing in recall and recognition. In S. Dornic & P.M.A. Rabbit (Eds.), *Attention and performance VI* (pp. 679–697). Hillsdale, NJ: Lawrence Erlbaum Associates Inc.

Craik, F.I.M., & Lockhart, R.S. (1972). Levels of processing: A framework for memory research. *Journal of Verbal Learning and Verbal Behavior*, 11, 671–684.

Craik, F.I.M., & Tulving, E. (1975). Depth of processing and the retention of words in episodic memory. *Journal of Experimental Psychology: General*, 104, 268–294.

Crowder, R.G. (1993). Systems and principles in memory theory: Another critique of pure memory. In A. Collins, S.E. Gathercole, M.A. Conway, & P.E. Morris (Eds.), *Theories of memory* (pp. 139–161). Hove, UK: Lawrence Erlbaum Associates Ltd.

Dronkers, N.F., Redfern, B.B., & Knight, R.T. (2000). The neural architecture of language disorders. In M.S. Gazzaniga (Ed.), *The new cognitive neurosciences (2nd Edn.)*, (pp. 949–958). Cambridge, MA: MIT Press.

Ebbinghaus, H. (1885/1964). *Memory: A contribution to experimental psychology* [H.A. Ruger & C.E. Bussenius, Trans.]. New York: Dover Publications.

Fisher, R.P., & Craik, F.I.M. (1977). Interaction between encoding and retrieval operations in cued recall. *Journal of Experimental Psychology: Human Learning and Memory*, 3, 701–711.

Geraci, L., & Rajaram, S. (in press). The orthographic distinctiveness effect on direct and indirect tests of memory: Delineating the awareness and processing requirements. *Journal of Memory and Language*.

Graf, P., & Ryan, L. (1990). Transfer-appropriate processing for implicit and explicit memory. *Journal of Experimental Psychology: Learning, Memory, & Cognition*, 16, 978–992.

Graf, P., & Schacter, D.L. (1985). Implicit and explicit memory for new associations in normal and amnesic subjects. *Journal of Experimental Psychology: Learning, Memory, & Cognition*, 11, 501–518.

Graf, P., Shimamura, A.P., & Squire, L.R. (1985). Priming across modalities and priming across category levels: Extending the domain of preserved function in amnesia. *Journal of Experimental Psychology: Learning, Memory, & Cognition*, 11, 386–396.

Habib, R., & Nyberg, L. (1997). Incidental retrieval processes influence explicit test performance with data-limited cues. *Psychonomic Bulletin & Review*, 4, 130–133.

Hayman, C.G., & Tulving, E. (1989). Is priming in fragment completion based on a "traceless" memory system? *Journal of Experimental Psychology: Learning, Memory, & Cognition*, 15, 941–956.

Hintzman, D.L. (1990). Human learning and memory: Connections and dissociations. *Annual Review of Psychology*, 41, 109–139.

Hunt, R.R., & Elliott, J.M. (1980). The role of nonsemantic information in memory: Orthographic distinctiveness effects on retention. *Journal of Experimental Psychology: General*, 109, 49–74.

Hunt, R.R., & Toth, J.P. (1990). Perceptual identification, fragment completion, and free recall: Concepts and data. *Journal of Experimental Psychology: Learning, Memory, & Cognition*, 16, 282–290.

Hyde, T.S., & Jenkins, J.J. (1969). Differential effects of incidental tasks on the organization of recall of a list of highly associated words. *Journal of Experimental Psychology, 82,* 472–481.

Jacoby, L.L. (1975). Physical features vs. meaning: A difference in decay? *Memory & Cognition, 3,* 247-251.

Jacoby, L.L. (1978). On interpreting the effects of repetition: Solving a problem versus remembering a solution. *Journal of Verbal Learning and Verbal Behavior, 17,* 649–667.

Jacoby, L.L. (1983). Remembering the data: Analyzing interactive processes in reading. *Journal of Verbal Learning & Verbal Behavior, 22,* 485–508.

Jacoby, L.L. & Dallas, M. (1981). On the relationship between autobiographical memory and perceptual learning. *Journal of Experimental Psychology: General, 110,* 306–340.

James, W. (1890). *The principles of psychology.* New York: Holt.

Kolers, P.A. (1973). Remembering operations. *Memory & Cognition, 1,* 347–355.

Kolers, P.A. (1975a). Memorial consequences of automatized encoding. *Journal of Experimental Psychology: Human Learning & Memory, 1,* 689–701.

Kolers, P.A. (1975b). Specificity of operations in sentence recognition. *Cognitive Psychology, 7,* 289–306.

Kolers, P.A. (1976). Pattern-analyzing memory. *Science, 191,* 1280–1281.

Kolers, P.A. (1978). On the representation of experience. In D. Gerver & W. Sinaiko (Eds.), *Language, interpretation, and communication.* (pp. 245–258). New York: Plenum.

Kolers, P.A. (1979). A pattern-analyzing basis of recognition. In L.S. Cermak & F.I.M. Craik (Eds.), *Levels of processing in human memory* (pp. 363–384). Hillsdale, NJ: Lawrence Erlbaum Associates Inc.

Kolers, P.A., & Ostry, D.J. (1974). Time course of loss of information regarding pattern analyzing operations. *Journal of Verbal Learning & Verbal Behavior, 13,* 599–612.

Kolers, P.A., & Perkins, D.N. (1975). Spatial and ordinal components of form perception and literacy. *Cognitive Psychology, 7,* 228–267.

Kolers, P.A., & Roediger, H.L. (1984). Procedures of mind. *Journal of Verbal Learning and Verbal Behavior, 23,* 425–449.

Lashley, K.S. (1950). In search of the engram. In *Symposia of the Society for Experimental Biology,* No. 4 (pp. 454–482). London: Cambridge University Press.

Masson, M.E.J. (1984). Memory for the surface structure of sentences: Remembering with and without awareness. *Journal of Verbal Learning and Verbal Behavior, 23,* 579–592.

McDaniel, M.A., Friedman, A., & Bourne, L.E. (1978). Remembering the levels of information in words. *Memory & Cognition, 6,* 156–164.

McDermott, K.B., & Roediger, H.L. (1994). Effects of imagery on perceptual implicit memory tests. *Journal of Experimental Psychology: Learning, Memory, & Cognition, 20,* 1379–1390.

McDermott, K.B., & Roediger, H.L. (1996). Exact and conceptual repetition dissociate conceptual memory tests: Problems for transfer appropriate processing theory. *Canadian Journal of Experimental Psychology, 50,* 57–71.

McDermott, K.B., & Watson, J.S. (2002). *Reactivation of phonemic and semantic brain regions used for encoding during episodic recognition.* Manuscript in preparation.

Morris, C.D., Bransford, J.D., & Franks, J.J. (1977). Levels of processing versus transfer-appropriate processing. *Journal of Verbal Learning and Verbal Behavior, 16,* 519–533.

Moscovitch, M. (1992). Memory and working-with-memory: A component process model based on modules and central systems. *Journal of Cognitive Neuroscience, 4,* 257–267.

Moscovitch, M. (1994). Memory and working with memory: Evaluation of a component process model and comparisons with other models. In D.L. Schacter & E. Tulving (Eds.), *Memory systems* (pp. 269–310). Cambridge, MA: MIT Press.

Moscovitch, M., Vriezen, E., & Goshen-Gottstein, Y. (1993). Implicit tests of memory in patients with focal lesions or degenerative brain disorders. In F. Boller & J. Grafman (Eds.), *Handbook of neuropsychology,* Vol. 8 (pp. 133–173). Amsterdam: Elsevier.

Nilsson, L., Nyberg, L., Klingberg, T., Aberg, C., Persson, J., & Roland, P.E. (2000). Activity in motor areas while remembering action events. *Neuroreport: For Rapid Communication of Neuroscience Research, 11,* 2199–2201.

Nyberg, L., Forkstam, C., Petersson, K.M., Cabeza, R., & Ingvar, M. (2002). Brain imaging of human memory systems: Between-systems similarities and within-systems differences. *Cognitive Brain Research, 13,* 281–292.

Nyberg, L., Habib, R., McIntosh, A.R., & Tulving, E. (2000). Reactivation of encoding-related brain activity during memory retrieval. *Proceedings of the National Academy of Sciences, 97,* 11120–11124.

Pilotti, M., Bergman, E.T., Gallo, D.A., Sommers, M., & Roediger, H.L. (2000). Direct comparison of auditory implicit memory tests. *Psychonomic Bulletin & Review, 7,* 347–353.

Pilotti, M., Gallo, D.A., & Roediger, H.L. (2000). Effects of hearing words, imagining hearing words, and reading on auditory implicit and explicit memory tests. *Memory & Cognition, 28,* 1406–1418.

Reingold, E.M. (2002). On the perceptual specificity of memory representations. *Memory, 10,* 365–379.

Richardson-Klavehn, A., & Bjork, R.A. (1988). Measures of memory. *Annual Review of Psychology, 39,* 475–543.

Rizzolatti, G., Fogassi, L., & Gallese, V. (2000). Cortical mechanisms subserving object grasping and action recognition: A new view on the cortical motor functions. In M.S. Gazzaniga (Ed.), *The new cognitive neurosciences (2nd Edn.),* (pp. 539–552). Cambridge, MA: MIT Press.

Roediger, H.L. (1984). Does current evidence from dissociation experiments favor the episodic/semantic distinction? *Behavior and Brain Sciences, 7,* 252–254.

Roediger, H.L. (1990). Implicit memory: Retention without remembering. *American Psychologist, 45,* 1043–1056.

Roediger, H.L., & Blaxton, T.A. (1987a). Retrieval modes produce dissociations in memory for surface information. In D.S. Gorfein & R.R. Hoffman (Eds.), *Memory and learning: The Ebbinghaus Centennial Conference* (pp. 349–379). Hillsdale, NJ: Lawrence Erlbaum Associates Inc.

Roediger, H.L., & Blaxton, T.A. (1987b). Effects of varying modality, surface features, and retention interval on priming in word-fragment completion. *Memory & Cognition*, *15*, 379–388.

Roediger, H.L., Buckner, R.L., & McDermott, K.B. (1999). Components of processing. In J.K. Foster & M. Jelicic (Eds.), *Memory: Systems, process, or function?* (pp. 31–65). Oxford: Oxford University Press.

Roediger, H.L., & Gallo, D.A. (2002). Levels of processing: Some unanswered questions. In M. Naveh-Benjamin, M. Moscovitch, & H.L. Roediger (Eds.), *Perspectives on human memory and cognitive aging: Essays in honour of Fergus Craik*. New York: Psychology Press.

Roediger, H.L., & McDermott, K.B. (1993). Implicit memory in normal human subjects. In F. Boller & J. Grafman (Eds.), *Handbook of neuropsychology*, Vol. 8 (pp. 63–131). Amsterdam: Elsevier.

Roediger, H.L., & McDermott, K.B. (1995). Creating false memories: Remembering words not presented in lists. *Journal of Experimental Psychology: Learning, Memory, & Cognition*, *21*, 803–814.

Roediger, H.L., & Srinivas, K. (1993). Specificity of operations in perceptual priming. In P. Graf & M.E.J. Masson (Eds.), *Implicit memory: New directions in cognition, development and neuropsychology*. (pp. 17–48). Hillsdale, NJ: Lawrence Erlbaum Associates Inc.

Roediger, H.L., Srinivas, K., & Weldon, M.S. (1989a). Dissociations between implicit measures of retention. In S. Lewandowsky, J.C. Dunn, & K. Kirsner (Eds.), *Implicit memory: Theoretical issues* (pp. 67–84). Hillsdale, NJ: Lawrence Erlbaum Associates Inc.

Roediger, H.L., Weldon, M.S., & Challis, B.H. (1989b). Explaining dissociations between implicit and explicit measures of retention: A processing account. In H.L. Roediger & F.I.M. Craik (Eds.), *Varieties of memory and consciousness: Essays in honor of Endel Tulving* (pp. 3–41). Hillsdale, NJ: Lawrence Erlbaum Associates Inc.

Schacter, D.L. (1990). Perceptual representation systems and implicit memory: Toward a resolution of the multiple memory systems debate. *Annals of the New York Academy of Sciences*, Vol. 608, (pp. 543–571).

Slamecka, N.J., & Graf, P. (1978). The generation effect: Delineation of a phenomenon. *Journal of Experimental Psychology: Human Learning and Memory*, *4*, 592–604.

Sommers, M.S., & Lewis, B.P. (1999). Who really lives next door: Creating false memories with phonological neighbors. *Journal of Memory & Language*, *40*, 83–108.

Squire, L.R. (1987). *Memory and the brain*. New York: Oxford University Press.

Srinivas, K., Greene, A.J., & Easton, R.D. (1997). Visual and tactile memory for 2-D patterns: Effects of changes in size and left–right orientation. *Psychonomic Bulletin & Review*, *4*, 535–540.

Srinivas, K., & Roediger, H.L. (1990). Classifying implicit memory tests: Category association and anagram solution. *Journal of Memory & Language*, *29*, 389–412.

Tenpenny, P.L., & Shoben, E.J. (1992). Component processes and the utility of the conceptually-driven/data-driven distinction. *Journal of Experimental Psychology: Learning, Memory, & Cognition*, *18*, 25–42.

Treisman, A. (1964). Monitoring and storage of irrelevant messages in selective attention. *Journal of Verbal Learning and Verbal Behavior*, *3*, 449–459.

Tulving, E. (1972). Episodic and semantic memory. In E. Tulving & W. Donaldson (Eds.), *Organization and memory* (pp. 381–403). New York: Academic Press.

Tulving, E. (1983). *Elements of episodic memory*. London: Oxford University Press.

Tulving, E. (1999). Study of memory: Processes and systems. In J.K. Foster & M. Jelicic (Eds.), *Memory: Systems, process, or function?* (pp. 11–30). New York: Oxford University Press.

Tulving, E. (2002). Does memory encoding exist? In M. Naveh-Benjamin, M. Moscovitch, & H.L. Roediger (Eds.), *Perspectives on human memory and cognitive aging: Essays in honour of Fergus Craik* (pp. 6–27). New York: Psychology Press.

Tulving, E., & Schacter, D.L. (1990). Priming and human memory systems. *Science*, *247*, 301–306.

Tulving, E., Schacter, D.L., & Stark, H.A. (1982). Priming effects in word-fragment completion are independent of recognition memory. *Journal of Experimental Psychology: Human Learning and Memory*, *8*, 336–342.

Tulving, E., & Thompson, D.M. (1973). Encoding specificity and retrieval processes in episodic memory. *Psychological Review*, *80*, 352–373.

Vaidya, C.J., Gabrieli, J.D.E., Keane, M.M., Monti, L.A., Gutierrez-Rivas, H., & Zarella, M.M. (1997). Evidence for multiple mechanisms of conceptual priming on implicit memory tests. *Journal of Experimental Psychology: Learning, Memory and Cognition*, *23*, 1324–1343.

Van Essen, D.C., Anderson, C.H., & Felleman, D.J. (1992). Information processing in the primate visual system: An integrated systems perspective. *Science*, *255*, 419–423.

Warrington, E.K., & Weiskrantz, L. (1968). A study of learning and retention in amnesic patients. *Neuropsychologia*, *6*, 283–291.

Warrington, E.K., & Weiskrantz, L. (1970). Amnesic syndrome: Consolidation or retrieval? *Nature*, *228*, 628–630.

Weldon, M.S. (1991). Mechanisms underlying priming on perceptual tests. *Journal of Experimental Psychology: Learning, Memory, & Cognition*, *17*, 526–541.

Weldon, M.S., & Coyote, K.C. (1996). Failure to find the picture superiority effect in implicit conceptual memory tests. *Journal of Experimental Psychology: Learning, Memory and Cognition*, *22*, 670–686.

Weldon, M.S., & Roediger, H.L. (1987). Altering retrieval demands reverses the picture superiority effect. *Memory and Cognition*, *15*, 269–280.

Wertsch, J.V. (1979). *The concept of activity in Soviet psychology*. New York: M.E. Sharpe, Inc.

Wheeler, M.A., & Roediger, H.L. (1992). Disparate effects of repeated testing: Reconciling Ballard's (1913) and Bartlett's (1932) results. *Psychological Science, 3*, 240–245.

Wheeler, M.E., Petersen, S.E., & Buckner, R.L. (2000). Memory's echo: Vivid recollection activates modality specific cortex. *Proceedings of the National Academy of Sciences, 97*, 11125–11129.

MEMORY, 2002, *10* (5/6), 333–338

Organisation: What levels of processing are levels of

George Mandler

University of California, San Diego, USA, and University College London, UK

The psychology of thought and memory has historically been concerned with a struggle between associationism and its opponents. Organisation theory—in part an offspring of Gestalt concepts—has been the most successful and vocal of these contenders. The levels-of-processing framework has been a part of the effort to overcome associationist predilections. Aspects of principles of organisation and of the recent history of organisation theory are presented, followed by an analysis of the levels-of-processing approach in terms of organisational concepts.

The history of human experimental psychology in the early 20th century was marked in the United States by the hegemony of behaviourism and in particular stimulus–response behaviourism (the theories of Hull and Spence rather than Skinner). I have suggested elsewhere that the so-called cognitive revolution was as much an attempt to overcome stimulus–response associationist positions as it was a struggle against classical behaviourism (Mandler, in press). However, the struggle against associationism was not new and was not confined to the United States. For example, George Humphrey suggested in 1951 that the history of the psychology of thinking consists mainly of an unsuccessful revolt against the doctrine of associationism. The attempt typically was one of trying to understand the appearance and observation of associative links and connections in terms of some underlying theory.[1] Solomon Asch once noted: "It may even be in order to entertain the possibility that it is not necessary, nor perhaps fruitful, to be an associationist in the study of associations" (Dixon &

Horton, 1968, p. 227). One such attempt to understand the appearance of associative phenomena was organisation theory which flourished briefly in the 1960s/70s.

In the early days of the 21st century when associationism has once again asserted its dominance and organisation has receded from public view, it is appropriate to review the levels-of-processing approach which is, in principle, another non-associationist development. This is apparently the third review of the relationship between organisation theory and levels of processing. The volume that first reviewed the levels approach in 1979 barely alluded to its relation to organisation theory (Cermak & Craik, 1979). That same year Battig and Bellezza (1979) presented the first review of that relationship, and the second review by Bower and Bryant followed in 1991. These reviews seem to recur every 10–12 years. It is possible that eventually their point will become obvious. I will not repeat the arguments made by my predecessors who had tried to show, as I will, that the levels project approaches and partially incorporates basic organisational processes. First I set the scene in which the levels approach emerged.

In the early 1970s the battles for the establishment of the not-so-new cognitive psychology (cf. Mandler, in press) were just about over. One

---

[1] Some years ago I suggested the possibility that structural characteristics may arise, under certain specified conditions, from associative links (Mandler, 1962). This may be true of some simple structures, but is unlikely for major meaningful units.

Requests for reprints should be sent to George Mandler, Department of Psychology, University of California, San Diego, 9500 Gilman Drive, La Jolla, CA 92093-0109, USA. Email: gmandler@ucsd.edu

DOI:10.1080/09658210244000153

sidelight of the dispute had been the attempt to overcome the strictures of associationism which had forever been the bane of a psychology of thinking. The notion that any set of words or items or mental representations (depending on one's particular theoretical predilections) could become "associated"—i.e., being given one would produce, generate, arouse the other one(s)—was rejected as reductionist and mechanical and not in keeping with apparent complexities of human memory. Associationism had been found wanting for some time, even by John Locke who noted that association of ideas was an inadequate explanation for human reasoning. The latter needed semantic connections among ideas derived from our experience and expressed in relations such as "union" and "correspondence" (Locke, 1690, II, xxxiii, 5). In the process of the cognitive (r)evolution a variety of notions were offered that were to replace both stimulus–response behaviourism and its blood cousin—classic associationism. Most of the developments of the 1950s and the rejection of the associationist S–R behaviourist approaches called themselves "cognitive" and had aspects of organisational principles in their structure. I shall argue that levels of processing was not only just one of these attempts but a specific instance of a movement to reinstate the notion of "meaning" and its progenitor—organisation.

I do not want to enumerate the specifics of Craik and Lockhart's (1972) levels-of-processing approach—that has been done extensively and repeatedly, and is implied by the various perspectives in this journal. Most generally the notion is that the orienting task specifies what aspects of an item will be encoded, so that tasks that require elaborate semantic encoding will have more complex encodings and retrieval aspects available than items that require only orthographic information during encoding. Specific details are not relevant here. In fact, as Bower (1991) suggests, successive developments of levels theory have brought it closer to general organisational principles (cf. Craik & Tulving, 1975; Jacoby & Craik, 1979). What is important is that levels of processing are effective—orienting tasks influence degree of recall. The specific relationship between the levels approach and principles of organisation starts with an introduction to the latter.

There were some earlier relevant forays towards the notion that organisation was important, one of the central ones being Thorndike's notion of "belongingness"—that words often have a meaningful sense of "belonging" together (Thorndike, 1932). The concept of organisation in human memory first appeared as a major concept in an application of Gestalt principles by George Katona (1940). However, an important forerunner was G.E. Müller in his pathbreaking monograph on memory (1911–13). Katona used many of Müller's insights on organisation in his book, and Wolfgang Köhler concluded from Müller's work that "...intentional memorizing amounts to intentional organizing" (Köhler, 1947, p. 263), which may well serve as the motto for this discussion.[2] Katona, following Wertheimer (1921), considered memorial material to be meaningful when the existence and quality of the parts are determined by the structure of the whole. Another presentation of organisation theory and attack on associationism by Köhler noted that "whatever factors favor organization in primary experience must at the same time favor association, retention, and therefore recall" (Köhler, 1941, p. 492). In general, meaning, organisation, and structure are used interchangeably in these suggestions. Take for example Garner's similar approach, though not in the field of memory. "By structure I mean the totality of the relations between events. Meaning ... refers to the entire set of relations ... [and] meaning as structure [implies] that the structure itself is meaningful" (Garner, 1962, p. 141). In his approach, Katona emphasised grouping and the notion that organisation is a process that establishes or discovers the formation and perception of groupings; it is a requirement for memorisation.

I was instrumental in introducing the next stage of interest in organisation. I presented a limited approach to the problem of organisation in 1967 by arguing for organisation, and the hierarchical organisation of words in particular, as determining factors in memory for sets of words (Mandler, 1967). The definition of organisation postulated the formation, availability, and use of consistent relations among the members of a set or subsets such as groups, concepts, categories, and chunks. This was accompanied by a series of experiments that demonstrated how people imposed organisation/categories on sets of items, and how the use of these categories constructed hierarchies and determined memorial performance. Ten years later I developed this theme further, dealt with possible criticisms, and added new evidence

---

[2] I am indebted to a paper by Murray and Bandomir (2000) for the insights into Müller's contribution to organisation theory.

(Mandler, 1977). My early attempts were followed by a number of experiments in the literature and in 1970 Bower reviewed these general principles together with additional experimental illustrations. In support of the notion of hierarchical organization, Bower (1970) concluded that such "...schemes ... are particularly effective retrieval plans" (p. 18).

The organisational approach not only rejected associationist approaches but also brought the problem of meaning back into experimental psychology. Meaning is—as Garner argued persuasively—identified with the structure of the material. The structure of a text, just as the structure in which the representation of a word is embedded, is its meaning. A mental event or object is meaningful to the extent that it is part of a larger, more extensive, and usually more intricate organisation. A nonsense syllable is "meaningless" only to the extent that it fails to provide obvious links or ties to groupings or other mental organisations. The notion of organisation was used extensively in the late 1960s and early 1970s in the psychology of memory, even generating a volume on the topic in 1972 (Tulving & Donaldson, 1972). "Organisation" was then used widely to include the organisational, i.e., categorical/grouping, approach, but also any other usually non-associative relations such as linguistic and semantic aspects of words and texts.

As Bower (1991) noted, the "Mandler Manifesto" ran out of steam in the later 1970s and was replaced in part by new models of the old (but enriched) associational processes. Although the levels-of-processing theory can be presented as part of this new development, I shall argue here that it was in fact another way of approaching truly organisational processes.

How can the levels approach be shown to be a variant of, or at least consistent with, principles of organisation? There are in fact indications that organisational notions were in the background of the levels approach. For example, in the original presentation we find, within a paragraph, the following locutions: "...meaningful stimuli are compatible ... with existing cognitive structure.... Retention is a function of depth ... and ... its compatibility with the analysing structures ... will determine the depth to which it is processed" (Craik & Lockhart, 1972, p. 676). Structures and meaning are allusions to organisation, although the commitment is not quite complete. For example, the paper also notes that categorisation of words involves incidental learning. The

reference (p. 677) is to an experiment in Mandler (1967) in which we showed that in terms of memory performance instruction to memorise words is equivalent to instruction to categorise them. The point was that categorisation established the appropriate organisation, as do instructions to memorise; no "learning" is involved.

Over the years there have been several attempts to produce a theoretical account for the levels approach to memory. Bradshaw and Anderson (1982) specified three kinds of theories that try to explain the levels approach: The first, which they called the *encoding-appropriateness* theory, claims that encoding and retrieval requirements are more similar during deep processing. This is related to Tulving's encoding specificity principle, which originally made the strong assertion that "...the properties of an effective retrieval cue are determined by the specific encoding operations performed by the system on the input stimuli" (Tulving & Thomson, 1973, p. 359). This strong version of the encoding specificity principle seems to violate both anecdotal and experimental evidence. In addition, remindings, unrelated to the initial situation (cf. Anderson & Pichert, 1978), lead us very often to information that not only is demanded by the often haphazard cues that are present at any one time, but that clearly was not encoded with them. The second set of models were called the *distinctiveness theories*. However, as Bradshaw and Anderson noted, there are a number of cases in the literature in which distinctiveness is changed or modified and memory improved when the material to be remembered is further elaborated. Which brings us to the third set, the *elaboration models*. Bradshaw and Anderson argued that elaboration, which develops relations between the target item and other mental contents either by network or referential redundancy, increases the probability of recall of to-be-remembered material. Central to the argument is the notion that "elaborative abilities are a function of what one knows about that domain" (p. 167). In a set of experiments with episodes of meaningful materials Bradshaw and Anderson showed that such elaboration in fact accounts for much of the levels phenomena. They concluded that interconnectedness and elaboration of facts is superior to any explanation based on encoding or distinctiveness. Facts to be remembered are best remembered when supported by related facts; another statement of the importance of the structure—the meaning—of the material.

With respect to the Anderson and Pichert (1978) study mentioned earlier, I should add that their demonstration has been relatively neglected in the experimental literature. They showed that changing the theme of the memory search also recovers previously apparently unreachable memorial items. For example, inspecting a house as a prospective buyer produces one set of memories, whereas later changing the search focus to being a potential robber produces additional memory items. If this can be shown to be generally true it suggests that structure not only organises material at the time of encounter (encoding) but also reorganises previously encountered material into new structures and new retrievals.

In general I want to defend the notion that all memorial phenomena that involve recall or search processes are examples of organisational processes. Or, to recall Asch's quote given earlier, organisation explains the appearance of associative phenomena. I have argued that most memorial representations involve one of several organisational structures: *coordinate* structures in which mutual and/or symmetric relations exist among the relevant events; *subordinate* structures in which the organisation is hierarchical and particular events are subordinate or superordinate to other parts of the structure; and *proordinate* structures that are serially organised, represented by many syntactic structures and lists (Mandler, 1979b; 1985b, p. 101). In addition to these organisations of memory there are retrieval-like processes that are not organisational but are more like perceptual pattern-matching processes. The major example is involved in the experience of familiarity that forms part of the recognition phenomena.[3]

One can approach all memory phenomena as a combination of integrative/perceptual processes on the one hand and elaborative/organisational ones on the other hand (Mandler, 1979a, 1980, 1982). Integrative processes involve the unitisation of mental units. Such integration is based in large part on the activation and interactive activation of the component part of some representation. Eventually the target item acts as a unit and is, for example, "recognised" as being familiar and having previously occurred. Elaboration assimilates a target unit into existing mental

structures. Elaboration, the relating of to-be-remembered material to other semantic or cognate mental contents, can be seen as a subcategory of general organisational principles. Elaboration always occurs, and can only occur, with respect to existing meaningful contents or structures. The target material is incorporated into existing structures, or—as is likely in many cases—its previously existing relations to existing structures are highlighted and emphasised. Elaboration is always consistent with existing or new meaningful units, never—as in basic associationist positions—haphazard or purely situational. The integration/elaboration position was recapitulated with additional experimental demonstrations by Bower (1996).

We have applied the general reasoning about organisational processes and the importance of meaning to a number of problems in the area of memory. In an extensive study of the coordinate structures represented in paired-associate acquisition (Mandler, Rabinowitz, & Simon, 1981) we demonstrated that pairs of words are acquired as whole, meaningful units. Among other results the data showed that retrieval of any one item implies the retrieval of the intact pair. It is encoding into a meaningful structure that provides recall, as the levels approach also insists. In Graesser and Mandler (1978) it was shown that retrieval from natural categories follows a topical and temporal pattern of access to subcategories, consistent with a hierarchical model of item retrieval. More specifically, as retrieval proceeds the "number of items per [categorical] cluster does not increase,... but rather, more clusters are emitted" (p.96). In other words memorial retrieval depends on the availability of structured subcategories.

There are some *caveats* that need be entered about the levels position. Craik and Lockhart (1972) made some assertions that I believe are too restrictive. First, they suggest repeatedly that different levels of processing are different levels of *perceptual* processing. There is now adequate evidence that processing of incoming material is frequently directly conceptual, apparently without perceptual analysis (see Marcel, 1980, 1983, and schema theory in general). Second, they note that "trace persistence is a function of depth of analysis, with deeper levels of analysis associated with more elaborate, longer lasting, and stronger traces. [And] ... the organism is normally concerned only with the extraction of meaning from the stimuli..." (p. 675). Organisation theory would

---

[3] Although recognition of previously encountered events is more complicated than this brief description (Mandler, 1980).

argue that any "deep" analysis at encoding is a process of finding structures (meanings) into which the target item "fits". It is this degree of organised fitness, of appropriateness of organised structures to the target item, that determines elaboration, time course, and "strength". There is no meaning to be extracted, whatever that may imply—meaning is in the structure in which the item is embedded. So-called shallow processing, e.g., the identification of letters, provides no access to meaningful structures and therefore fails in the retrieval of target items. However, it may be useful for perceptual, pattern-matching purposes (cf. Mandler, 1980).

In summary, organisation and the resulting structures and meanings are an important aspect of memory retention and retrieval. Organisation is also relevant to an understanding of memory as it functions in daily life. Memory does not primarily involve the situational encoding of stimuli, nor the learning of lists, nor the identification of previously encountered events. All of these may occur in everyday life, although some of these events that once seemed simple are in fact complicated. Our memories occur in the speech and thoughts of daily life as we interact with others and (internally) with ourselves. The father of the more artificial aspects of memory experiments, Hermann Ebbinghaus, already noted that everyday memory is not represented by the experimental approach (Ebbinghaus, 1885; see also Mandler, 1985a). As we speak and retrieve what we know, we are primarily concerned with conveying meanings—not words or lists or items. Meanings require organisation as I have defined it here. Unfortunately associationism never directly addressed problems of meaning, and its current incarnation—connectionism—tends to avoid it, just like its predecessors.

REFERENCES

Anderson, R.C., & Pichert, J.W. (1978). Recall of previously unrecallable information following a shift in perspective. *Journal of Verbal Learning and Verbal Behavior, 17,* 1–12.

Battig, W.F., & Bellezza, F.S. (1979). Organization and levels of processing. In C.R. Puff (Ed.), *Memory organization and structure* (pp. 321–346). New York: Academic Press.

Bower, G.H. (1970). Organizational factors in memory. *Cognitive Psychology, 1,* 18–46.

Bower, G.H. (1996). Reactivating a reactivation theory of implicit memory. *Consciousness and Cognition, 5,* 27–72.

Bower, G.H., & Bryant, D.J. (1991). On relating the organizational theory of memory to levels of processing. In W. Kessen, A. Ortony, & F. Craik (Eds.), *Memories, thoughts, and emotions: Essays in honor of George Mandler* (pp. 149–168). Hillsdale, NJ: Lawrence Erlbaum Associates Inc.

Bradshaw, G.L., & Anderson, J.R. (1982). Elaborative encoding as an explanation of levels of processing. *Journal of Verbal Learning and Verbal Behavior, 21,* 165–174.

Cermak, L.S., & Craik, F.I.M. (Eds.). (1979). *Levels of processing in human memory.* Hillsdale, NJ: Lawrence Erlbaum Associates Inc.

Craik, F.I.M., & Lockhart, R.S. (1972). Levels of processing: A framework for memory research. *Journal of Verbal Learning and Verbal Behavior, 11,* 671–684.

Craik, F.I.M., & Tulving, E. (1975). Depth of processing and the retention of words in episodic memory. *Journal of Experimental Psychology: General, 104,* 268–294.

Dixon, T.R., & Horton, D.L. (Eds.). (1968). *Verbal behavior and general behavior theory.* Englewood Cliffs, NJ: Prentice Hall.

Ebbinghaus, H. (1885). *Ueber das Gedächtnis: Untersuchungen zur experimentellen Psychologie.* Leipzig: Duncker und Humblot.

Garner, W.R. (1962). *Uncertainty and structure as psychological concepts.* New York: Wiley.

Graesser, A.C.II., & Mandler, G. (1978). Limited processing capacity constrains the storage of unrelated sets of words and retrieval from natural categories. *Journal of Experimental Psychology: Human Learning and Memory, 4,* 86–100.

Humphrey, G. (1951). *Thinking; an introduction to its experimental psychology.* New York: John Wiley.

Jacoby, L.L., & Craik, F.I.M. (1979). Effects of elaboration of processing at encoding and retrieval: Trace distinctiveness and recovery of initial context. In L.S. Cermak & F.I.M. Craik (Eds.), *Levels of processing in human memory.* Hillsdale, NJ: Lawrence Erlbaum Associates Inc.

Katona, G. (1940). *Organizing and memorizing.* New York: Columbia University Press.

Köhler, W. (1941). On the nature of associations. *Proceedings of the American Philosophical Society, 84,* 489–502.

Köhler, W. (1947). *Gestalt psychology.* New York: Liveright.

Locke, J. (1690). *An essay concerning humane understanding* (Book 2). London: Thomas Basset.

Mandler, G. (1962). From association to structure. *Psychological Review, 69,* 415–427.

Mandler, G. (1967). Organization and memory. In K.W. Spence & J.T. Spence (Eds.), *The psychology of learning and motivation: Advances in research and theory* (pp. 328–372). New York: Academic Press.

Mandler, G. (1977). Commentary on "Organization and memory". In G.H. Bower (Ed.), *Human memory: Basic processes* (pp. 297–308). New York: Academic Press.

Mandler, G. (1979a). Organization and repetition: Organizational principles with special reference to rote learning. In L.-G. Nilsson (Ed.), *Perspectives on memory research* (pp. 293–327). Hillsdale, NJ: Lawrence Erlbaum Associates Inc.

Mandler, G. (1979b). Organization, memory, and mental structures. In C.R. Puff (Ed.), *Memory organization and structure*. New York: Academic Press.

Mandler, G. (1980). Recognizing: The judgment of previous occurrence. *Psychological Review, 87*, 252–271.

Mandler, G. (1982). The integration and elaboration of memory structures. In F. Klix, J. Hoffmann, & E.v.d. Meer (Eds.), *Cognitive research in psychology*. Amsterdam: North Holland.

Mandler, G. (1985a). From association to structure. *Journal of Experimental Psychology: Learning, Memory, and Cognition, 11*, 464–468.

Mandler, G. (1985b). *Cognitive psychology: An essay in cognitive science*. Hillsdale, NJ: Lawrence Erlbaum Associates Inc.

Mandler, G. (in press). Origins of the cognitive (r)evolution. *Journal of the History of the Behavioral Sciences*.

Mandler, G., Rabinowitz, J.C., & Simon, R.A. (1981). Coordinate organization: The holistic representation of word pairs. *American Journal of Psychology, 94*, 209–222.

Marcel, A.J. (1980). Conscious and preconscious recognition of polysemous words: Locating the selective effects of prior verbal context. In R.S. Nickerson (Ed.), *Attention and performance VIII*. Hillsdale, NJ: Lawrence Erlbaum Associates Inc.

Marcel, A.J. (1983). Conscious and unconscious perception: An approach to the relations between phenomenal experience and perceptual processes. *Cognitive Psychology, 15*, 238–300.

Müller, G.E. (1911–1913). Zur Analyse der Gedächtnistätigkeit und des Vorstellungsverlaufes, I., II., III. Teil. *Zeitschrift für Psychologie, Ergänzungsband 5,8,9*.

Murray, D.J., & Bandomir, C.A. (2000). G.E. Müller (1911, 1913, 1917) on memory. *Psychologie et Histoire, 1*, 208–232. [Also available at http://lpe.psycho.univ-paris5.fr/membres/Murray.htm]

Thorndike, E.L. (1932). *The fundamentals of learning*. New York: Teacher's College.

Tulving, E., & Donaldson, W. (Eds.). (1972). *Organization of memory*. New York: Academic Press.

Tulving, E., & Thomson, D.M. (1973). Encoding specificity and retrieval processes in episodic memory. *Psychological Review, 80*, 359–380.

Wertheimer, M. (1921). Untersuchungen zur Lehre von der Gestalt. I. *Psychologische Forschung, 1*, 47–58.

MEMORY, 2002, *10* (5/6), 339–343

Limits and province of levels of processing: Considerations of a construct

Michael J. Watkins

Rice University, Texas, USA

The limitations and the proper domain of the levels-of-processing construct are considered. Following a sketch of the historical context in which the construct was proposed, some of its empirical and conceptual shortcomings are noted. The argument is then advanced that the notion of memory being determined by depth of processing should be regarded as a functional or purely psychological heuristic, immune to certain criticisms appropriate to the realms of cognitive science and cognitive neuroscience.

The idea that memory depends on depth of processing (Craik & Lockhart, 1972) was proposed in the wake of the cognitive revolution of the 1950s and 1960s. One effect of the revolution was a relocation of the locus of control of behaviour. Such control had, at least in the USA, long been vested in environmental stimuli, but with remarkable rapidity it became entrusted to the organism itself, now ennobled as an "information processor". Another, and more practical, effect was to return memory, and indeed cognition generally, to the forefront of the research agenda.

Control over memory was attributed to three key mental capacities. The first was attention. Some stimuli could be selected for processing and others largely ignored, according to the direction of the experimenter and, presumably, the desires of the subject (Broadbent, 1958; Cherry, 1953). Next, the rememberer was endowed with the ability to rehearse. Rehearsal served not only to retain in mind events no longer present in the outside world, but also to enhance the likelihood of these events being subsequently remembered (Johnson, 1980). The third key development in the evolution of memory control was Craik and Lockhart's (1972) proposal that the likelihood of remembering something depended not merely on its having gained our attention during its occurrence or on how much it had been rehearsed after its occurrence, but also on how deeply it was processed.

The standard paradigm for demonstrating the effects of processing level entails presenting subjects with a list of items, such as random words, and requiring a response to an orienting question about each item in turn (Craik, 1973; Craik & Tulving, 1975; Hyde & Jenkins, 1969, 1973). The critical manipulation is the nature of the question posed. Specifically, this question may call for processing that is assumed to be shallow ("Is this word in upper case?"), moderate ("Does this word rhyme with 'care'?"), or deep ("Does this word fit into the sentence, 'She put the ~ into her pocket'?"). A subsequent test shows that memory is typically strongest for words subjected to a deep orienting task and weakest for words subjected to a shallow orienting task. For the examples given, level of processing is likely to be confounded with processing time, but its effect persists when the confound is removed (Craik & Tulving, 1975). Importantly, the effect tends to be large relative to those of most other variables of concern to researchers.

Requests for reprints should be sent to Michael J. Watkins, Department of Psychology, Rice University, 6100 Main, Houston, Texas 77005, USA. Email: watkins@rice.edu

http://www.tandf.co.uk/journals/pp/09658211.html

DOI:10.1080/09658210244000162

LIMITATIONS

Craik and Lockhart's (1972) paper has been extraordinarily influential. According to one thoughtful review, it has been recently suggested that it has been the most influential cognitive psychology paper since at least as far back as Miller's (1956) magical number seven paper (Roediger & Gallo, 2001). At the same time, it has not been free of criticism. Indeed, it would be a good bet for the most criticised cognitive psychology paper since the cognitive revolution. The criticisms are of two kinds, empirical and conceptual.

Empirically, limitations of the levels-of-processing construct are not hard to identify. The proportion of established memory findings explicable in terms of levels of processing is, in fact, extremely small. For example, it does not include the fundamental fact that memory for a given event tends to fade over time or that the rate at which it does so depends on the would-be rememberer's prior and subsequent experiences. Nor does the levels-of-processing construct shed light on the dependence of memory at any given moment on prevailing conditions. For example, it says nothing about why a word's prior presentation as a member of a list is more likely to be recollected in response to its re-presentation as a reminder than in response to an instruction to report as many words from the list as possible, or why the latter instruction would be more effective than a situation in which no reference is made to the prior list presentation and instead the subject's clothes are set afire.

Moreover, the levels-of-processing construct fails to account even for a variety of findings that also arise from the very orienting procedure in which the construct is grounded. Roediger and Gallo (2001) identified six such findings: (i) recall is more likely for words given a positive response to the orienting question than for words given a negative response, (ii) the levels-of-processing effect occurs even if the subjects are aware that their memory will be subsequently tested and so might reasonably be expected to supplement the processing called for by a comparatively shallow task with covert deep processing, (iii) the levels-of-processing effect occurs even if the orienting questions are withheld for several seconds after the presentation of their respective target words, (iv) orienting tasks that might reasonably be expected to require the same level of processing may give rise to appreciably different levels of recall, (v) items subjected to a shallow orienting task often have an appreciable probability of being recalled, and (vi) the effect of orienting task is modulated by type of memory test.

Of the more conceptual criticisms of the levels-of-processing construct, perhaps the most familiar is the charge that it is circular: Level of recall depends on depth of processing, and depth of processing is gauged from level of recall. There is some validity to this charge, for there is no principled metric of depth of processing independent of memory. But just as Darwin's theory of natural selection has utility despite a similar problem (propagation depends on adaptation, and adaptation is gauged from propagation), so too has the levels-of-processing construct. Even if unprincipled, it is intuitively plausible that judging a written word according to its sound is a deeper process than saying whether it is in upper case but not so deep as a judgement on the basis of its meaning. To the extent that the relative levels of processing occasioned by two or more orienting tasks are more obvious than their effects on memory, the levels-of-processing construct can be said to have explanatory power.

A second conceptual criticism is, perhaps, more serious. Although the relative processing levels for the three standard orienting tasks are obvious enough, it is harder to identify tasks that recruit other levels. Consequently, it is questionable whether levels of processing can be properly regarded as a continuum.

Such scepticism could be taken one step further by challenging the assumption that the processing engendered by structural, phonemic, and semantic orienting tasks are linearly related. Many years ago, when the levels-of-processing notion was still young, I explored this assumption by presenting words in combinations of orienting tasks. Some words were presented once and others twice. Some once-presented words were presented in the context of a structural orienting task, and others were presented in the context of a semantic orienting task. For some twice-presented words both orienting tasks were structural, for others both were semantic, and for yet others one was structural and the other semantic. If structural, phonemic, and semantic processing are linearly related, and if recall is strictly a function of depth of processing, then the probability of recalling a twice-presented item should be determined solely by the task requiring the deeper processing. I expected that the effects of processing at one level would be only partially subsumed by the effects of processing at a deeper level, and I worked out what I thought was a foolproof method for specifying the functional relation between the two orienting tasks. Suffice it to say that the method was not foolproof, for it could not take account of the effect of repeating an item even with the same orienting task. I was, of course, expecting mere repetition of presentation to enhance memory. Strictly speaking, such an enhancement is at variance with levels-of-processing theory, but the essence of the theory can be maintained by ascribing the variance to a random element that each act of encoding superimposes on an average depth of processing for the encoding conditions. Probability of recalling a twice-presented item would then correspond to the deeper of two encodings, and so on average it would be greater than the probability of recalling a once-presented item. The problem that arose in my study was that the effect of repetition was superadditive—greater than would have arisen if the two presentations functioned completely independently. I see no way of accommodating such a finding within the levels-of-processing perspective.

As Craik and Lockhart (1972) freely conceded from the outset, any notion of the levels-of-processing construct as a comprehensive account of memory is absurd. Any one of the limitations of the construct just noted could be regarded as fatal to such a notion, and countless other limitations could be added. Why, then, has it not succumbed to the neglect that has been the fate of most other memory constructs, older and younger? Why, indeed, is it being celebrated in this volume?

One way of accounting for at least some of the resilience of the levels-of-processing construct is to appeal to what might be loosely characterised as its power-to-complexity ratio. As we have seen, the power of the levels-of-processing construct is very strong within a limited domain and non-existent beyond, a state of affairs that might be crudely captured with a designation of moderate power. There is nothing moderate about its complexity—it is trivial. The idea of some items or events being processed more deeply than others is intuitive and nontechnical, and so readily grasped. Thus, its power-to-complexity ratio is high. The idea can of course be elaborated to increase its power—by appeal, for example, to the notion of spread or elaboration of processing (Craik & Tulving, 1975)—but only at the cost of increasing its complexity.

Also, even the shortcomings of levels-of-processing theory can be instructive. Thus, to the extent that performance varies with depth of orienting task, removal of this variance brings the residual variance to the fore and changes our idea of what is most in need of explanation. The finding that words eliciting a positive response to orienting questions are better recalled than words eliciting a negative response is an excellent case in point. And even the finding of supperadditive effects of repetition, though unaccountable in levels-of-processing terms, arose from an exploration of levels-of-processing theory and led to further research and eventually to an interesting conclusion, namely that as few as two presentations of an item no more than a minute ago can be recalled generically (i.e., as a pair) rather than individually (Watkins & Kerkar, 1985).

PROVINCE

Its limitations aside, what is the proper place or function of the levels-of-processing construct in the conceptual scheme of things? Craik and Lockhart (1972) stressed that it should be regarded as a framework and not as a theory. Their reasons, however, were not entirely clear on either count. Given the sharply limited range of findings it addresses, framework seems too expansive; principle might be more apt. But whether framework or principle, it serves to organise a set of findings and, as we have seen, it submits to testable predictions. Why, then, would it be denied the status of theory?

An answer may be sought in the culture of cognitive research. With the advent of the cognitive revolution, the concept of theory became fused with that of model. People became information-processing machines, and the explanation of a finding came to mean devising a mechanism that would, at least in principle, simulate the finding. The result was an era of personalised theorising. As noted elsewhere (Watkins, 1990), a psychology student was allowed to borrow his or her advisor's theory for the purpose of a master's thesis, but a model of his or her own became a requirement for a PhD dissertation.

Naturally, personalised theorising is immensely satisfying. But does it bring wider or more permanent benefits? Does it even contribute to the public enterprise that is science? There may be close to universal agreement that psychology is the science of mind and behaviour, but mechanistic information-processing models are not inherently psychological or even scientific. Whereas psychology is concerned with mind and behaviour, information processing has to do with the material world of mechanism. Whether cast as a system of stores, as traces of experiences or of the processing associated with experiences, or as activations of specific sites within some sort of permanent structure, memory is transformed from a mental state or behavioural propensity into a tangible thing, and as such is conceptualised from what is essentially an artificial intelligence perspective. The conception is thus more one of engineering than of science (Watkins, 1991).

The dominance of the information-processing conception of memory has not gone unchallenged. Over the past 10 or 15 years, memory has been increasingly cast in neurological terms. The identification of the neurological underpinnings of memory is as scientific as it is exciting, but it is not psychology. Memory should not be confused with its physical substrate. No matter how successful this field may prove, it is unlikely to shed much light on either the experience of memory or its behavioural consequences.

What about the status of the levels-of-processing construct? Is its province that of reified memory, whether of the engineering realm of hypothetical information-processing constructs or of the natural science realm of neurological substrate? Or is it of the psychological, or functional, realm?

Like virtually all other memory researchers since the cognitive revolution, Craik and Lockhart (1972) reified memory. Thus, they assumed that the processing they invoked was captured and preserved over time by a memory trace. On the other hand, their focus was confined to the processing itself. They considered the memory trace to be merely a byproduct of perceptual and cognitive analysis; as Tulving (2001) has vigorously complained, they postulated no separate process for encoding the products of the perceptual or cognitive analysis into the memory trace. In short, Craik and Lockhart reified with a marked lack of enthusiasm, but enough to run into trouble.

The memory trace forms the core of any reification of memory, for it serves to bridge the temporal gap between an event and its recollection. For memory *per se*, on the other hand, the notion of memory trace simply does not arise (Watkins, 1990). To assume that the idea of a memory trace is necessary for an adequate account of memory just because it is necessary for

a mechanical simulation of memory or for an account of its physical substrate is to confuse the realms of mind and matter. Craik and Lockhart (1972) appear to have made this confusion. The idea that memory for an item or event depends on the depth to which it is processed is best considered as a relatively powerful psychological principle. Of course, it can be reified in any number of hypothetical mechanical systems, and it can even be applied to the physiological substrate of memory (Velichkovsky, 2001). Such applications would be open to criticisms of the sort levelled by Tulving (2001), but conceived as a purely psychological theory or principle, the notion of memory being determined by level of processing would not. Its role in organising findings and formulating research would be undiminished. We might still ask whether the changes in the ability to remember that occur over the course of a lifetime, or the differences among individuals at a given stage of life, are attributable to different levels of processing; or how far memory deficiencies can be mediated through strategies of deepening perceptual and cognitive analyses; and so on. With its power undiminished, formulating the levels-of-processing notion in purely psychological or functional terms would reduce its complexity to a minimum and thereby raise its power-to-complexity ratio to an even higher level.

REFERENCES

Broadbent, D.E. (1958). *Perception and communication*. London: Pergamon Press.

Cherry, E.C. (1953). Some experiments on the recognition of speech with one and with two ears. *Journal of the Acoustical Society of America, 25*, 975–979.

Craik, F.I.M. (1973). A "levels of analysis" view of memory. In P. Pliner, L. Krames, & T.M. Alloway (Eds.), *Communication and affect: Language and thought* (pp. 45–65). New York: Academic Press.

Craik, F.I.M., & Lockhart, R.S. (1972). Levels of processing: A framework for memory research. *Journal of Verbal Learning and Verbal Behavior, 11*, 671–684.

Craik, F.I.M., & Tulving, E. (1975). Depth of processing and the retention of words in episodic memory. *Journal of Experimental Psychology: General, 104*, 268–294.

Hyde, T.S., & Jenkins, J.J. (1969). Differential effects of incidental tasks on the organization of recall of a list of highly associated words. *Journal of Experimental Psychology, 82*, 472–481.

Hyde, T.S., & Jenkins, J.J. (1973). Recall for words as a function of semantic, graphic, and syntactic orienting tasks. *Journal of Verbal Learning and Verbal Behavior, 12*, 471–480.

Johnson, R.E. (1980). Memory-based rehearsal. In G. Bower (Ed.), *The psychology of learning and motivation* (Vol. 14). New York: Academic Press.

Miller, G.A. (1956). The magical number seven, plus or minus two: Some limits on our capacity for processing information. *Psychological Review, 63,* 81–97.

Roediger, H.L.III., & Gallo, D.A. (2001). Levels of processing: Some unanswered questions. In M. Naveh-Benjamin, M. Moscovitch, & H.L. Roediger III (Eds.), *Perspectives on human memory and cognitive aging: Essays in honour of Fergus Craik* (pp. 28–47). New York: Psychology Press.

Tulving, E. (2001). Does memory encoding exist? In M. Naveh-Benjamin, M. Moscovitch, & H.L. Roediger III (Eds.), *Perspectives on human memory and cognitive aging: Essays in honour of Fergus Craik* (pp. 6–27). New York: Psychology Press.

Velichkovsky, B.M. (2001). Levels of processing: Validating the concept. In M. Naveh-Benjamin, M. Moscovitch, & H.L. Roediger III (Eds.), *Perspectives on human memory and cognitive aging: Essays in honour of Fergus Craik* (pp. 48–71). New York: Psychology Press.

Watkins, M.J. (1990). Mediationism and the obfuscation of memory. *American Psychologist, 45,* 328–335.

Watkins, M.J. (1991). An experimental psychologist's view of cognitive science. In R.G. Lister & H.J. Weingartner (Eds.), *Perspectives on cognitive neuroscience* (pp. 132–144). New York: Oxford University Press.

Watkins, M.J., & Kerkar, S.P. (1985). Recall of a twice-presented item without recall of either presentation: Generic memory for events. *Journal of Memory and Language, 24,* 666–678.

MEMORY, 2002, *10* (5/6), 345–348

Levels of processing:
A view from functional brain imaging

Lars Nyberg

Umeå University, Sweden

This paper briefly reviews two central assumptions of the levels-of-processing framework in the light of findings from recent PET and fMRI studies: First, to address the suggestion that memory traces can be seen as records of analyses carried out for the purposes of perception and comprehension, studies on encoding–retrieval overlap in brain activation patterns are considered. Second, to address the suggestion that deeper, more semantic, processing results in more durable traces, studies of how encoding activity relates to processing depth and subsequent memory performance are examined. The results show that some of the sensory regions that are activated during initial perception are subsequently reactivated during retrieval, and activity in frontal and medial-temporal brain regions is related to depth of processing and level of memory performance. Collectively, these results provide support for central components of the levels framework.

In their classical paper on levels of processing, Craik and Lockhart (1972) suggested that memory traces can be seen as records of analyses carried out for the purposes of perception and comprehension, and that deeper, more semantic, processing results in more durable traces. In the present review, these suggestions will be discussed in the light of findings from recent PET and fMRI studies. First, findings from studies on encoding-retrieval overlap in brain activation patterns will be considered. If a memory trace is a record of processes recruited during initial perception and comprehension, then the activation of a trace during subsequent retrieval should involve reactivation of processes that were engaged during the original experience. Accordingly, encoding–retrieval overlap in brain activation patterns is expected. Second, studies of brain activity associated with deeper, more semantic, processing will be considered. If there are different levels of processing, then the activity in some brain regions should vary as a function of the depth of processing. Moreover, given that deeper processing results in more durable traces, activity in regions associated with deeper processing should predict subsequent memory performance.

ENCODING–RETRIEVAL OVERLAP IN BRAIN ACTIVITY

Several recent PET and fMRI studies have examined the relation between brain activity during intial encoding/acquisition and subsequently during episodic memory retrieval (see Nyberg, 2002). Collectively, these studies provide converging evidence that some of the brain regions that are activated during encoding are reactivated during retrieval. As summarised in Table 1, overlap is observed in different brain regions depending on the specific type of event information. However, regardless of type of information, the emerging view is that only a subset of the encoding-related activation pattern is reactivated during retrieval, and the sites where overlap is observed tend to be in secondary rather than in primary areas (Nyberg, 2002; see also Wheeler, Petersen, & Buckner, 2000).

Requests for reprints should be sent to Lars Nyberg, Department of Psychology, Umeå, Sweden. Email: Lars.Nyberg@psy.umu.se
Supported by the Swedish Science Council. I am grateful to Roberto Cabeza for help with the illustrations.

DOI:10.1080/09658210244000171

TABLE 1

Functional brain imaging studies of episodic encoding–retrieval overlap

Type of event information	Select overlap sites
Auditory information	
Nyberg et al. (2000)	Bilateral auditory responsive cortex (BA 21/22)
Wheeler et al. (2000)	Left superior temporal cortex (BA 22)
Visual information	
Roland & Gulyás (1995)	Precuneus & angular gyrus
Wheeler et al. (2000)	Precuneus (7) & left fusiform cortex (19)
Spatial information	
Köhler et al. (1998)	Right inferior parietal cortex (BA 39/40)
Moscovitch et al. (1995)	Right inferior parietal cortex (BA 39/40)
Persson & Nyberg (2000)	Bilateral inferior parietal cortex (BA 39/40)
Motor information	
Nyberg et al. (2001)	Left ventral motor cortex (BA 4/6)

BA = Brodmann area

In several of the studies on encoding–retrieval overlap, reactivation of encoding-related activity has been demonstrated when the test required the subjects to retrieve specific perceptual information. For example, Persson and Nyberg (2000) contrasted retrieval of spatial event information (trying to remember if centrally presented stimuli had appeared on the left or right side of the computer screen at encoding) with conditions that did not involve retrieval of spatial information. It was found that regions in the dorsal visual stream were differentially activated during retrieval of spatial information. These regions overlapped with regions that were activated when subjects tried to memorise location information. While such findings of encoding–retrieval overlap provide some support that memory traces can be seen as records of analyses carried out for the purpose of perception and comprehension, there is also evidence that the act of directing one's attention to a certain modality can lead to activation of brain regions that are engaged during real perception (see Cabeza & Nyberg, 2000). Therefore, in order to provide strong evidence that it is the actual process of remembering that accounts for the reactivation pattern, it is critical to control for potential confounding effects of selective attention. This has been done in several studies.

One example comes from an experiment by Nyberg, Habib, McIntosh, and Tulving (2000) on "incidental reactivation". In that study, subjects encoded single visual words and visual words paired with sounds. Subsequently, they were given yes/no recognition tests of visually presented words. It was found that recognition of words that had been encoded in the context of auditory sounds was associated with increased activity in auditory regions of the temporal lobes. This was so despite the fact that there was no demand to try to remember auditory information (hence the term "incidental"). These and related findings (e.g., Nyberg et al., 1995) provide strong evidence that perceptual information is part of memory traces and that the brain regions where such information is stored are spontaneously reactivated at retrieval.

Findings that sensory brain regions are recruited during episodic memory tests can be related to the original proposal in the levels-of-processing framework that "there is usually no need to store the products of preliminary analyses" (Craik & Lockhart, 1972, p. 675). "Preliminary analyses" referred to analyses of various sensory features (e.g., brightness and loudness). However, subsequent studies showed that records of sensory information can persist to affect later performance over a long retention interval (e.g., Conway & Gathercole, 1987). Indeed, in later developments of the framework, it was concluded that "sensory or surface aspects of stimuli are not always lost rapidly as we claimed in 1972" (Lockhart & Craik, 1990, p. 98). Thus, functional brain imaging findings of activation of sensory brain regions during standard episodic memory tests are consistent with the levels framework.

LEVELS OF BRAIN ACTIVITY

The preceding discussion concerned recruitment of sensory brain regions during encoding. In addition, a number of PET and fMRI studies have found that intentional as well as incidental encoding processes are associated with prefrontal brain regions. In an early study (Kapur et al., 1994), brain activity associated with semantic processing (living/nonliving classification) was contrasted with activity associated with a more shallow processing task (detecting the presence or absence of the letter a). It was found that deeper, semantic processing was associated with increased activity in left prefrontal regions (BAs 10, 45, 46, 47). Similar findings have been observed in a number of studies (e.g., Grady, McIntosh, Rajah, & Craik, 1998; Kapur et al., 1996, for reviews, see Buckner, Logan, Donaldson, & Wheeler, 2000; Cabeza & Nyberg, 2000), and it has been suggested that encoding processes are more strongly associated with the left than the right frontal lobe (Nyberg, Cabeza & Tulving, 1996, 1998; Tulving, Kapur, Craik, Moscovitch, & Houle, 1994; see Figure 1). It should be noted, however, that regions of the right frontal lobe have been engaged during encoding of nonverbal information such as unfamiliar faces (e.g., Kelley et al., 1998).

In their early study on neuroanatomical correlates of the levels-of-processing effect (Kapur et al., 1994), Kapur, Craik and colleagues proposed that increased activity in left inferior frontal regions leads to more readily retrievable memory traces. This proposal was supported by the results from an event-related fMRI study (Wagner et al., 1998). In that study, brain activity was measured while subjects made semantic decisions (abstract or concrete word?). After a retention interval, they were given a recognition memory test. The event-related design permitted identification of

brain regions that showed increased activity during encoding of words subsequently remembered compared with those subsequently forgotten. It was found that correct recognition that was accompanied by high confidence was associated with increased activity in several left prefrontal regions, and also in left temporal regions (parahippocampal/fusiform gyri). The results of a related event-related fMRI study on encoding of indoor and outdoor scences provided additional support that level of prefrontal and medial temporal (parahippocampal) activity predicted subsequent memory performance (Brewer, Zhao, Desmond, Glover, & Gabrieli, 1998). In the latter study the frontal activation was right-lateralised and the temporal activity was bilateral, which likely reflected the nonverbal nature of the stimuli. These event-related fMRI findings provide strong support that increased activity in frontal regions leads to more readily retrievable memory traces.

CONCLUSION

In conclusion, functional brain imaging studies have identified neuroanatomical correlates of two central components of the levels-of-processing framework; that memory traces are records of analyses related to perception and comprehension, and that deeper semantic processing yields more durable records. Specifically, brain-imaging findings suggest that input from frontal regions to medial temporal regions affects the binding of sensory information into memory traces (cf., Buckner et al., 2000). Clearly, levels-of-processing has proven to be a useful framework not only

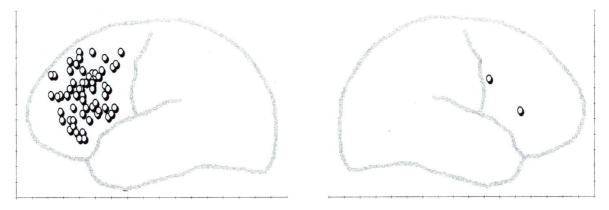

Figure 1.   Results from published PET and fMRI studies of intentional and incidental encoding (based on Cabeza & Nyberg, 2000). Each circle represents the result of one experimental contrast. Only frontal peaks are plotted. Courtesy of Roberto Cabeza.

for memory research but also for cognitive neuroscience.

REFERENCES

Brewer, J.B., Zhao, Z., Desmond, J.E., Glover, G.H., & Gabrieli, J.D.E. (1998). Making memories: Brain activity that predicts how well visual experience will be remembered. *Science, 281,* 1185–1187.

Buckner, R.L., Logan, J.M., Donaldson, D.I., & Wheeler, M.E. (2000). Cognitive neuroscience of episodic memory encoding. *Acta Psychologica, 105,* 127–139.

Cabeza, R., & Nyberg, L. (2000). Imaging cognition II: An empirical review of 275 PET and fMRI studies. *Journal of Cognitive Neuroscience, 12,* 1–47.

Conway, M.A., & Gathercole, S.E. (1987). Modality and long-term memory. *Journal of Memory and Language, 26,* 341–361.

Craik, F.I.M., & Lockhart, R.S. (1972). Levels of processing: A framework for memory research. *Journal of Verbal Learning and Verbal Behavior, 11,* 671–684.

Grady, C.L., McIntosh, A.R., Rajah, M.N., & Craik, F.I.M. (1998). Neural correlates of the episodic encoding of pictures and words. *Proceedings of the National Academy of Sciences, USA, 95,* 2703–2708.

Kapur, S., Craik, F.I.M., Tulving, E., Wilson, A.A., Houle, S., & Brown, G.M. (1994). Neuroanatomical correlates of encoding in episodic memory: Levels of processing effect. *Proceedings of the National Academy of Sciences, USA, 91,* 2008–2011.

Kapur, S., Tulving, E., Cabeza, R., McIntosh, A.R., Houle, S., & Craik, F.I.M. (1996). The neural correlates of intentional learning of verbal materials: A PET study in humans. *Cognitive Brain Research, 4,* 243–249.

Kelley, W.M., Miezin, F.M., McDermott, K.B., Buckner, R.L., Raichle, M.E., Cohen, N.J., Ollinger, J.M., Akbudak, E., Centuro, T.E., Snyder, A.Z., & Petersen, S.E. (1998). Hemispheric specialization in human dorsal frontal cortex and medial temporal lobe for verbal and nonverbal memory encoding. *Neuron, 20,* 927–936.

Köhler, S., Moscovitch, M., Winocur, G., Houle, S., & McIntosh, A.R. (1998). Networks of domain-specific and general regions involved in episodic memory for spatial location and object identity. *Neuropsychologia, 36,* 129–142.

Lockhart, R.S., & Craik, F.I.M. (1990). Levels of processing: A retrospective commentary on a framework for memory research. *Canadian Journal of Psychology, 44,* 87–112.

Moscovitch, M., Kapur, S., Köhler, S., & Houle, S. (1995). Distinct neural correlates of visual long-term memory for spatial location and object identity: A positron emission tomography study in humans. *Proceedings of the National Academy of Sciences, USA, 92,* 3721–3725.

Nyberg, L. (2002). Where encoding and retrieval meet in the brain. In L.R. Squire & D.L. Schacter (Eds.), *Neuropsychology of memory* (pp. 193–203). New York: The Guilford Press.

Nyberg, L., Cabeza, R., & Tulving, E. (1996). PET studies of encoding and retrieval: The HERA model. *Psychonomic Bulletin & Review, 3,* 134–147.

Nyberg, L., Cabeza, R., & Tulving, E. (1998). Asymmetric frontal activation during episodic memory: What kind of specificity? *Trends in Cognitive Sciences, 2,* 419–420.

Nyberg, L., Habib, R., McIntosh, A.R., & Tulving, E. (2000). Reactivation of encoding-related brain activity during memory retrieval. *Proceedings of the National Academy of Sciences, USA, 97,* 11120–11124.

Nyberg, L., Petersson, K.-M., Nilsson, L.-G., Sandblom, J., Åberg, C., & Ingvar, M. (2001). Reactivation of motor brain areas during explicit memory for actions. *NeuroImage, 14,* 521–528.

Nyberg, L., Tulving, E., Habib, R., Nilsson, L.-G., Kapur, S., Houle, S., Cabeza, R., & McIntosh, A.R. (1995). Functional brain maps of retrieval mode and recovery of episodic memory. *NeuroReport, 7,* 249–252.

Persson, J., & Nyberg, L. (2000). Conjunction analysis of cortical activations common to encoding and retrieval. *Microscopy Research and Technique, 51,* 39–44.

Roland, P.E., & Gulyás, B. (1995). Visual memory, visual imagery, and visual recognition of large field patterns by the human brain: Functional anatomy by positron emission tomography. *Cerebral Cortex, 5,* 79–93.

Tulving, E., Kapur, S., Craik, F.I.M., Moscovitch, M., & Houle, S. (1994). Hemispheric encoding/retrieval asymmetry in episodic memory: Positron emission tomography findings. *Proceedings of the National Academy of Sciences, USA, 91,* 2016–2020.

Wagner, A.D., Schacter, D.L., Rotte, M., Koutsaal, W., Maril, A., Dale, A.M., Rosen, B.R., & Buckner, R.L. (1998). Building memories: Remembering and forgetting of verbal experiences as predicted by brain activity. *Science, 281,* 1188–1191.

Wheeler, M.E., Petersen, S.E., & Buckner, R.L. (2000). Memory's echo: Vivid remembering reactivates sensory-specific cortex. *Proceedings of the National Academy of Sciences, USA, 97,* 11125–11129.

MEMORY, 2002, *10* (5/6), 349–364

Level of processing and the process-dissociation procedure: Elusiveness of null effects on estimates of automatic retrieval

Alan Richardson-Klavehn

Goldsmiths College, University of London, UK

John M. Gardiner

University of Sussex, UK

Cristina Ramponi

MRC Cognition and Brain Sciences Unit, Cambridge, UK

We describe two experiments that used the process-dissociation procedure to investigate the effects of level of processing on estimates of controlled and automatic retrieval processes in word-stem completion tasks. Despite our best endeavours, we found the null effect of level of processing on estimates of automatic retrieval reported by Toth, Reingold, and Jacoby (1994) elusive. Estimates of automatic retrieval were not independent of level of processing but inversely related to it. In part, the reason was that, following deeper levels of processing, instructions to exclude recollected words led to floor effects. But the inverse relationship persisted even when floor effects were avoided. Only participants who were not given strict instructions in the exclusion task—and who also qualified as lax responders based on answers in a structured post-test interview—showed no effect of level of processing on estimates of automatic retrieval. This null effect apparently occurred because these participants failed to exclude words that they in fact recollected from the study list. This finding violates the critical assumption that in this task participants exclude recollected words. The results are therefore paradoxical. Successful replication of the null effect occurred only under conditions that preclude the very use of the procedure. This paradox has important implications for views on how consciousness should be conceived in relation to memory.

The levels-of-processing approach has been a dominant one in the science of memory ever since its inception some 30 years ago (Craik & Lockhart, 1972). This achievement is remarkable, considering not only the many trenchant criticisms the approach attracted almost immediately, and which it still continues to attract (e.g., Roediger & Gallo, 2001; Tulving, 2001), but also the empirical refutations, quite soon after the approach was launched, of most of its initial assumptions. Few theoretical approaches have proved so robust. What survives in current theorising, however, is not the form the approach initially took, but its essence. The essential ideas are that memory is a by-product of ongoing cognitive processing—so that memory can only be understood in the context of other cognitive functions—and that encoding of new memories and retrieval of pre-existing knowledge are intimately interlinked. These core ideas continue to have profound

Requests for reprints should be sent to Alan Richardson-Klavehn, Department of Psychology, Goldsmiths College, University of London, New Cross, London SE14 6NW, UK. Email: a.richardson-klavehn@gold.ac.uk

This research was supported by Grant 000236225 from the Economic and Social Research Council to the second and first authors. The first author's work on this article was also facilitated by a senior research fellowship at the Department of Neurology II, University of Magdeburg, Germany, funded by the Wissenschaftsgemeinschaft Gottfried Wilhelm Leibniz.

DOI:10.1080/09658210244000180

implications, not least for the understanding of higher-order brain processes. But the levels-of-processing approach has also proved to be of continuing value in a much more pragmatic role. In this latter role, level-of-processing manipulations act as tools for determining the presence or absence of other components of memory—both processing components, and components of consciousness.

This critical pragmatic role for level of processing is well exemplified in relation to the validation of memory estimates from the process-dissociation procedure (Jacoby, 1991, 1998). This procedure is designed to distinguish between the processes of controlled retrieval, which is held to be associated with recollection, and of automatic retrieval, which is held to be associated with familiarity. The contributions the two processes make to performance are estimated from inclusion and exclusion tasks. For example, in the inclusion version of a word-stem completion task, participants are instructed to use word stems (i.e., the first three letters of words) as cues to recollect studied words but, if recollection fails, to complete the stems with the first word that comes to mind. In the exclusion version of a word-stem completion task, participants are also instructed to use the stems as cues to recollect studied words, but are told not to produce those words, and instead to complete the stems with first different word that comes to mind (Jacoby, 1998). Because recollection acts in opposing ways in these two tasks, it follows that subtracting the proportion of studied words produced in the exclusion task from the proportion of studied words produced in the inclusion task gives an estimate of the controlled retrieval process. Studied words produced in the exclusion task are attributed to the automatic retrieval process. But the two processes are assumed to be independent, so that automatic retrieval may also occur in conjunction with controlled retrieval, and studied words associated with both processes would be excluded rather than produced. It follows that automatic retrieval must be estimated by dividing the proportion of studied words produced in the exclusion task by one minus the estimate for controlled retrieval, thus boosting observed exclusion performance to take account of the probability that the two processes co-occur. The probability of automatic retrieval, thus estimated, is compared to the baseline probability of completing a stem with a target word in the absence of prior study. This baseline probability is often estimated by averaging the proportions of stems completed with unstudied target words in the inclusion and exclusion conditions (e.g., Jacoby, Toth, & Yonelinas, 1993). If the probability of automatic retrieval exceeds baseline, automatic retrieval is said to have occurred.

A common way of validating the estimates from a new measurement procedure is to compare them with some benchmark. With regard to controlled and automatic retrieval processes, level of processing has become something of a gold standard. Level of processing has very well-known effects on performance in traditional intentional memory tests, as well as on recollective experiences (e.g., Gardiner, Java, & Richardson-Klavehn, 1996). And it has been widely believed that level of processing does not influence perceptual priming in traditional incidental memory tests, including incidental word-stem completion tests (e.g., Roediger, Weldon, Stadler, & Riegler, 1992; for reviews, see Richardson-Klavehn & Bjork, 1988; Roediger & McDermott, 1993). Thus estimates of automatic retrieval from the process-dissociation procedure in word-stem completion would be validated if they showed no level-of-processing effect. Toth et al. (1994) reported just such an outcome. They found similar estimates of automatic retrieval for deep and shallow study processing, and greater estimates of controlled retrieval for deep compared with shallow study processing. In the same experiment, they found a significant level-of-processing effect on priming in a traditional incidental word-stem completion test—a result implying that this test had been contaminated by controlled retrieval.

By contrast, we have generally not found level-of-processing effects in incidental word-stem completion tests (see Richardson-Klavehn, Clarke, & Gardiner, 1999, Table 2; see also Schott, Richardson-Klavehn, Heinze, & Düzel, 2002). And we have found null effects of level of processing on estimates of automatic retrieval from the process-dissociation procedure elusive. In a series of experiments (Richardson-Klavehn & Gardiner, 1995, 1996, 1998) we have encountered floor effects in attempting to use the process-dissociation procedure in conjunction with level-of-processing manipulations. That is, our participants have been excellent at suppressing deeply studied words in exclusion tasks, resulting in low exclusion proportions, and low estimates of automatic retrieval. The estimates of automatic retrieval were consequently below the baseline for unstudied words, and hence uninterpretable, because such an outcome corresponds to negative repetition priming. In the most recent study (Richardson-Klavehn & Gardiner, 1998), this result was particularly puzzling, because we had taken special care to avoid a floor effect. We had used normative data to obtain a high baseline stem-completion rate, we had used the deep study task that Toth et al. (1994) had used, we had given participants more words to study than Toth et al. (1994) had, and we had delayed the test with a filler test in an effort to make exclusion more difficult, in contrast to the immediate test used by Toth et al. (1994).

Given this puzzling failure, the goal of the experiments described in the present article was to make further attempts to replicate the null effect of level of processing on estimates of automatic retrieval found by Toth et al. (1994). In our 1998 experiment there were additional procedural differences from Toth et al.'s (1994) experiment that could have made exclusion performance easier rather than more difficult. Most notably, inclusion and exclusion trials were blocked, rather than randomised within the test list. Because of our uncertainty about the cause of the difference in results, here we elected to implement the design reported by Toth et al. (1994) more closely, and we report the results of two experiments using this design.

EXPERIMENT 1

As in Toth et al. (1994, Expt. 1), our participants studied words at a deep and a shallow level of processing, after which half received standard incidental test instructions, and the other half received inclusion and exclusion test instructions, with the inclusion and exclusion trials mixed randomly in the test list. The deep (pleasantness rating) and shallow (vowel comparison) study tasks, the study and test list length and construction, and the counterbalancing procedures all followed the design reported by Toth et al. (1994). We deviated from the procedure reported by Toth et al. (1994) in three respects, but none of these differences should have made replication of their results less likely. Most notably, the exclusion test instructions used by Toth et al. (1994) were to treat exclusion trials as a test of creativity that involved responding with nonstudied words, but *direct retrieval* instructions have now been recommended instead (e.g., Jacoby, 1998; Toth et al., 1994), so we elected to use these. The critical

feature of the direct retrieval instructions appears to be that participants are told to use each stem as a cue to recall a studied word on both inclusion and exclusion trials, and then to include or exclude, depending on the instruction for that trial. Only if unable to recall a studied word are they to use the first word coming to mind. These instructions are designed to avoid the possibility that participants use a *generate–recognise strategy* which, on exclusion trials, consists of responding with the first word coming to mind, and omitting studied words only if the first word coming to mind is a studied one. Such a strategy is held to have two effects (e.g., Jacoby, 1998): First, it makes consciously controlled retrieval redundant with automatic retrieval, thus violating the assumption that these forms of retrieval are independent. Second, it induces participants to exclude words, whether studied or unstudied, that spring to mind automatically, thus causing a feeling of familiarity, but which are not specifically recollected as belonging to the study list. It is an assumption of the procedure that words automatically retrieved, but not recollected as belonging to the study list, appear in overt exclusion responses, even if they are associated with feelings of familiarity.

There were two further differences from the procedure reported by Toth et al. (1994). First, in the shallow study task Toth et al. (1994) had participants give a yes/no response to whether the currently presented word shared any vowels with the preceding word, whereas we had them count the number of vowels the two words had in common. Second, we used a small number of practice test trials, to check that participants had understood the test instructions, whereas Toth et al. (1994) had administered the critical test immediately following the test instructions.

Method

Participants and design. A total of 48 male and female student volunteers from City University, London, were paid to participate. All participants studied a list of 96 words, which consisted of 80 critical words and 16 filler words. They then received a test consisting of 160 three-letter word stems, half of which could be completed with the critical studied target words. Study task was manipulated within subjects, with each participant performing a deep study task for one half of the studied words (i.e., for 40 critical and 8 filler words) and a shallow study task for the other half. Test instructions were manipulated between subjects, with 24 participants receiving incidental test instructions for all of the test items, and 24 participants receiving inclusion test instructions for one half of the test items and exclusion test instructions for the other half. The 96 study trials were presented in four blocks of 24, with 20 critical and 4 filler words in each block. Half the participants in each test condition performed the deep study task for the words in Blocks 1 and 3, and the shallow study task for the words in Blocks 2 and 4; the other half performed the shallow study task for the words in Blocks 1 and 3, and the deep study task for the words in Blocks 2 and 4. In the group that received inclusion and exclusion test instructions, the order of inclusion and exclusion test trials was randomised separately for each participant.

Materials. The critical materials were 160 five-letter words, mostly singular nouns, with a median frequency of 20.0 per million words of print (interquartile range = 5.0–80.5), according to the Kucera and Francis (1967) count. They were assembled from materials developed on the basis of normative data by Richardson-Klavehn and Gardiner (1998), and materials published by Graf and Williams (1987), Jacoby (1998), and Roediger et al. (1992). The filler words were 16 five-letter words selected from the *Concise Oxford English Dictionary* (Allen, 1990). The three-letter stems corresponding to all these words were non-overlapping, and could be completed with at least one five-letter word besides the target word. The 160 stems corresponding to the critical words were presented to all participants in the test phase. The critical words were assigned into eight sets of 20 words each (Sets A–H), and each participant studied only four of these sets. One set was presented in each block of 24 study trials, together with four filler words. The fillers were always the first two and the last two words in a block, and the order of the critical words within each block was randomised separately for each participant. Which four sets of critical words were studied was counterbalanced across participants. Either Sets A–D or Sets E–H were studied, and the four sets that were studied were presented in a fixed order (i.e., A, B, C, D or E, F, G, H). Because order of study tasks was counterbalanced, each word appeared in each study task across participants, and was also an unstudied target word at test. Crossing the two counterbalancing variables

resulted in four unique study formats, and six participants in the incidental test group were assigned to each format. For participants in the group receiving inclusion and exclusion instructions, the critical words in one of the two deep study blocks were tested with inclusion instructions, and words in the other study block were tested with exclusion instructions. The same procedure was followed for the words in the shallow study blocks. In addition, two of the four unstudied sets of words were assigned to inclusion instructions, and the other two were assigned to exclusion instructions. Assignment of words to test instructions was counterbalanced, and this counterbalancing variable was crossed with the two counterbalancing variables at study, resulting in eight unique study–test formats within the inclusion/exclusion group. Three participants were assigned to each of these formats. The test stems were presented in an order randomised separately for each participant. Because words were assigned to test instructions prior to randomization in the inclusion/exclusion group, this procedure ensured that the order of inclusion test and exclusion test trials was also randomised for each participant in that group.

Apparatus and procedure. All study and test stimuli were presented on a Macintosh Powerbook 5300 computer controlled by Hypertalk software and equipped with an external mouse. The participants were tested individually, and were told that the experiment involved simple verbal tasks. On each study trial a word appeared on the screen, and the participant responded by using the mouse to click on one of seven buttons labelled 0–6, whereupon the next word appeared. Instructions on the screen informed the participants which kind of judgement to make for each block of trials. In the deep study task they were to judge the pleasantness of the word on a 7-point scale (0 = very unpleasant; 6 = very pleasant), and in the shallow study task they were to judge how many vowels the current word shared with the previous word (0 = no shared vowels). For the latter task, they were instructed select zero for the first word in the block (which was a filler word), because there was no previous word.

Instructions for the test phase immediately followed the last study block. The participants in the incidental group were instructed to complete each stem with the first five-letter word that came to mind, or to pass if none came to mind. They were told that overlap in materials meant that some of

TABLE 1

Mean proportions of stems completed with studied and unstudied target words, and mean estimates of controlled and automatic retrieval in Experiment 1

Measure	Estimate	Studied		Unstudied
		Deep	Shallow	
Incidental		.51	.49	.34
Inclusion		.58	.50	.31
Exclusion		.06	.34	.31
	Controlled	.52	.16	–
	Automatic	.10 (.18)	.41 (.40)	–

Means in parentheses were computed omitting participants with exclusion proportions of zero in the deep study condition. For comparison with the current data, Toth et al. (1994) reported deep, shallow, and unstudied completion proportions of .51, .45, and .30 (incidental), .60, .47, and .29 (inclusion), and .33, .43, and .26 (exclusion); controlled retrieval estimates of .27 (deep) and .03 (shallow); and automatic retrieval estimates of .42 (deep) and .45 (shallow).

the stems corresponded to words seen earlier, but that it was absolutely critical that they simply use the first word coming to mind, regardless of whether that word was seen earlier or not. The participants in the inclusion/exclusion group were told to use the stem as a cue to recall a five-letter word shown earlier, and that each stem would be accompanied by the message "OLD" or "NEW". If the message was "OLD", they were to complete the stem with the studied word. If the message was "NEW", they were not to use the studied word, but they were to complete the stem with a different five-letter word, or to pass if no alternative five-letter word came to mind. Regardless of the instruction accompanying the stem, if they could not recall a studied word, they were to complete the stem with the first word coming to mind, or to pass if no completion at all came to mind. All participants were additionally instructed not to respond with names of people, places, or products. The stems appeared on the screen in uppercase letters, accompanied by the "OLD"/"NEW" instruction only for participants in the inclusion/exclusion group. All participants typed two letters to complete each stem, and these letters appeared on the screen just to the right of the stem. They then pushed the "return" key to initiate the next trial. If they entered only one letter, or more than two letters, the computer prompted them to enter exactly two letters. To pass, they pushed the "return" key without entering any letters. Just prior to the critical test trials, all participants were asked to complete eight stems, which all corresponded to filler items shown in the study phase. For participants in the inclusion/exclusion group,

half of these practice trials were inclusion trials and half were exclusion trials, presented in random order. After these practice trials, the experimenter checked that participants in the inclusion/exclusion group had understood the instructions, and reiterated to participants in the incidental group that it was critical to respond with the first word coming to mind.

Results and discussion

The mean proportions of stems completed with target words are shown in Table 1, together with the mean estimates of controlled and automatic retrieval. For comparison with the current data, the values reported by Toth et al. (1994) are listed in the note to the table. The significance criterion for inferential tests was .05, with two-tailed tests where applicable. The results from the incidental and inclusion tests were similar to those of Toth et al. (1994), except that priming in the current incidental test did not show a significant level-of-processing effect. The proportion of target words used to complete stems when the targets had not been previously studied (henceforth referred to as baseline performance) did not differ between the tests, $t(46) = 1.26$, $SEM = .02$. Inclusion test performance was higher in the deep than in the shallow study condition, $t(23) = 6.57$, $SEM = .03$. By contrast, incidental test performance showed no difference between the deep and shallow study conditions, $t(23) = 1.05$, $SEM = .02$, although priming resulted in higher-than-baseline performance in both of these conditions, $t(23)s$ = 6.52 and 6.23, SEMs = .03 and .02, respectively.[1]

Baseline performance was identical for the inclusion and exclusion tests. The mean estimate of controlled retrieval was significantly higher for the deep than for the shallow study condition, $t(23)$ = 7.90, SEM = .04. Estimates of automatic retrieval were compared to a baseline obtained by averaging the inclusion and exclusion baselines for each participant. The mean estimate of automatic retrieval exceeded baseline only in the shallow study condition, $t(23)$ = 3.44, SEM = .03. The low mean estimate of automatic retrieval in the deep study condition occurred because 10 out of 24 participants excluded studied words perfectly (i.e., their exclusion proportion was zero), and because the remainder produced very few studied words. When participants with exclusion proportions of zero in the deep study condition were omitted, the mean estimate of automatic retrieval was still well below the unstudied baseline, and hence uninterpretable. (Note that we do not report tests of significance for uninterpretable estimates.)

In summary, the current results differed from those of Toth et al. (1994) in two respects. First, the level-of-processing effect on priming in the incidental test was small and nonsignificant, whereas it was significant in the prior experiment. The difference in results cannot reflect instructions which informed participants that they were likely to notice responding with studied words, but requested that they nevertheless always respond with the first word coming to mind, as Toth et al. (1994) also used these instructions. Second, exclusion performance in the deep study condition was much lower than in Toth et al.'s (1994) experiment, leading to an uninterpretable (i.e., below baseline) estimate of automatic retrieval.

Thus, null effects of level of processing on estimates of automatic retrieval continued to prove elusive, despite other close similarities between our experiment and that reported by Toth et al. (1994). Our participants studied exactly the same number of words as theirs, under very similar study conditions. Inclusion task performance levels were similar to theirs, as were baseline performance levels. The estimate of automatic retrieval in our shallow study condition was similar to the one they reported, and the incidental test data show similar levels of priming

to theirs. Nor do our data suggest that our participants adopted a generate–recognise strategy, despite receiving direct retrieval instructions. Jacoby (1998) argued that a generate–recognise strategy has two signatures: (a) inclusion test performance resembles incidental test performance, because participants are responding with the first word coming to mind; and (b) the baseline for the exclusion condition is lower than the baseline for the inclusion condition, because unstudied target words that come to mind fluently are excluded based on the feelings of familiarity caused by this fluency. These signatures, however, were absent.

EXPERIMENTS 2A AND 2B

In Experiments 2a and 2b we tested two groups of participants with the inclusion and exclusion instructions published by Toth et al. (1994). The critical difference relates to the exclusion instructions, which were to attempt to be creative by using nonstudied words, and are henceforth referred to as *creativity exclusion instructions*. For these groups, all other aspects of the design and procedure were also changed so as to conform *exactly* to those reported by Toth et al. (1994).

Experiments 2a and 2b also addressed the question of the basis on which studied words were suppressed on exclusion test trials. According to Jacoby (1998), studied words should only be excluded on the basis of recollection of the study episode, and not on the basis of familiarity, which is thought to accompany automatic retrieval. Exclusion on the basis of familiarity is thought to occur when participants adopt a generate–recognise strategy, and might be a cause of a floor effect on exclusion performance. To further check on this possibility, Experiment 2a also incorporated a group of participants who received Jacoby's (1998) *remember/know* instructions. The instructions regarding stem completion are similar to direct retrieval instructions for inclusion test trials. After completing each stem, the participants are instructed to indicate either (a) that they remember that they studied the word (i.e., they recollect contextual detail about the study event), or (b) that they know that they studied the word (i.e., the word seems familiar in the experimental context, but they do not recollect the study event), or (c) that the word was not studied. The assumption is that a direct retrieval strategy on exclusion trials would lead to remembered words,

---

[1] For brevity, we omit omnibus analyses of variance where specific comparisons were planned for theoretical reasons.

but not known or unstudied words, being suppressed. Exclusion performance is then estimated by subtracting the proportion of target words remembered from the overall proportion of target words produced. Jacoby (1998; see also Jacoby, Yonelinas, & Jennings, 1997) has argued that this procedure leads to similar results to the inclusion/exclusion procedure.

Experiment 2b incorporated a further group of participants who received the creativity exclusion instructions, but with the addition of a single sentence emphasising that it was necessary to pass on exclusion trials when they could not think of a nonstudied word. These instructions are henceforth referred to as *strict creativity instructions*. This modification was made on the basis of informal post-test reports by the inclusion/exclusion participants in Experiment 2a, some of whom reported that they had responded with studied words on exclusion trials because they could not think of an unstudied five-letter word. It is possible that the creativity exclusion instructions may have produced a desire to respond and not to pass, because passing could be seen as reflecting a lack of creativity. Alternatively, because the test was long (160 items), it is possible that the desire to be creative may have waned as it progressed. Finally, in Experiment 2b, reports of strategy on exclusion trials were elicited from all participants via a structured post-test interview. These reports were quantified using a blind rating system, and their relationship to exclusion performance was examined.

Method

Participants, design, and materials. A total of 96 male and female student volunteers from City University, London, were paid to participate, 48 in Experiment 2a and 48 in Experiment 2b. In Experiment 2a, 24 participants were assigned to inclusion/exclusion creativity instructions, and 24 were assigned to remember/know instructions. In Experiment 2b, all participants were assigned to inclusion/exclusion instructions, with 24 receiving exactly the same instructions as the inclusion/exclusion group in Experiment 2a, and 24 receiving the strict creativity instructions. Within experiments, assignment to groups was random.

The other aspects of the design and materials were identical to Experiment 1, with the exception that the assignment of study words to inclusion and exclusion test conditions was performed dif-

ferently.[2] Each of the eight sets of words (Sets A–H) used in Experiment 1 was further divided into two subsets (e.g., Sets A1 and A2). For half of the participants in the inclusion/exclusion group, subsets designated 1 were tested on inclusion trials, and subsets designated 2 were tested on exclusion trials. For the other half, subsets designated 2 were tested on inclusion trials, and subsets designated 1 were tested on exclusion trials. This procedure meant that half the words within each study block were tested with inclusion instructions and the other half were tested with exclusion instructions. With the counterbalancing of order of study conditions (Deep, Shallow, Deep, Shallow vs Shallow, Deep, Shallow, Deep), and of which sets of words were studied (A–D vs E–H), this procedure resulted in eight study–test formats, as in Experiment 1. Three participants in the inclusion/exclusion groups received each format. The inclusion/exclusion manipulation did not apply to the remember/know group in Experiment 2a, so that there were four counterbalancing formats for this group (as for the incidental test group in Experiment 1), and six participants were assigned to each format.

Apparatus and procedure. These were identical to Experiment 1, with the following exceptions: (a) The shallow study task involved judging whether or not each word shared any vowels with the previous word on the study list, and buttons labelled "yes" and "no" appeared on the screen. Participants were instructed to respond "no" for the first word in each study block (which was a filler word) given that there was no previous word. The buttons for the deep (pleasantness-rating) task were also changed so that responses ranged between 1 (least pleasant) and 7 (most pleasant). (b) There were no practice test trials following the test instructions. (c) The test instructions were either the inclusion/exclusion instructions published by Toth et al. (1994, p. 303), the remember/know instructions published by Jacoby (1998, pp. 24–25), or the inclusion/exclusion instructions published by Toth et al. (1994) with the addition of a sentence at the end stressing that participants should pass on exclusion trials when unable to think of a nonstudied word. (d) In the remember/

---

[2] We learned that Toth et al. (1994) had used a different method for assigning words to inclusion and exclusion trials than we had used in Experiment 1 (J.P. Toth, personal communication, November 1996). The Toth et al. (1994) article had not specified this detail.

TABLE 2
Mean proportions of stems completed with studied and unstudied target words, and mean
estimates of controlled and automatic retrieval in Experiments 2a and 2b

		Studied		
Measure	Estimate	Deep	Shallow	Unstudied
Inclusion/exclusion test: Creativity exclusion instructions (n = 48)				
Inclusion		.58	.48	.33
Exclusion		.21	.38	.31
	Controlled	.38	.10	–
	Automatic	.30 (.34)	.44 (.44)	–
Inclusion test: Remember/know instructions (n = 24)				
Inclusion		.62	.54	.36
"Remember"		.53	.10	.01
"Know"		.07	.18	.07
"New"		.03	.27	.29
	Exclusion	.09	.44	.35
	Controlled	.53	.10	–
	Automatic	.18 (.23)	.49 (.48)	–
Inclusion/exclusion test: Strict creativity exclusion instructions (n = 24)				
Inclusion		.60	.48	.31
Exclusion		.13	.35	.30
	Controlled	.48	.12	–
	Automatic	.21 (.27)	.41 (.42)	–

Means in parentheses were computed omitting participants with exclusion proportions
of zero in the deep study condition (six in the creativity group, five in the remember/know
group, and six in the strict creativity group).

know group, when participants typed in two letters
and pushed the "return" key on each trial, three
buttons labelled "remember", "know", and
"new" appeared on the screen, and participants
clicked on the appropriate button to indicate their
judgement. On "pass" trials (i.e., when participants pushed the "return" key without entering
any letters), these buttons did not appear. (e)
During debriefing of the remember/know group in
Experiment 2a, the experimenter asked participants for justifications of "remember" and
"know" responses, to check that these responses
had been used correctly (as, e.g., in Gardiner,
Ramponi, & Richardson-Klavehn, 1998). (f)
During debriefing of all participants in Experiment
2b there was a structured interview. Following two
introductory questions about difficulty of recalling
words on inclusion trials, the critical questions
were as follows: (i) When the message was
"NEW", did you find it difficult to come up with
new words? (ii) When the message was "NEW",
did the old words interfere with you coming up with
a novel completion? (iii) When the message was
"NEW", did you ever leave an old word in, maybe
because you pressed "return" and then realised it
was an old word, or maybe because you could not

think of a new word so you left the old one in, or
maybe at other times because you were not entirely
sure that it was an old word, but thought that it
might have been? The statements made in
response to these questions were noted by the
experimenter and then transcribed. The resulting
protocols were quantified by two independent
raters as to the care with which participants had
followed the exclusion instructions.

Results and discussion

The mean proportions of stems completed with
target words in Experiments 2a and 2b are shown
in Table 2, together with the mean estimates of
controlled and automatic retrieval. For the
remember/know test in Experiment 2a, Table 2
also shows the division of inclusion proportions
into "remember", "know", and "new" proportions, and the mean of the estimated exclusion
proportions. The exclusion proportions were
estimated for each participant by subtracting the
proportion of "remember" responses from the
total proportion of stems completed with target
words (see Jacoby, 1998).

For the first set of analyses we report, we merged the creativity exclusion groups from Experiments 2a and 2b, which were treated identically, in order to gain more stable data. Moreover, because inclusion and baseline performance was similar across the creativity, remember/know, and strict creativity groups, we report overall analyses of the inclusion and exclusion proportions with test instructions (creativity vs remember/know vs strict creativity) as a factor. The baseline proportions were subjected to a 3 (test instructions) by 2 (inclusion vs exclusion) mixed analysis of variance (ANOVA), which revealed only a marginal main effect of test instructions, $F(2, 93) = 2.74$, $MSE = .01$, reflecting somewhat higher overall baseline performance in the remember/know group compared with the other two groups. A further 3 (test instructions) by 2 (deep vs shallow) ANOVA on the inclusion proportions for studied words revealed only a main effect of level of processing, $F(1, 93) = 43.84$, $MSE = .01$, reflecting higher performance in the deep than in the shallow study condition. By contrast, a similar ANOVA on the exclusion proportions revealed an interaction between level of processing and test instructions, $F(1, 93) = 8.08$, $MSE = .01$, in addition to a main effect of level of processing, $F(1, 93) = 181.32$, $MSE = .01$. To analyse the interaction, separate one-way ANOVAs with test instructions (creativity vs remember/know vs strict creativity) as the factor were conducted on the exclusion proportions in the deep and shallow study conditions. Test instructions influenced exclusion performance in the deep study condition, $F(2, 93) = 5.51$, $MSE = .02$, and a Newman-Keuls test showed that this effect was attributable to a higher mean exclusion proportion in the creativity group than in the remember/know and strict creativity groups, with the latter two groups not differing from each other. The effect of test instructions in the shallow study condition was marginal, $F(2, 93) = 2.75$, $MSE = .05$, reflecting a somewhat higher mean exclusion proportion in the remember/know group compared with the other two groups, but no differences survived the Newman-Keuls test. A difference in this direction was to be expected, given the somewhat higher baseline performance in the remember/know group. Note that the lower exclusion mean in the deep study condition for the remember/know group compared with the creativity group occurred despite the somewhat higher scores in the shallow and baseline conditions.

Mean estimates of controlled retrieval were greater for the deep than the shallow study condition for the creativity group, $t(47) = 7.52$, $SEM = .04$, the remember/know group, $t(23) = 14.01$, $SEM = .03$, and the strict creativity group, $t(23) = 7.49$, $SEM = .05$. Mean estimates of automatic retrieval in the shallow study condition exceeded baseline for the creativity group, $t(47) = 7.03$, $SEM = .02$, the remember/know group, $t(23) = 5.64$, $SEM = .02$, and the strict creativity group, $t(23) = 3.72$, $SEM = .03$. By contrast, mean estimates of automatic retrieval in the deep study condition did not approach or exceed baseline in the remember/know and strict creativity groups, and were therefore uninterpretable. In the creativity group, however, the mean estimate was similar to the baseline, and did not differ from it statistically, $t(47) = 0.80$, $SEM = .03$. The pattern of estimates was not changed when the estimates were recomputed excluding participants with zero exclusion scores in the deep study condition, with one exception: In the strict creativity group, the mean estimate of automatic retrieval in the deep study condition approached baseline, and did not differ from it statistically, $t(17) = 0.76$, $SEM = .04$. Notably, the estimate of automatic retrieval in the deep study condition for the creativity group still did not exceed baseline when zero exclusion scores were eliminated, $t(41) = 0.63$, $SEM = .03$, and thus this estimate was below the estimate of automatic retrieval in the shallow study condition for that group, $t(41) = 3.42$, $SEM = .03$.

In summary, when we exactly followed the design and procedure reported by Toth et al. (1994, Expt. 1), including the use of the creativity exclusion instructions reported in that article, there was no longer a floor effect on exclusion performance in the deep study condition. The inclusion and exclusion baselines did not differ, and there was a significant advantage of deep over shallow processing in the inclusion test, so that the two signatures of a generate–recognise strategy (Jacoby, 1998) were absent. Moreover, the results satisfied a further boundary condition of the process-dissociation procedure, which is that estimates of automatic retrieval should not be below the unstudied baseline. Thus the mean estimate of automatic retrieval in the deep study condition was interpretable (see, e.g., Toth et al., 1994, Expt. 2). The outcome nevertheless did not agree with that reported by Toth et al. (1994, Expt. 1), because automatic retrieval in the deep study condition was still lower than in the shallow study condition—and in that it did not exceed baseline, would have to be taken as indicating that there was no automatic retrieval in the deep study condition. Note that this difference in results occurred even though inclusion and baseline performance levels, and the mean estimate of automatic retrieval in the shallow study condition, were again similar across the experiments (see the note to Table 1).

The remember/know instructions provided information concerning the basis of exclusion performance with the creativity exclusion instructions. The estimated exclusion values for remember/know instructions reflected words that were familiar or that were believed to be unstudied, and did not reflect words that were recollected as studied. For present purposes, therefore, the most important results were that baseline performance, inclusion performance, and exclusion performance in the shallow study condition were similar with creativity and remember/know instructions. In the deep study condition, inclusion performance with remember/know instructions was largely associated with recollection and estimated exclusion performance with remember/know instructions was significantly lower than actual exclusion performance with creativity instructions. Instead, it resembled exclusion performance with the direct retrieval instructions used in Experiment 1. This last result suggests that, with the creativity exclusion instructions, some of the overt exclusion responses in the deep study condition were words that participants recollected having encountered in the study phase, and that a floor effect in the deep study condition was avoided only for that reason.[3]

The strict creativity exclusion instructions provide further information relevant to this hypothesis. The addition of a sentence stressing that participants should pass on exclusion trials if they were only able to think of a studied word had a significant impact, such that exclusion performance in the deep study condition was below exclusion performance with the creativity instructions. Indeed, exclusion performance displayed a floor effect, as observed with estimated exclusion performance in the remember/know test, and with exclusion performance with direct retrieval instructions in Experiment 1, so that the mean estimate of automatic retrieval was again

uninterpretable. Only when participants with zero scores in the deep study condition were omitted did performance resemble performance with the creativity exclusion instructions (i.e., estimates of automatic retrieval in the deep study condition were similar to baseline), suggesting that the strict creativity instructions may have influenced some, but not all, participants not to respond with recollected words when they were unable to think of unstudied words.

The post-test protocols obtained in Experiment 2b were quantified by two raters with respect to the care with which participants had excluded studied words, using a 6-point scale, where 1 represented strict adherence to the exclusion instructions, and 6 represented very loose adherence. Critical features of the rating criteria were what participants said that they had done when only able to think of a studied word as a completion (i.e., whether they had knowingly responded with studied words in this situation), and the extent to which they reported having made mistakes by entering a word and then remembering that it was in fact a studied word. The rating criteria are reproduced in Appendix A. The raters were blind to the test performance of the participants, and to each other's ratings. Inter-rater reliability was high, whether computed for all participants (Spearman's $\rho = 0.96$, $n = 48$), or separately for the creativity ($\rho = 0.96$, $n = 24$) and strict creativity ($\rho = 0.96$, $n = 24$) groups, so the ratings for each protocol were averaged across raters before further analysis. The mean rating for the creativity group was 3.02, $SEM = 0.30$, range 1–6, and the mean rating for the strict creativity group was 2.48, $SEM = 0.23$, range 1–5.

Table 3 shows the inclusion and exclusion data and process-dissociation procedure estimates with the creativity and strict creativity groups each split into approximately equal groups (labelled as careful and lax) based on the ratings, with ratings of 3 and above resulting in assignment into the lax groups. We do not report a full analysis of these data owing to the small group sizes. The most important finding was that there were, at last, null effects of level of processing on estimates of automatic retrieval. But only for the participants in the creativity group rated as more lax did the estimates of automatic retrieval replicate this result. With the omission of the single participant in that group with an exclusion score of zero in the deep study condition, the mean estimate of automatic retrieval for these participants was significantly above baseline in both the deep study

---

[3] This conclusion held whether the remember/know data were compared to the pooled creativity exclusion data from Experiments 2a and 2b, or just to the creativity exclusion data from Experiment 2a.

TABLE 3

Mean proportions of stems completed with studied and unstudied target words, and mean estimates of controlled and automatic retrieval for participants rated as careful and lax excluders on the basis of post-test reports in Experiment 2b

Measure	Estimate	Studied		Unstudied
		Deep	Shallow	
Creativity exclusion instructions: Careful participants (n = 11)				
Inclusion		.55	.45	.35
Exclusion		.14	.33	.29
	Controlled	.40	.12	–
	Automatic	.20 (.24)	.38 (.37)	–
Creativity exclusion instructions: Lax participants (n = 13)				
Inclusion		.61	.44	.31
Exclusion		.29	.33	.27
	Controlled	.32	.10	–
	Automatic	.40 (.43)	.39 (.39)	–
Strict creativity exclusion instructions: Careful participants (n = 13)				
Inclusion		.61	.47	.33
Exclusion		.10	.36	.32
	Controlled	.50	.12	–
	Automatic	.16 (.26)	.40 (.41)	–
Strict creativity exclusion instructions: Lax participants (n = 11)				
Inclusion		.59	.48	.29
Exclusion		.15	.35	.27
	Controlled	.44	.13	–
	Automatic	.26 (.29)	.41 (.43)	–

Means in parentheses were computed omitting participants with exclusion proportions of zero in the deep study condition (two in the creativity/careful group, one in the creativity/lax group, five in the strict creativity/careful group, and one in the strict creativity/lax group).

condition, $t(11) = 2.56$, $SEM = .05$, and the shallow study condition, $t(11) = 2.64$, SEM = .04, and there was no significant difference between these mean estimates, $t(11) = 0.84$, $SEM = .06$. The mean rating for this subgroup (not including the participant who scored zero for deep exclusion) was 4.13, $SEM = 0.34$, which—in terms of the rating criteria—corresponds with "not very strict adherence" to the exclusion instructions. The other subgroups showed patterns similar to those previously reported for the overall data, with mean estimates of automatic retrieval in the deep study condition that were either similar to or below baseline.

GENERAL DISCUSSION

To summarise the results, in two close replications of Toth et al. (1994, Expt. 1) we generally failed to obtain null effects of level of processing on estimates of automatic retrieval. Our participants were usually well able to exclude studied words following deep study conditions, sometimes resulting in floor effects on exclusion performance, with estimates of automatic retrieval falling below baseline and hence being uninterpretable. But even when floor effects were avoided, so that estimates were not below baseline, and hence were interpretable (see, e.g., Toth et al., 1994, Expt. 2), there was an inverse relationship between level of processing and estimates of automatic retrieval. The use of remember/know instructions, as in Jacoby (1998), as well as reports of strategy elicited after the tests, indicated that participants were sometimes failing to exclude recollected words following deep study conditions, resulting in higher estimates of automatic retrieval, and that floor effects were avoided only for that reason. Partitioning data according to whether participants given creativity exclusion instructions could be classified as careful or lax in their adherence to those instructions showed that null effects of level of processing on estimates of automatic retrieval did occur, but only for participants who received the less strict exclusion instructions and who also qualified as lax in their adherence to those instructions. Thus the Toth et al. (1994) result was replicated eventually, but only in paradoxical circumstances; that is, when participants failed to exclude recollected words. This failure violates one of the key assumptions of the process-dissociation procedure and so renders the use of the procedure to assess the effect of level of processing on perceptual priming in word-stem completion invalid—hence the paradox.

What are we to make of these results? To begin with, some disclaimers are in order, if only to put our results into perspective. We note that we are not alone in having encountered problems in obtaining null effects on estimates of automatic retrieval in situations where results from standard incidental tests of priming would lead one to expect null effects (e.g., Bodner, Masson, & Caldwell, 2000; Curran & Hintzman, 1995; Russo, Cullis, & Parkin, 1998). But on the other hand there is a substantial set of evidence to show that various manipulations that might be expected to have no effects on automatic retrieval (e.g., divided vs undivided attention) do indeed have null effects on estimates of automatic retrieval (e.g., Jacoby, 1998; Jacoby et al., 1993, 1997). Nor is it the case that the null effect of level of processing obtained by Toth et al. (1994) has been unreplicable under conditions that appear to meet the requirements for use of the process-dissociation procedure, because Toth et al. (1995) reported just such a replication. That fact, however, makes it even harder to understand why even our most exact replication of the Toth et al. (1994) experiment failed to yield the expected outcome, except under the paradoxical circumstances that invalidate the procedure.

Use of a generate–recognise retrieval strategy might be thought to explain the floor effects in the exclusion tasks, as well as the inverse relationship between level of processing and estimates of automatic retrieval that persisted even when floor effects were avoided. But the two signatures of a generate–recognise strategy discussed by Jacoby (1998) were not evident in our data. Inclusion test performance did not resemble incidental test performance, nor were the baselines in exclusion tasks lower than the baselines in inclusion tasks. According to Jacoby (1998), a generate–recognise strategy leads to smaller level-of-processing effects in inclusion tasks because participants are responding with the first word that comes to mind. And it leads to exclusion on the basis of familiarity, rather than recollection, hence reducing baselines in exclusion tasks relative to those in inclusion tasks. Additional individual-difference analyses conducted on the pooled data from the creativity and strict creativity groups in Experiment 2b also provided no evidence for the use of a generate–recognise strategy by participants who excluded carefully. We found no significant correlation between the ratings of adherence to exclusion task instructions and the size of the level-of-processing effect in the inclusion task. Nor were lower ratings (indicating more careful adherence to instructions) associated with larger differences between inclusion and exclusion baselines. The only aspect of performance significantly correlated with the ratings was exclusion following deep study processing (Spearman's $\rho = 0.45$, $n = 48$, $p = .001$), with exclusion proportions being lower for participants rated more careful and higher for participants rated more lax.[4]

If anything, our results suggest precisely the reverse of the conclusion that a generate–recognise retrieval strategy led to floor effects following deep study processing, or to inverse relationships between level of processing and automatic retrieval (see also Bodner et al., 2000). It was the lax participants, whose automatic retrieval estimates replicated the invariance reported by Toth et al. (1994), for which the post-test responses could be taken to suggest a generate–recognise retrieval strategy. These were the participants who most frequently reported making exclusion "mistakes" by entering words prior to recognising that these words had occurred earlier. Thus our results are bound to raise the question of the extent to which previously published findings of invariance in estimates of automatic retrieval might reflect the output of recollected words in exclusion tasks.

It might be suggested that failure to find invariance in estimates of automatic retrieval, where invariance is expected based on priming results from incidental tests, *in itself* indicates that participants have used an inappropriate test strategy—regardless of the lack of evidence from independent, objective indicators of strategy, such as those delineated by Jacoby (1998). Such a suggestion would, however, be deeply proble-

---

[4] Correlations among the behavioural measures also provided no evidence for a generate–recognise strategy. Exclusion performance following deep study processing did not correlate with the size of the level-of-processing effect in the inclusion task, or with the difference between inclusion and exclusion baselines.

matic. For example, in examinations of the effect of modality match between study and test (e.g., Jacoby et al., 1993), and in contrasts of study conditions involving generating versus reading words (e.g., Toth et al., 1994, Expt. 2), estimates of automatic retrieval in word-stem completion have not shown invariance and—as in the deep study condition for the creativity groups in Experiments 2a and 2b—have been similar to baseline in the cross-modal and generate conditions. Such results could then also be explained away as reflecting an inappropriate test strategy. Moreover, it would then be difficult to establish new findings: If estimates of automatic retrieval failed to show invariance when invariance was expected, it would be unclear whether this was a new result, advancing theory, or whether it was an artefact of an inappropriate test strategy. Such unexpected outcomes have, however, occurred in studies using standard incidental tests of priming: For example, it is now apparent that there can be genuine deficits in perceptual and conceptual priming following highly superficial shallow study conditions (Gardiner, Richardson-Klavehn, Ramponi, & Brooks, 2001; Richardson-Klavehn & Gardiner, 1998). In these circumstances, level-of-processing effects on priming reflect the importance of "whole word" lexical processing, not contamination of the priming measure by controlled retrieval.

Why should we have had such difficulty achieving invariance in estimates of automatic retrieval, except under the paradoxical circumstances in which participants were responding with recollected words in exclusion tasks? We suggest that the reason is that, contrary to what is assumed in two-process models, automatic retrieval may be associated with recollective experiences, and not just feelings of familiarity or a complete absence of memory awareness (e.g., Richardson-Klavehn, Gardiner, & Java, 1994, 1996; see also Moscovitch, 1994, 2000; Whittlesea, 1997, 2002). Given that participants follow exclusion instructions, such automatic recollection will contribute to the withholding of studied items, contrary to the critical assumption that automatically retrieved items are produced in these tasks. In our view, therefore, the two-process approach to memory and consciousness is itself too simple, regardless of whether the relationship between the processes is conceived as one of independence, as in the process-dissociation model, or one of redundancy, as in generate–recognise models (e.g., Bodner et al., 2000).

Consistent with our view, there is evidence that conscious control of retrieval—that is, whether studied words are retrieved *with that purpose in mind or with some other purpose in mind*—is systematically dissociable from conscious recollection that studied words have been previously encountered. The evidence comes both from behavioural studies (e.g., Richardson-Klavehn & Gardiner, 1995, 1996) and studies of brain electrical activity (e.g., Curran, 1999; Paller & Kutas, 1992; Paller, Kutas, & McIsaac, 1995; Richardson-Klavehn, Düzel, Schott, Heinze, & Gardiner, 2001).

Our view predicts that there should be situations in which the boundary conditions for the use of the process-dissociation procedure cannot legitimately be met, because floor effects on exclusion performance will be unavoidable, assuming that participants follow instructions. Such situations would tend to involve study conditions that promote automatic recollection, such as the deep study conditions used here. Inability to meet the boundary conditions for the use of the process-dissociation procedure in tasks involving conceptual priming, such as category exemplar production, is likely to prove a further particularly telling example (e.g., Mecklenbräuker, Wippich, & Mohrhusen, 1996). This difficulty contrasts markedly with the clear evidence for conceptual priming in amnesic patients obtained using standard incidental tests (e.g., Graf, Shimamura, & Squire, 1985; Keane et al., 1997).

Our view also predicts that there should be other situations in which the boundary conditions for the use of the process-dissociation procedure are apparently met, but in which automatic retrieval is systematically underestimated. There is now clear evidence that the predicted underestimation can occur. For example, the process-dissociation procedure has led to the conclusion that perceptual priming is entirely modality-specific (e.g., Toth & Reingold, 1996), because estimates of automatic retrieval in word-stem completion do not exhibit transfer across modalities (e.g., Jacoby et al., 1993), and do not show an impact of generating words at study (Toth et al., 1994, Expt. 2). However, in standard incidental tests of perceptual priming, amnesic patients have exhibited normal levels of cross-modal priming (e.g., Graf et al., 1985), and priming from generating at study has been observed despite drug-induced amnesia (Hirshman, Passannante, & Arndt, 1999, 2001). Other research with non-amnesic participants using the logic of the retrieval intentionality criterion (Schacter, Bowers, & Booker, 1989) also shows that cross-modal priming and priming from generating at study can reflect automatic retrieval (Richardson-Klavehn & Gardiner, 1996; Richardson-Klavehn et al., 1999). In these situations, in view of the abstract memory representations involved, priming in non-amnesic participants is again likely to be associated with automatic recollection, and consequently with withholding of studied items in exclusion tasks.

Within the context of two-process models, it is usually assumed that controlled retrieval, and hence recollection, is a relatively slow process and that automatic retrieval, and hence familiarity, is a relatively fast process. In recognition memory a response deadline procedure has been used to partially separate the relative contributions of the two processes (e.g., Toth, 1996). A short response deadline forces rapid responding that is likely to depend more on automatic processes. A long response deadline forces delayed responding that allows controlled processes to come more fully into play. However, Gardiner, Ramponi, and Richardson-Klavehn (1999) showed in the remember/know paradigm that even with a short deadline and rapid responding, recognition memory was still associated with substantial proportions of remembered words. Moreover, both remembering and knowing increased with a long deadline and delayed responding. Those results also support the view that recollective experiences may sometimes be associated with relatively automatic processing and, moreover, that feelings of familiarity, as well as recollective experiences, may sometimes depend on more controlled processing (see also Dewhurst & Conway, 1994).

Thus, the thrust of our conclusion is that what at first blush might have been thought to be a methodological problem—the elusiveness of null effects of level of processing on estimates of automatic retrieval—has in fact turned out to be a theoretical problem, with important implications for views of how consciousness should be conceived in relation to memory. Whether or not this resolution of the problem is persuasive, the presence or absence of level-of-processing effects has been absolutely essential to the argument. And, whatever the fate of level-of-processing ideas with respect to their intrinsic theoretical value, the more pragmatic use of level of processing in regard to what it can contribute to our understanding of other components of processing, and of consciousness, is likely to constitute an enduring legacy.

REFERENCES

Allen, R.E. (Ed.) (1990). *The concise Oxford English dictionary* (8th Edn.). Oxford: Oxford University Press.

Bodner, G.E., Masson, M.E., & Caldwell J.I. (2000). Evidence for a generate-recognize model of episodic influences on word-stem completion. *Journal of Experimental Psychology: Learning, Memory, and Cognition, 26,* 267–293.

Craik, F.I.M., & Lockhart, R.S. (1972). Levels of processing: A framework for memory research. *Journal of Verbal Learning and Verbal Behavior, 11,* 671–684.

Curran, T. (1999). The electrophysiology of incidental and intentional retrieval: ERP old/new effects in lexical decision and recognition memory. *Neuropsychologia, 37,* 771–785.

Curran, T., & Hintzman, D.L. (1995). Violations of the independence assumption in process dissociation. *Journal of Experimental Psychology: Learning, Memory, and Cognition, 21,* 531–547.

Dewhurst, S.A., & Conway, M.A. (1994). Pictures, images, and recollective experience. *Journal of Experimental Psychology: Learning, Memory, and Cognition, 20,* 1088–1098.

Gardiner, J.M., Java, R.I., & Richardson-Klavehn, A. (1996). How level of processing really influences awareness in recognition memory. *Canadian Journal of Experimental Psychology, 50,* 114–122.

Gardiner, J.M., Ramponi, C., & Richardson-Klavehn, A. (1998). Experiences of remembering, knowing, and guessing. *Consciousness and Cognition, 7,* 1–26.

Gardiner J.M., Ramponi, C., & Richardson-Klavehn, A. (1999). Response deadline and subjective awareness in recognition memory. *Consciousness and Cognition, 8,* 484–496.

Gardiner, J.M., Richardson-Klavehn, A., Ramponi, C., & Brooks, B.M. (2001). Involuntary level-of-processing effects in perceptual and conceptual priming. In M. Naveh-Benjamin, M. Moscovitch, & H.L. Roediger III (Eds.), *Perspectives on human memory and cognitive aging: Essays in honor of Fergus Craik* (pp. 71–82). New York: Psychology Press.

Graf, P., Shimamura, A.P., & Squire, L.R. (1985). Priming across modalities and priming across category levels: Extending the domain of preserved function in amnesia. *Journal of Experimental Psychology: Learning, Memory, and Cognition, 11,* 386–396.

Graf, P., & Williams, D. (1987). Completion norms for 40 three-letter word stems. *Behavior Research Methods, Instruments, & Computers, 19,* 422–445.

Hirshman, E., Passannante, A., & Arndt, J. (1999). The effect of midazolam on the modality-match effect in implicit memory. *Cognitive Brain Research, 7,* 473–479.

Hirshman, E., Passannante, A., & Arndt, J. (2001). Midazolam amnesia and conceptual processing in implicit memory. *Journal of Experimental Psychology: General, 130*, 453–465.

Jacoby, L.L. (1991). A process-dissociation framework: Separating automatic from intentional uses of memory. *Journal of Memory and Language, 30*, 513–541.

Jacoby, L.L. (1998). Invariance in automatic influences of memory: Toward a user's guide for the process-dissociation procedure. *Journal of Experimental Psychology: Learning, Memory, and Cognition, 24*, 3–26.

Jacoby, L.L., Toth, J.P., & Yonelinas, A.P. (1993). Separating conscious and unconscious influences of memory: Measuring recollection. *Journal of Experimental Psychology: General, 122*, 139–154.

Jacoby, L.L., Yonelinas, A.P., & Jennings, J.M. (1997). The relation between conscious and unconscious (automatic) influences: A declaration of independence. In J.D. Cohen & J.W. Schooler (Eds.), *Scientific approaches to the question of consciousness* (pp. 13–47). Hillsdale, NJ: Lawrence Erlbaum Associates Inc.

Keane, M.M., Gabrieli, J.D., Monti, L.A., Fleischman, D.A., Cantor, J.M., & Noland, J.S. (1997). Intact and impaired conceptual memory processes in amnesia. *Neuropsychology, 11*, 59–69.

Kucera, H., & Francis, W. (1967). *Computational handbook of present-day American English.* Providence, RI: Brown University Press.

Mecklenbräuker, S., Wippich, W., & Mohrhusen, S.H. (1996). Conscious and unconscious influences of memory in a conceptual task: Limitations of a process-dissociation procedure. *Swiss Journal of Psychology, 55*, 34–48.

Moscovitch, M. (1994). Memory and working-with-memory: Evaluation of a component process model and comparison with other models. In D.L. Schacter & E. Tulving (Eds.), *Memory systems* (pp. 269–310). Cambridge, MA: MIT Press.

Moscovitch, M. (2000). Theories of memory and consciousness. In E. Tulving & F.I.M. Craik (Eds.), *Oxford handbook of memory* (pp. 609–625). New York: Oxford University Press.

Paller, K.A., & Kutas, M. (1992). Brain potentials during memory retrieval provide neurophysiological support for the distinction between conscious recollection and priming. *Journal of Cognitive Neuroscience, 4*, 375–391.

Paller, K.A., Kutas, M., & McIsaac, H. (1995). Monitoring conscious recollection via the electrical activity of the brain. *Psychological Science, 6*, 107–111.

Richardson-Klavehn, A., & Bjork, R.A. (1988). Measures of memory. *Annual Review of Psychology, 39*, 475–543.

Richardson-Klavehn, A., Clarke, A.J.B., & Gardiner, J.M. (1999). Conjoint dissociations reveal involuntary "perceptual" priming from generating at study. *Consciousness and Cognition, 8*, 271–284.

Richardson-Klavehn, A., Düzel, E., Schott, B., Heinze, H.-J., & Gardiner, J.M. (2001, July). *What do we mean by "consciousness" in memory? Evidence from the event-related brain potential.* Presented at the Third International Conference on Memory, Valencia, Spain.

Richardson-Klavehn, A., & Gardiner, J.M. (1995). Retrieval volition and memorial awareness in stem completion: An empirical analysis. *Psychological Research, 57*, 166–178.

Richardson-Klavehn, A., & Gardiner, J.M. (1996). Cross-modality priming in stem completion reflects conscious memory, but not voluntary memory. *Psychonomic Bulletin & Review, 3*, 238–244.

Richardson-Klavehn, A., & Gardiner, J.M. (1998). Depth-of-processing effects on priming in stem completion: Tests of the voluntary-contamination, conceptual-processing, and lexical-processing hypotheses. *Journal of Experimental Psychology: Learning, Memory, and Cognition, 24*, 593–609.

Richardson-Klavehn, A., Gardiner, J.M., & Java, R.I. (1994). Involuntary conscious memory and the method of opposition. *Memory, 2*, 1–29.

Richardson-Klavehn, A., Gardiner, J.M., & Java, R.I. (1996). Memory: Task dissociations, process dissociations and dissociations of consciousness. In G. Underwood (Ed.), *Implicit cognition* (pp. 85–158). Oxford: Oxford University Press.

Roediger, H.L.III, & Gallo, D.A. (2002). Levels of processing: Some unanswered questions. In M. Naveh-Benjamin, M. Moscovitch, & H.L. Roediger III (Eds.), *Perspectives of human memory and cognitive aging: Essays in honor of Fergus Craik* (pp. 28–47). New York: Psychology Press.

Roediger, H.L.III, & McDermott, K.B. (1993). Implicit memory in normal human subjects. In F. Boller & J. Grafman (Eds.), *Handbook of neuropsychology* (Vol. 8, pp. 63–131). Amsterdam: Elsevier.

Roediger, H.L.III, Weldon, M.S., Stadler, M.L., & Riegler, G.L. (1992). Direct comparison of two implicit memory tests: Word fragment and word stem completion. *Journal of Experimental Psychology: Learning, Memory, and Cognition, 18*, 1251–1269.

Russo, R., Cullis, A.M., & Parkin, A.J. (1998). Consequences of violating the assumption of independence in the process dissociation procedure: A word fragment completion study. *Memory & Cognition, 26*, 617–632.

Schacter, D.L., Bowers, J., & Booker, J. (1989). Intention, awareness, and implicit memory: The retrieval intentionality criterion. In S. Lewandowsky, J.C. Dunn, & K. Kirsner (Eds.), *Implicit memory: Theoretical issues* (pp. 47–65). Hillsdale, NJ: Lawrence Erlbaum Associates Inc.

Schott, B., Richardson-Klavehn, A., Heinze, H.-J., & Düzel, E. (2002). Perceptual priming versus explicit memory: Dissociable neural correlates at encoding. *Journal of Cognitive Neuroscience, 14*, 578–592.

Toth, J.P. (1996). Conceptual automaticity in recognition memory: Levels-of-processing effects on familiarity. *Canadian Journal of Experimental Psychology, 50*, 123–138.

Toth, J.P., Levine, B., Stuss, D.T., MacDonald, R., Schwartz, M., & Snow, W.G. (1995). Dissociation of automatic and controlled uses of memory in TBI patients (Abstract). *Journal of Neurotrauma, 12*, 394.

Toth, J.P., & Reingold, E.M. (1996). Beyond perception: Conceptual contributions to unconscious influences of memory. In G. Underwood (Ed.), *Implicit cognition* (pp. 41–84). Oxford: Oxford University Press.

Toth, J.P., Reingold, E.M., & Jacoby, L.L. (1994). Toward a redefinition of implicit memory: Process dissociation following elaborative processing and self-generation. *Journal of Experimental Psychology: Learning, Memory, and Cognition, 20*, 290–303.

Tulving, E. (2001). Does memory encoding exist? In M. Naveh-Benjamin, M. Moscovitch, & H.L. Roediger III (Eds.), *Perspectives on human memory and cognitive aging: Essays in honor of Fergus Craik* (pp. 6–27). New York: Psychology Press.

Whittlesea, B.W.A. (1997). Production, evaluation, and preservation of experiences: Constructive processing in remembering and performance tasks. In D.L. Medin (Ed.), *The psychology of learning and motivation* (Vol. 37, pp. 211–264). New York: Academic Press.

Whittlesea, B.W.A. (2002). False memory and the discrepancy-attribution hypothesis: The prototype-familiarity illusion. *Journal of Experimental Psychology: General, 131*, 96–115.

APPENDIX A

Six-point scale used to rate post-test protocols in Experiment 2b, with rating criteria

(1) Strict adherence to the exclusion instructions with no element of doubt regarding the status of the words
- Did not knowingly enter any old words
- If unsure that words were new, they were not used as completions, but omitted
- No remembered mistakes

(2) Strict adherence to the exclusion instructions with an element of doubt regarding the status of the words
- Did not knowingly enter any old words
- If unsure that words were new, they tended to be entered
- No remembered mistakes but some doubts

(3) Fairly strict adherence to the exclusion instructions but some mistakes
- Did not knowingly enter any old words, only by mistake
- If unsure that words were new, they tended to be entered
- One to three remembered or assumed mistakes (e.g., hit "return" too early)

(4) Not very strict adherence to the exclusion instructions
- Did not knowingly enter any old words, only by mistake
- If unsure that words were new, they were entered with little concern
- Four to eight remembered or assumed mistakes (e.g., hit "return" too early)

(5) Fairly loose adherence to the exclusion instructions
- Knowingly entered old words because of sloppy adherence to the instructions, it was easier to do so, etc., but tried most of the time to complete stems with new words
- If unsure that words were new, they were entered with no concern
- Eight or more remembered mistakes (e.g., hit "return" too early) or old words knowingly entered

(6) Very loose adherence to the exclusion instructions
- Knowingly entered old words out of boredom, tiredness, or misinterpretation of the instructions, etc.
- Did not try much to comply with the instructions
- Eight or more remembered mistakes (e.g., hit "return" too early) or old words knowingly entered

MEMORY, 2002, *10* (5/6), 365–379

On the perceptual specificity of memory representations

Eyal M. Reingold

University of Toronto, Canada

The present paradigm involved manipulating the congruency of the perceptual processing during the study and test phases of a recognition memory task. During each trial, a gaze-contingent window was used to limit the stimulus display to a region either inside or outside a $10°$ square centred on the participant's point of gaze, constituting the Central and Peripheral viewing modes respectively. The window position changed in real time in concert with changes in gaze position. Four experiments documented better task performance when viewing modes at encoding and retrieval matched than when they mismatched (i.e., perceptual specificity effects). Viewing mode congruency effects were demonstrated with both verbal and non-verbal stimuli. The present research is motivated and discussed in terms of theoretical views proposed in the 1970s including the levels-of-processing framework and the proceduralist viewpoint. In addition, implications for current processing and multiple systems views of memory are outlined.

According to the levels-of-processing (LOP) framework, memory is a by-product of cognitive operations performed on stimuli, ranging from "shallow" encoding (surface characteristics) to "deep" semantic processing (Craik & Lockhart, 1972). From semantic processing ensues a more durable and elaborate representation than from surface analysis (Craik & Tulving, 1975). According to this view, the by-products of surface analysis are lost comparatively rapidly. In a typical LOP experiment, participants are presented with single words at encoding and asked to focus their attention on either semantic (meaningful) or non-semantic (e.g., orthographic or phonological) aspects of the word. LOP effects in memory performance (i.e., better memory for words encoded semantically than superficially) are thought to provide conclusive evidence of semantic or conceptual influences on memory because perceptual encoding is assumed to be equated across the semantic and non-semantic encoding conditions and only the degree of meaningful elaboration is hypothesised to vary.

As pointed out by Kolers and Roediger (1984), a key assumption underlying the LOP framework, as well as other memory theories, is the assumption of semantic primacy. Namely, that "the representation of the linguistic meaning of events is primary and that other aspects of experience are not coded with, or as durably as, meaning" (p. 428). Meaning is abstracted from the stimulus's surface form, and thus represented in memory. After the embedded meaning is extracted, surface characteristics are not long retained. The origin of this assumption lies in the abstractionist approach to language processing. In particular, Chomsky's (1957, 1965) work was instrumental in promoting the notion of semantic primacy in cognitive psychology. Chomsky analysed the structure of sentences, isolating a semantic "deep structure" and a shallow "surface structure". The deep structure, he argued, may be derived from the surface structure by applying a specifiable set of transformations. However, as different surface forms may represent the same underlying meaning, the surface structure serves only to convey the "deeper" meaning.

Requests for reprints should be sent to Eyal M. Reingold, Department of Psychology, University of Toronto, 100 St. George Street, Toronto, Ontario, Canada M5S 3G3. Email: reingold@psych.utoronto.ca

This research was supported by a grant to Eyal Reingold from the Natural Science and Engineering Research Council of Canada (NSERC). The author is grateful to Elizabeth Bosman, Fergus Craik, David Gallo, Colleen Ray, Jennifer Ryan, Dave Stampe, Boris Velichkovsky and Martin Wainwright for their comments on earlier drafts of this manuscript.

http://www.tandf.co.uk/journals/pp/09658211.html

DOI:10.1080/09658210244000199

Thus, in attempting to evaluate the LOP framework it is important to examine alternative theoretical proposals and empirical evidence suggesting perceptual specificity of memory representations (i.e., long-term retention of surface characteristics). The present research was inspired by one such theoretical framework developed by Paul Kolers and his colleagues (e.g., Kolers, 1968, 1973, 1975, 1976, 1978, 1979; Kolers & Magee, 1978; Kolers, Palef, & Stelmach, 1980; Kolers & Perkins, 1975; Kolers & Roediger, 1984; Kolers & Smythe, 1979, 1984). Accordingly, in the first part of this paper Kolers' work is briefly reviewed. Next, the current status of the perceptual specificity hypothesis is discussed. Finally, four experiments extending Kolers' findings are reported. These experiments demonstrate robust perceptual specificity effects in a recognition memory task.

PAUL KOLERS AND THE PROCEDURALIST VIEWPOINT

Historically, the most powerful challenge to the semantic primacy assumption originated from the work of Paul Kolers and his proceduralist viewpoint. He advocated a radical departure from the contemporaneous emphasis on memory traces and structure. In lieu, he advanced accounts of memory (and of cognitive functioning in general) that emphasised procedures or skills. For instance, Kolers (1973) argued that "what is recognized or remembered are the analytical operations themselves that have been used to transform an optical output into a perceptual experience.... We remember in terms of the operations or activities of encoding as well as, sometimes, their results" (p. 347). Importantly, within the proceduralist framework knowledge is conceptualised as the skilled manipulation of symbols. This conception leads to analysis of the nature of symbols, and of systems of symbols (Kolers & Smythe, 1979, 1984). A critical consequence is that knowledge is dependent on the means of acquisition. As Kolers (1978) argues, our "knowledge depends upon the symbol system ... used for encoding the information of interest" and therefore, "our means of acquisition are part of our representation" (p. 257). This declaration of the means-dependent nature of knowledge constitutes another fundamental tenet of the proceduralist viewpoint.

Clearly, the means-dependence of knowledge logically entails the repudiation of semantic primacy. For if the means of acquisition cannot be entirely divorced from the acquired meaning, then surface form cannot serve merely as a vehicle for semantic content. Thus, according to the proceduralist account, "features of the message that most theorists consider superficial—cadence or pitch of a voice, typography, spacing, or orientation of a written text, and the like— ... should play a prominent role in forming the representation of the message in memory" (Kolers & Roediger, 1984, p. 430). Therefore, the proceduralist denies meaning its traditional privileged status: that of an abstracted and necessarily propositional representation. Moreover, according to Kolers and Roediger (1984), "semantic" means, "the relation between a symbol and its referent, [a relation which] is always specific to a system of symbols" (p. 430). While pertinent to language processing, such a definition applies equally to manipulations of other (non-linguistic) symbol types. In fact, underlying many models of cognitive psychology is a generalised semantic primacy assumption: namely "that in dealing with pictorial, graphemic, verbal, or other symbols, people abstract out the meaning from the symbol and perform cognitive operations on this representation" (Gonzalez & Kolers, 1982; p. 308). It is precisely this "pearl-in-the-oyster" view of memory (i.e., extract the semantic pearl and discard the surface shell) that Kolers rejects (see Kolers, 1979). In contrast, he contends that meaning does not exist independently of the symbol-manipulating procedures through which it is expressed.

Furthermore, the argument that representations depend on the means of acquisition motivates the investigation of the specificity of transfer in learning and memory (Kolers & Magee, 1978; Kolers et al., 1980; Kolers & Perkins, 1975). In particular, the proceduralist proposes that the amount of transfer between tasks is a function of the relative concordance between the procedures activated by the tasks. Kolers and Roediger (1984) contend that memory tasks should be studied "in terms of the procedures used to acquire or express knowledge" (p. 436). An elegant theoretical shift, one rendered especially poignant by contemporary emphasis on task dissociations, results from these two preceding propositions in conjunction: "It is not dissociation that needs to be explained, for that is the natural state of affairs; it is the characteristics of tasks—and *relations among their underlying procedures*—that needs explaining" (p. 439; emphasis added). Thus, Kolers and Roediger (1984) criticise the proliferation of different memory systems, wryly and prophetically remarking that one "may anticipate the invention of still more memory systems to explain still other dissociations encountered experimentally" (p. 437).

To study the specificity of transfer in memory Paul Kolers introduced the use of spatially transformed text. Such text is derived from normal text by applying certain geometrical transformations, such as rotation about axes, inversion, and mirror reflection (Kolers, 1968). Normal text is processed so fluently as to render difficult the task of isolating the components of language processing. Employing transformed typographies, Kolers felt, could disentangle the relative contributions to reading of graphemic and semantic analyses. In a seminal series of studies, Kolers (1975, 1976, 1979) demonstrated that through practice, participants develop skills at reading transformed texts, and that these skills may be transferred to subsequent readings. Furthermore, he claimed that such skills are both instance-specific (i.e., linked to the acquisitive instance) and pattern-analytic (i.e., directed at the graphemic level). In particular, Kolers (1976) provided a demonstration of perceptual influences that was particularly startling given the 1970s emphasis on semantic factors. Kolers trained participants in reading unfamiliar typography by requiring them to read aloud many pages of inverted text. After an interval ranging from 13 to 15 months, participants then read a mixture of previously read passages and new passages, all in inverted orientation. Kolers reported that previously read passages were re-read 5–6% faster than new passages. Furthermore, Kolers found participants' familiarity judgements about the passages were not well correlated with their reading speed of these passages. On this basis, he concluded that readers were retaining highly specific pattern-analysing operations for over a year. Note that this demonstration of memory for superficial features (such as typography) undermines the semantic primacy assumption. In particular, the results of this study seemed to directly violate a primary tenet of semantic primacy: that "superficial" properties (such as typography) are not long preserved in memory.

PERCEPTUAL SPECIFICITY OF MEMORY REPRESENTATION: CURRENT STATUS

Not surprisingly, Kolers' inference of perceptual specificity in re-reading facilitation has been the object of intense scrutiny (Craik, 1989; Graf, 1981; Graf & Levy, 1984; Horton, 1985, 1989; Tardif & Craik, 1989; Masson, 1984, 1986; Masson & Sala, 1978). A detailed review of the ensuing controversies is beyond the scope of the present paper (for such a review see Levy, 1993). Irrespective of these controversies, the last three decades have seen a dramatic theoretical shift away from the hegemony of the semantic primacy assumption and towards greater appreciation of the importance of the perceptual specificity of memory representations. Specifically, current processing theories of memory incorporate core concepts such as "transfer appropriate processing" (for a review see Roediger, Weldon, & Challis, 1989) and "perceptual fluency" (for a review see Jacoby, Kelley, & Dywan, 1989), which reject the notion advocated by the LOP framework that elaborating the meaning of an event always leads to better memory, and instead echo Kolers' view that memory performance reflects the overlap in processing requirements at encoding and retrieval. Similarly, in a clear opposition to the semantic primacy assumption, several dominant multiple memory systems theories were extended to include a "presemantic, perceptual representation system" that mediates the long-term retention of specific perceptual or surface descriptions of stimuli without representing their meaning (e.g., Moscovitch, 1992; Schacter, 1994; Schacter & Tulving, 1994; Schacter, Wagner, & Buckner, 2000; Squire, 1992; Tulving & Schacter, 1990).

This theoretical shift coincided with findings that were emerging in studies with amnesic patients (for a review see Moscovitch, Vriezen, & Gottstein, 1993) and with normal participants (for reviews see Roediger & McDermott, 1993; Schacter, 1987), which employed indirect or implicit memory tests. In contrast to direct or explicit memory tests such as recognition and recall, in which participants are instructed to refer back to the study episode, implicit tests of memory attempt to disguise the relation between the study and test phases of the experiment by presenting them as unrelated tasks. For example, in a perceptual identification task, masked study words are briefly presented and participants are simply instructed to identify these stimuli. In this task, memory is expressed as facilitation in the identification of study words. Similarly, in a stem completion task, participants are provided with the first few letters corresponding to study words (e.g., BLA_ _ for BLANK) and are asked to complete them with the first word that comes to mind. Memory is measured as an increased tendency to complete stems with study words.

Implicit tests such as perceptual identification and stem completion that employ physically degraded (i.e., data-limited) retrieval cues have been labelled perceptual implicit tests and memory facilitation measured by such tasks is often referred to as perceptual priming. This terminology reflects the fact that in direct opposition to the semantic primacy assumption there is now ample convergent evidence for perceptual specificity effects on performance when such memory tests are employed (for reviews see Roediger & McDermott, 1993; Roediger & Srinivas, 1993; Roediger et al., 1989; Schacter, 1987).

However, it should be acknowledged that during the 1970s when the LOP framework was proposed, recognition and recall were the dominant tasks used to assess memory performance. Could it be that the semantic primacy assumption holds true for performance measured by these explicit memory tasks? Support for this hypothesis comes from findings that recognition and recall performance is strongly influenced by semantic factors and is relatively immune to perceptual or "surface" manipulations (for a detailed review see Richardson-Klavehn & Bjork, 1988).

Robust LOP effects routinely demonstrated with recognition and recall provide clear evidence for the influence of semantic or conceptual factors on performance. An even stronger indication for the dominant influence of semantic factors on recognition and recall performance is derived from the sizeable "generation effects" obtained with these tasks (Slamecka & Graf, 1978). In the generation paradigm, during the study phase, participants read some words in isolation and generate others on the basis of semantic cues. Given that items that are read are fully specified perceptually, whereas generated items lack complete perceptual specification, better memory performance in the latter than in the former condition (i.e., a generation effect) is thought to reflect conceptual rather than perceptual transfer. Consequently, Roediger et al. (1989) proposed an operational definition according to which generation effects such as the ones demonstrated with

recognition and recall would serve as the basis for classifying these tasks as conceptual memory tasks.

Additional support for the semantic primacy assumption in the context of recognition and recall performance is derived from experimental manipulations in which the test stimulus is perceptually dissimilar from the stimulus originally presented at study. Such manipulations include changing presentation modality (e.g., auditory vs visual), typography, and language from study to test. In general, study/test mismatches on such "surface" variables do not result in a substantial decrement in recognition and recall performance (for a review see Richardson-Klavehn & Bjork, 1988).

Findings obtained with a recognition memory task provide a particularly powerful illustration of the general pattern just described. Specifically, when contrasting performance across the standard condition in which words are presented at both study and test with a condition in which pictures are presented at study and words are presented at test, recognition performance has been consistently shown to be better in the latter than in the former condition (for a review see Roediger & Weldon, 1987). Note that as is the case with the generation effect, in the picture–word effect, recognition is better when the physical cues provided at study and test are different than when they are the same.

The major goal of the present study was to explore whether despite the prior findings summarised earlier, it is in fact possible to demonstrate substantial perceptual specificity effects in recognition memory performance with normal participants.

OVERVIEW OF THE PRESENT METHODOLOGY

The experimental strategy used in the present research involved directly manipulating the congruency of the perceptual processing during the study and test phases of a recognition memory task, to examine Kolers' hypothesis that performance should be better when the processing at encoding and retrieval match than when they mismatch (see also the encoding/retrieval paradigm—Roediger et al., 1989; Tulving, 1983). To vary the nature of the perceptual processing at encoding and retrieval a gaze-contingent window paradigm was employed (e.g., McConkie & Rayner, 1975; Pomplun, Reingold, & Shen, 2001; Reingold, Charness, Pomplun, & Stampe, 2001; for a review see Rayner, 1998). Throughout the experiments, participants' eye movements were monitored and the stimulus display was modified in real time contingent on changes in gaze position. As shown in Figure 1, during encoding and retrieval a 10° square gaze-contingent window was displayed centred on the participants' point of gaze. The window position changed across fixations to follow the gaze position. Two viewing modes were used at encoding and retrieval. In the Central viewing mode, stimuli were only visible inside the window and the rest of the display was replaced by a uniform grey background image (see Row A in Figure 1). Consequently, this viewing mode selectively impaired the use of peripheral visual processing while permitting normal foveal and parafoveal processing (i.e., central vision was unaffected). In contrast, in the Peripheral viewing mode, stimuli were only visible outside the window and a uniform grey image was displayed inside the window (see Row B in Figure 1). Thus, this viewing mode selectively impaired the use of foveal and parafoveal processing while permitting normal peripheral processing. Given the qualitatively different characteristics of central and peripheral visual processing it was expected that the viewing mode manipulation would dramatically influence the nature of visual behaviour resulting in differential memory representations.

In a pilot study, the Central and Peripheral viewing modes were contrasted with a Normal viewing mode in which the entire stimulus display was visible throughout the trial. As shown in Figure 2, saccades, high-velocity eye movements required to align the point of gaze with the display area of interest, produced in the Central viewing mode were shorter than normal, as the majority of saccades were aimed at the visible (i.e., inside the window) rather than the invisible (i.e., outside the window) regions of the stimulus display. In contrast, the saccades produced in the Peripheral viewing mode were longer than normal as the visible parts of the display were outside the window and participants were forced to fixate more than 5° away from any stimulus detail that they attempted to process.

In the present experiments, by orthogonally manipulating Viewing mode (Central, Peripheral) at encoding and retrieval, four experimental combinations were created (Central encoding/Central retrieval, Peripheral encoding/Central retrieval, Central encoding/Peripheral retrieval, and Peripheral encoding/Peripheral retrieval). Findings of better recognition memory performance when viewing modes matched across encoding and retrieval (henceforth, the Congruent condition) than when they mismatched (henceforth, the Incongruent condition) would constitute a prerequisite for demonstrating perceptual specificity effects in the present paradigm. Based on this logic, four experiments documented a variety of perceptual specificity effects with both verbal and non-verbal stimuli.

EXPERIMENT 1

In this experiment, natural scenes from four broad categories (Animals, Buildings, Interiors, and Landscapes) were used as stimuli, and each participant viewed only one category type. Viewing mode was manipulated at both encoding and retrieval, and recognition memory performance was contrasted across the four experimental conditions.

Method

Participants. A total of 44 paid participants took part in the present study. All participants had normal or corrected-to-normal vision.

Apparatus. Eye movements were measured with an SR Research Ltd EyeLink system. Following calibration, gaze-position error was less than 0.5 degrees. The temporal resolution of the system was 4 ms. During each trial in the study and test phases of the experiment, a gaze-contingent window was used to limit the stimulus display to a region either inside or outside a 10° square centred on the participant's point of gaze, constituting the Central and Peripheral viewing modes respectively (see Figure 1). The gaze-contingent window followed the participant's gaze position with an average delay of 14 ms.

Stimuli were displayed on a 17″ ViewSonic 17PS monitor from a distance of 60 centimetres, which subtended a visual angle of 30° horizontally and 22.5° vertically. The display was generated using an S3 VGA card, and the frame rate was 120 Hz.

Materials and design. Stimuli were greyscale images with 360 by 240 pixels resolution. To avoid recognition memory ceiling effects, each partici-

370

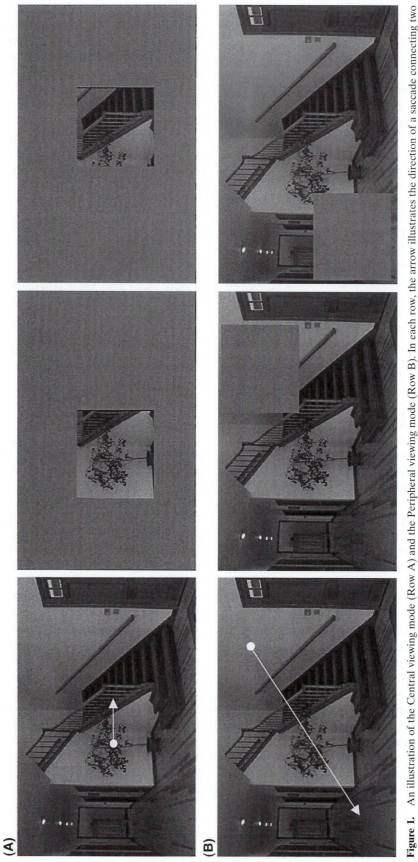

Figure 1. An illustration of the Central viewing mode (Row A) and the Peripheral viewing mode (Row B). In each row, the arrow illustrates the direction of a saccade connecting two consecutive gaze locations of a viewer looking at an image. The corresponding gaze-contingent displays are also shown. See text for details.

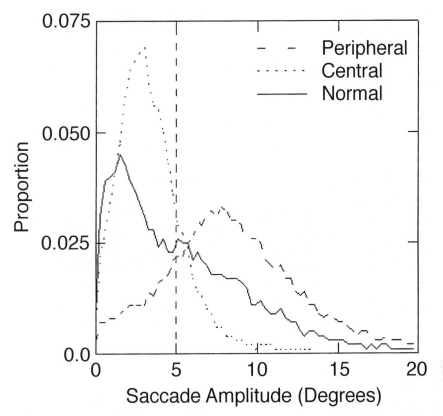

Figure 2.   The distribution of saccadic amplitudes as a function of viewing mode in a pilot study. See text for details.

pant was shown scenes from one of four categories of images (Animals, Buildings, Interiors, or Landscapes), for a total of 11 participants per scene type. During the study phase of the experiment, each participant was shown 36 images in the Central viewing mode and 36 images in the Peripheral viewing mode for a total of 72 trials. During the test phase of the experiment, 36 new images were added (18 shown in each viewing mode) and the 72 study or "old" images were shown as follows: 18 with Central encoding and Central retrieval, 18 with Peripheral encoding and Central retrieval, 18 with Central encoding and Peripheral retrieval, and 18 with Peripheral encoding and Peripheral retrieval. In addition, to help participants become familiar with the two viewing modes, before the experiment they were shown 12 images as practice (6 shown in each viewing mode). For each participant, the pairing of scenes to conditions and trial order was determined randomly

Procedure. A 9-point calibration was performed at the start of the experiment followed by a 9-point calibration accuracy test. Calibration was repeated if the error at any point was more than 1°,

or if the average error for all points was greater than 0.5°. During the study phase participants were instructed to memorise the scenes, each of which was shown for 5 seconds. During the test phase participants were instructed to judge, regardless of viewing mode, whether the images shown were old (i.e., seen in the study phase) or new. Participants were told that the speed of responding was not important and they were asked to be as accurate as possible. In each test trial, images were shown until the participant provided a response.

Results and discussion

For each participant and condition, recognition memory accuracy and reaction time measures were computed. In all of the experiments reported here there was no evidence of a speed—accuracy tradeoff. In order to derive a measure of memory sensitivity independent of response bias, recognition performance was computed as the proportion of hits minus the proportion of false alarms (see Snodgrass & Corwin, 1988).

The results of the experiment were analysed using a 4 × 2 × 2 mixed ANOVA, which crossed scene type (Animals, Buildings, Interiors, or Landscapes) as a between-participants factor with viewing modes at encoding (Central, Peripheral) and retrieval (Central, Peripheral) as within-participant factors. As shown in Figure 3, there was a large variation in recognition performance as a function of scene types, $F(3, 40) = 20.31$, $p < .001$, but this factor did not interact with any of the other factors in the experiment (all Fs < 1). Most importantly, a very powerful encoding viewing mode by retrieval viewing mode interaction was observed, $F(1, 40) = 126.88$, $p < .001$, reflecting better recognition memory when viewing modes were congruent than when they were incongruent (Central/Central and Peripheral/Peripheral > Central/Peripheral and Central/Peripheral; All $t(43)$s > 5.38, $p < .001$; see also Table 1). Thus, the present experiment documented a robust viewing mode congruency effect that generalised across the four different stimulus sets employed.

EXPERIMENT 2

The goal of this experiment was to further establish that the pattern documented in Experiment 1 reflects perceptual rather than semantic influences. As illustrated in Figure 4, a new stimulus set was created that included pairs of scenes (depicting activities, animals, or objects), with strong semantic similarity and weak visual similarity across pairs. Participants performed one of two retrieval tasks: (1) The "repeated scenes" condition—this condition was identical to the old/new recognition task used in the previous experiment; and (2) The "semantic associates" condition—in this condition participants were asked to classify scenes as semantically related or unrelated to the scenes shown during study. The perceptual specificity hypothesis predicts that the encoding by retrieval interaction observed in Experiment 1 should occur in the former, but not in the latter, condition.

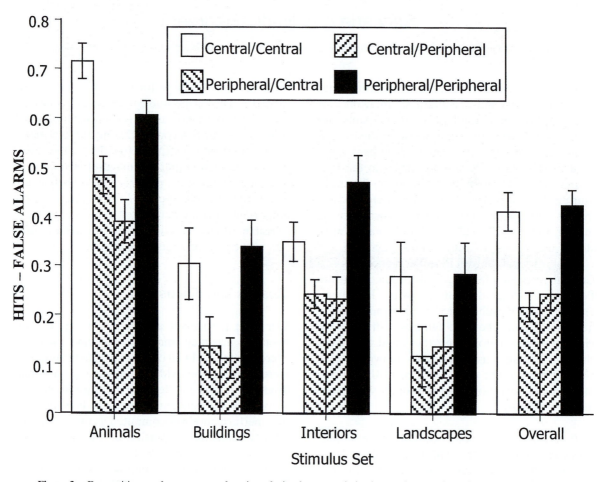

Figure 3.   Recognition performance as a function of stimulus set and viewing mode at study and test in Experiment 1.

Figure 4. An illustration of semantically related scene pairs used in Experiment 2 depicting activities (Row A), animals (Row B), and objects (Row C).

Method

General. Two groups, (the repeated scenes group and the semantic associates group) with 23 paid participants in each, took part in the experiment. None of the participants had taken part in Experiment 1. All participants had normal or corrected-to-normal vision.

The stimulus set included 24 pairs of scenes depicting activities, 48 pairs of scenes depicting animals, and 36 pairs of scenes depicting objects (see Figure 4). During the study phase of the experiment, in the Central and Peripheral viewing mode trials, each participant was shown 36 images (8 activities, 16 animals, and 12 objects) for a total of 72 trials. To avoid recognition memory ceiling

TABLE 1
Recognition performance in the congruent and incongruent
conditions in Experiments 1, 2, 3 and 4

Condition	Congruent	Incongruent
Experiment 1		
Animals	0.661 (0.022)	0.435 (0.029)
Buildings	0.321 (0.047)	0.124 (0.040)
Interiors	0.409 (0.034)	0.237 (0.030)
Landscapes	0.280 (0.051)	0.126 (0.047)
Overall	0.418 (0.030)	0.231 (0.026)
Experiment 2		
Repeat scenes	0.712 (0.028)	0.605 (0.029)
Semantic associates	0.523 (0.038)	0.499 (0.037)
Experiment 3		
Same typography	0.589 (0.026)	0.513 (0.031)
Different typography	0.480 (0.030)	0.500 (0.027)
Experiment 4		
Same orientation	0.398 (0.022)	0.285 (0.023)
Different orientation	0.219 (0.022)	0.141 (0.024)

effects in the repeated scenes condition study images were shown for only 2 seconds. Study images were shown for 5 seconds in the semantic associates condition. During the test phase, study images were presented in the repeated scenes condition while their counterparts were presented in the semantic associates condition. All other aspects of the experiment were identical to Experiment 1.

Results and discussion

Recognition memory performance in the congruent and incongruent viewing mode conditions in both the repeated scenes group and the semantic associates group are shown in Table 1. As can be clearly seen by an inspection of the Table, in the repeated scenes group recognition memory was better when viewing modes were congruent than when they were incongruent, $t(22) = 6.72, p < .001$, replicating the congruency effect demonstrated in Experiment 1. In contrast such an effect was not found in the semantic associates group, $t(22) = 1.31, p = .20$. This pattern resulted in a significant group by viewing mode congruency interaction, $F(1, 44) = 11.64, p < .001$. Thus, a viewing mode congruency effect did not occur despite the strong semantic resemblance between images presented at encoding and their associates presented at retrieval. This indicates the impor-

tance of perceptual encoding/retrieval overlap in mediating this effect.

EXPERIMENT 3

Using words as stimuli permits an even stronger test of the hypothesis that the congruency effects reported in the earlier experiments represent perceptual specificity effects. As illustrated in Figure 5, the stimulus set in the present study included words presented in one of two visually dissimilar typographies. Following Kolers' logic, the meaning of words is identical across typographies and therefore superior memory performance when the typography is matched across encoding and retrieval must be due to perceptual specificity effects. Based on the results of Experiment 2 it was expected that the viewing mode congruency effect would be obtained when the same typography was used at study and test (same typography condition) but would be absent when typography was different at study and test (different typography condition).

Method

General.   A total of 36 paid participants took part in the experiment. None of the participants had taken part in previous experiments. All participants had normal or corrected-to-normal vision.

As illustrated in Figure 5, words were presented in either an uppercase outline font or in lowercase bold font. During the study phase of the experiment, each participant was shown a total of 96 words, 24 in each combination of font (uppercase, lowercase) by viewing mode (Central, Peripheral). During the test phase of the experiment, 48 new words were added (12 shown in each font by viewing mode combination). In addition, half of the study words were shown in same font at test and the other half were shown in a different font corresponding to the same versus different typography conditions respectively.

In this experiment, the width of the gaze-contingen window was adjusted to be 4° corresponding to the approximate average width of a single character in either font. Throughout the trial, the window was extended vertically to cover the entire height of the screen (i.e., it was insensitive to vertical gaze position). All other

Figure 5.   An illustration of the typographies used in Experiment 3.

aspects of the experiment were identical to Experiment 1.

Results and discussion

Recognition memory performance in the congruent and incongruent viewing mode conditions in both the same typography and different typography conditions is shown in Table 1. Replicating previous experiments, in the same typography condition recognition memory was better when viewing modes were congruent than when they were incongruent, $t(35) = 3.50$, $p < .001$. In contrast, such an effect was not found in the different typography condition ($t < 1$). This pattern resulted in a significant typography match by viewing mode congruency interaction, $F(1, 35) = 10.64$, $p < .01$. Thus, consistent with the results of Experiment 2, when the semantic object (i.e., word) was held constant but the visual object (i.e., typography) changed, the viewing mode congruency effect disappeared. This strongly suggests that perceptually specific memory representations mediate the viewing mode congruency effect.

EXPERIMENT 4

This experiment further explored the degree to which the perceptual processing at encoding and retrieval must overlap as a prerequisite for demonstrating the viewing mode congruency effect. The mismatch conditions used in Experiment 2 (semantic associates) and Experiment 3

(different typography) eliminated the viewing mode congruency effect. In the present experiment, a more subtle perceptual mismatch condition was employed. Specifically, during the study phase of this experiment, in each viewing mode, scenes were shown to participants rotated 90° clockwise or 90° counterclockwise. During test, scenes were shown either in the same orientation as in the study phase (same orientation condition) or in the normal upright orientation (different orientation condition).

Method

General.   A total of 32 paid participants took part in the experiment. None of the participants had taken part in previous experiments. All participants had normal or corrected-to-normal vision.

Greyscale images with 240 by 240 pixels resolution depicting animals were used as stimuli. During the study phase of the experiment, each participant was shown a total of 96 scenes, 24 in each combination of orientation (90° clockwise, 90° counterclockwise) by viewing mode (Central, Peripheral). During the test phase of the experiment, half of the scenes presented during study were shown in same orientation at test and the other half were shown in a normal upright orientation corresponding to the same versus different orientation conditions respectively. In addition, 48 new scenes were shown during the test phase (12 in each orientation by viewing mode combination). All other aspects of the experiment were identical to Experiment 1.

Results and discussion

Recognition memory performance in the congruent and incongruent viewing mode conditions in both the same orientation and different orientation conditions is shown in Table 1. Recognition memory was substantially better when scene orientation was matched than when it was mismatched across study and test, $F(1, 31) = 71.38, p < .001$. However, in both the same and different orientation conditions, recognition memory was better when viewing modes were congruent than when they were incongruent: same orientation, $t(31) = 5.04, p < .001$; different orientation, $t(31) = 3.44, p < .01$. The orientation match by viewing mode congruency interaction was not significant, $F(1, 31) = 1.07, p = .31$. Thus, the present experiment documented two independent specificity effects, demonstrating that recognition memory is likely influenced by multiple levels of perceptual representations, both ones that are orientation-specific (accounting for the effect of orientation match) and ones that are orientation-invariant (accounting for the effect of viewing mode congruency).

GENERAL DISCUSSION

Extending the methodology developed by Kolers, the present study clearly demonstrated that in addition to the well-documented conceptual influences on recognition memory (e.g., LOP effects and generation effects), performance on this task is partially mediated by a variety of perceptually specific memory representations. The present results are consistent with several recent reports demonstrating that a mismatch in the size, rotation, contrast, illumination, or colour of objects across study and test led to poorer recognition memory performance (Beiderman & Cooper, 1992; Cave, Bost, & Cobb, 1996; Cooper, Schacter, Ballesteros, & Moore, 1992; Jolicoeur, 1987; Kolers, Duchnicky, & Sundstroem, 1985; Milliken & Jolicoeur, 1992; Rajaram, 1996; Srinivas, 1995, 1996). The present study established that such effects are reliably obtained across a wide range of stimulus material and can be very substantial in magnitude (e.g., Experiment 1).

The present findings are also consistent with the results from a recent series of studies examining recognition memory performance of patients with semantic dementia (Graham, Becker, & Hodges, 1997; Graham, Simons, Pratt, Patterson, & Hodges, 2000; Simons & Graham, 2000; Simons, Graham, Galton, Patterson, & Hodges, 2001). These studies demonstrated that despite strong conceptual and semantic deficits, patients show normal recognition memory for pictures of nameable objects provided that identical exemplars are presented at study and test (Graham et al., 2000). In marked contrast, when the exemplars of objects differ across study and test, recognition memory is severely impaired. Thus, recognition memory performance in semantic dementia patients must be mediated at least in part by perceptually specific memory representations. The present study demonstrated that such representations are also a factor in recognition memory with normal participants.

As mentioned earlier, findings of perceptual specificity effects documented with indirect or implicit memory tasks had a marked influence on both processing views of memory (e.g., Jacoby, 1983; Roediger & Blaxton, 1987; Roediger & Srinivas, 1993; Roediger et al., 1989) and multiple memory systems views (e.g., Moscovitch, 1992; Schacter, 1994; Schacter & Tulving, 1994; Schacter et al., 2000; Squire, 1992; Tulving & Schacter, 1990). It is argued here that any comprehensive theory of memory must also account for perceptual specificity effects on recognition performance such as the ones demonstrated in the present study.

Taken together, the conceptual and perceptual influences reported in the literature clearly indicate that any "single process" view of recognition memory is untenable (see also Gardiner, 1988; Jacoby, 1991; Mandler, 1980; Tulving 1985). More generally, the present findings point to the danger of assuming a one-to-one mapping between tasks and processes/systems (see Jacoby, 1991; Reingold & Merikle, 1988, 1990; Reingold & Toth, 1996; Richardson-Klavehn & Bjork, 1988; Ryan & Cohen, 2002; Toth & Reingold, 1996; Toth, Reingold, & Jacoby, 1994). Indeed, semantic primacy is an extreme illustration of such an assumption.

Consequently, exploring the experimental and participant variables that may determine the precise mixture of conceptual and perceptual influences on recognition performance is an important goal for future research. The present findings suggest that one potentially important factor is related to the use of verbal versus nonverbal stimulus material. This is the case as the magnitude of the perceptual specificity effects was larger with non-verbal stimuli (Experiments 1, 2,

4) than with verbal stimuli (Experiment 3). Interestingly, this variable also seems to be important in the context of LOP effects. Specifically, whereas LOP effects are very robust with verbal material, they are not easily documented with non-verbal stimuli (see Baddeley, 1978; Velichkovsky, 2002). One possible explanation for this difference in results as a function of stimulus type may be that non-verbal stimulus material often provides far richer and more distinctive perceptual context than verbal stimuli containing different combinations of the same basic units (i.e., letters) and resulting in relatively impoverished and indistinct perceptual environment.

Thus, it appears that in addition to the nature of the task (e.g., indirect or implicit vs direct or explicit; see Challis, Velichovsky, & Craik, 1996) the type of the stimulus material (i.e., verbal vs non-verbal) may mediate the magnitude of perceptual and conceptual memory influences. The fact that the vast majority of memory research prior to the last three decades involved the use of recognition and recall tasks with verbal stimuli undoubtedly contributed to the pervasiveness of the semantic primacy assumption. Thirty years later it is now evident that such a "pearl-in-the-oyster" theory of memory—according to which perceptual analysis serves only as a tool to extract the semantic pearl, after which the surface shell is discarded—is ill-founded.

REFERENCES

Baddeley, A.D. (1978). The trouble with levels: A reexamination of Craik and Lockhart's framework for memory research. *Psychological Review*, *85*, 139–152.

Beiderman, I., & Cooper, E.E. (1992). Size invariance in visual priming. *Journal of Experimental psychology: Human Perception & Performance*, *18*, 121–133.

Cave, C.B., Bost, P.R., & Cobb, R.E. (1996). Effects of color and pattern on implicit and explicit picture memory. *Journal of Experimental Psychology: Learning, Memory, & Cognition*, *22*, 639–653.

Challis, B.H., Velichovsky, B.M., & Craik, F.I.M. (1996). Levels-of-processing effects on a variety of memory tasks: New findings and theoretical implications. *Consciousness & Cognition: An International Journal*, *5*, 142–164.

Chomsky, N. (1957). *Syntactic structures*. The Hague: Mouton.

Chomsky, N. (1965). *Aspects of the theory of syntax*. Cambridge, MA: MIT Press.

Cooper, L.A., Schacter, D.L., Ballesteros, S., & Moore, C. (1992). Priming and recognition of transformed three-dimensional objects: Effects of size and reflection. *Journal of Experimental Psychology: Learning, Memory, & Cognition*, *18*, 43–57.

Craik, F.I.M. (1989). On the making of episodes. In H.L. Roediger & F.I.M. Craik (Eds.), *Varieties of memory and consciousness: Essays in honour of Endel Tulving* (pp. 43–57). Hillsdale, NJ: Lawrence Erlbaum Associates Inc.

Craik, F.I.M., & Lockhart, R.S. (1972). Levels of processing: A framework for memory research. *Journal of Verbal Learning and Verbal Behavior*, *11*, 671–684.

Craik, F.I.M., & Tulving, E. (1975). Depth of processing and the retention of words in episodic memory. *Journal of Experimental Psychology: General*, *104*, 268–294.

Gardiner, J.M. (1988). Functional aspects of recollective experience. *Memory & Cognition*, *16*, 309–313.

Gonzalez, E.G., & Kolers, P.A. (1982). Mental manipulation of arithmetic symbols. *Journal of Experimental Psychology: Learning, Memory and Cognition*, *8*, 308–319.

Graf, P. (1981). Reading and generating normal and transformed sentences. *Canadian Journal of Psychology*, *35*, 293–308.

Graf, P., & Levy, B.A. (1984). Remembering and reading: Conceptual and perceptual processing involved in reading rotated passages. *Journal of Verbal Learning and Verbal Behavior*, *23*, 405–424.

Graham, K.S., Becker, J.T., & Hodges, J.R. (1997). On the relationship between knowledge and memory for pictures: Evidence from the study of patients with semantic dementia and Alzheimer's disease. *Journal of the International Neuropsychological Society*, *3*, 534–544.

Graham, K.S., Simons, J.S., Pratt, K.H., Patterson, K., & Hodges, J.R. (2000). Insights from semantic dementia on the relationship between episodic and semantic memory. *Neuropsychologia*, *38*, 313–324.

Horton, K.D. (1985). The role of semantic information in reading spatially transformed text. *Cognitive Psychology*, *17*, 66–88.

Horton, K.D. (1989). The processing of spatially transformed text. *Memory & Cognition*, *17*, 283–291.

Jacoby, L.L. (1983). Remembering the data: Analyzing interactive processes in reading. *Journal of Verbal Learning and Verbal Behavior*, *22*, 485–508.

Jacoby, L.L. (1991). A process dissociation framework: Separating automatic from intentional uses of memory. *Journal of Memory and Language*, *30*, 513–541.

Jacoby, L.L., Kelley, C.M., & Dywan, J. (1989). Memory attributions. In H.L. Roediger, & F.I.M. Craik (Eds.), *Varieties of memory and consciousness: Essays in honour of Endel Tulving* (pp. 391–422). Hillsdale, NJ: Lawrence Erlbaum Associates Inc.

Jolicoeur, P. (1987). A size-congruency effect in memory for visual shape. *Memory & Cognition*, *15*, 531–543.

Kolers, P.A. (1968). The recognition of geometrically transformed text. *Perception & Psychophysics*, *3*, 57–64.

Kolers, P.A. (1973). Remembering operations. *Memory & Cognition*, *1*, 347–355.

Kolers, P.A. (1975). Specificity of operations in sentence recognition. *Cognitive Psychology, 7,* 289–306.

Kolers, P.A. (1976). Reading a year later. *Journal of Experimental Psychology: Human Learning and Memory, 2,* 554–565.

Kolers, P.A. (1978). On the representations of experience. In D. Gerver & W. Sinaiko (Eds.), *Language interpretation and communication.* New York: Plenum.

Kolers, P.A. (1979). A pattern-analyzing basis of recognition. In L.S. Cermak & F.I.M. Craik (Eds.), *Levels of processing in human memory.* Hillsdale, NJ: Lawrence Erlbaum Associates Inc.

Kolers, P.A., Duchnicky, R.L., & Sundstroem, G. (1985). Size in the visual processing of faces and words. *Journal of Experimental Psychology: Human Perception & Performance, 11,* 726–751.

Kolers, P.A., & Magee, L.E. (1978). Specificity of pattern-analyzing skills in reading. *Canadian Journal of Psychology, 32,* 43–51.

Kolers P.A., Palef, S.R., & Stelmach, L.B. (1980). Graphemic analysis underlying literacy. *Memory & Cognition, 8,* 322–328.

Kolers P.A., & Perkins, D.N. (1975). Spatial and ordinal components of form perception and literacy. *Cognitive Psychology, 7,* 228–267.

Kolers, P.A., & Roediger, H.L. (1984). Procedures of mind. *Journal of Verbal Learning and Verbal Behaviour, 23,* 425–449.

Kolers, P.A., & Smythe, W.E. (1979). Images, symbols and skills. *Canadian Journal of Psychology, 33,* 158–184.

Kolers, P.A., & Smythe, W.E. (1984). Symbol manipulation: Alternatives to the computational view of mind. *Journal of Verbal Learning and Verbal Behaviour, 23,* 289–314.

Levy, B.A. (1993). Fluent rereading: An implicit indicator of reading skill development. In P. Graf & M. Masson (Eds.), *Implicit memory: New directions in cognition, development and neuropsychology.* Hillsdale, NJ: Lawrence Erlbaum Associates Inc.

Mandler, G. (1980). Recognizing: The judgment of previous occurrence. *Psychological Review, 87,* 252–271.

Masson, M.E.J. (1984). Memory for the surface structure of sentences: Remembering with and without awareness. *Journal of Verbal Learning and Verbal Behaviour, 23,* 579–592.

Masson, M.E.J. (1986). Identification of typographically transformed words: Instance-based skill acquisition. *Journal of Experimental Psychology: Learning, Memory and Cognition, 12,* 479–488.

Masson, M.E.J., & Sala, L.S. (1978). Interactive processes in sentence comprehension and recognition. *Cognitive Psychology, 10,* 244–270.

McConkie, G.W., & Rayner, K. (1975). The span of the effective stimulus during a fixation in reading. *Perception & Psychophysics, 17,* 578–586.

Milliken, B., & Jolicoeur, P. (1992). Size effects in visual recognition memory are determined by perceived size. *Memory & Cognition, 20,* 83–95.

Moscovitch, M. (1992). Memory and working-with-memory: A component process model based on modules and central systems. *Journal of Cognitive Neuroscience (Special Issue: Memory Systems), 4,* 257–267.

Moscovitch, M., Vriezen, E.R., & Gottstein, J. (1993). Implicit tests of memory in patients with focal lesions or degenerative brain disorders. In H. Spinnler & F. Boller (Eds.), *Handbook of neuropsychology* (Vol. 8). Amsterdam: Elsevier.

Pomplun, M., Reingold, E.M., & Shen, J. (2001). Investigating the visual span in comparative search: The effects of task difficulty and divided attention. *Cognition, 81,* B57–B67.

Rajaram, S. (1996). Perceptual effects on remembering: Recollective processes in picture recognition memory. *Journal of Experimental Psychology: Learning, Memory, & Cognition, 22,* 365–377.

Rayner, K. (1998). Eye movements in reading and information processing: 20 years of research. *Psychological Bulletin, 124,* 372–422.

Reingold, E.M., Charness, N., Pomplun, M., & Stampe, D.M. (2001). Visual span in expert chess players: Evidence from eye movements. *Psychological Science, 12,* 49–56.

Reingold, E.M., & Merikle, P.M. (1988). Using direct and indirect measures to study perception without awareness. *Perception & Psychophysics, 44,* 563–575.

Reingold, E.M., & Merikle, P.M. (1990). On the interrelatedness of theory and measurement in the study of unconscious processes. *Mind and Language, 5,* 9–28.

Reingold, E.M., & Toth, J.P. (1996). Process dissociations versus task dissociations: A controversy in progress. In G.D.M. Underwood (Ed). *Implicit cognition* (pp. 159–202). New York: Oxford University Press.

Richardson-Klavehn, A., & Bjork, R.A. (1988). Measures of memory. *Annual Review of Psychology, 39,* 475–543.

Roediger, H.L., & Blaxton, T.A. (1987). Effects of varying modality, surface features, and retention interval on priming in word-fragment completion. *Memory & Cognition, 15,* 379–388.

Roediger, H.L., & McDermott, K.B. (1993). Implicit memory in normal human subjects. In H. Spinnler & F. Boller (Eds.), *Handbook of neuropsychology* (Vol. 8, pp. 63–131). Amsterdam: Elsevier.

Roediger, H.L., & Srinivas, K. (1993). Specificity of operations in perceptual priming. In P. Graf & M.E.J. Masson (Eds.), *Implicit memory: New directions in cognition, development, and neuropsychology* (pp. 17–48). Hillsdale, NJ: Lawrence Erlbaum Associates Inc.

Roediger, H.L., & Weldon, M.S. (1987). Reversing the picture superiority effect. In M.A. McDaniel & M. Pressley (Eds.), *Imagery and related mnemonic processes: Theories, individual differences, applications* (pp. 151–174). New York: Springer-Verlag.

Roediger, H.L., Weldon, M.S., & Challis, B.H. (1989). Explaining dissociations between implicit and explicit measures of retention: A processing account. In H.L. Roediger & F.I.M. Craik (Eds.), *Varieties of memory and consciousness: Essays in honour of Endel Tulving* (pp. 3–41). Hillsdale, NJ: Lawrence Erlbaum Associates Inc.

Ryan, J.D., & Cohen, N.J. (2002). *On the evidence for multiple memory systems*. Manuscript submitted for publication.

Schacter, D.L. (1987). Implicit memory: History and current status. *Journal of Experimental Psychology: Learning, Memory, and Cognition, 13*, 501–518.

Schacter, D.L. (1994). Priming and multiple memory system: Perceptual mechanisms of implicit memory. In D.L. Schacter & E. Tulving (Eds.), *Memory systems 1994* (pp. 233–268). Cambridge, MA: The MIT Press.

Schacter, D.L., & Tulving, E. (1994). What are the memory systems of 1994? In D.L. Schacter & E. Tulving (Eds.), *Memory systems 1994* (pp. 1–38). Cambridge, MA: The MIT Press.

Schacter, D.L., Wagner, A.D., & Buckner, R.L. (2000). Memory systems of 1999. In E. Tulving & F.I.M. Craik (Eds.), *The Oxford handbook of memory* (pp. 627–643). New York: Oxford University Press.

Simons, J.S., & Graham, K.S. (2000). New learning in semantic dementia: Implications for cognitive and neuroanatomical models of long-term memory. *Revue de Neuropsychologie, 10*, 199–215.

Simons, J.S., Graham, K.S., Galton, C.J., Patterson, K., & Hodges, J.R. (2001). Semantic knowledge and episodic memory for faces in semantic dementia. *Neuropsychology, 15*, 101–114.

Slamecka, N.J., & Graf, P. (1978). The generation effect: Delineation of a phenomenon. *Journal of Experimental Psychology: Human Learning & Memory, 4*, 592–604.

Snodgrass, J.G., & Corwin, J. (1988). Pragmatics of measuring recognition memory: Applications to dementia and amnesia. *Journal of Experimental Psychology: General, 117*, 34–50.

Squire, L.R. (1992). Memory and the hippocampus: A synthesis from findings with rats, monkeys, and humans. *Psychological Review, 99*, 195–231.

Srinivas, K. (1995). Representation of rotated objects in explicit and implicit memory. *Journal of Experimental Psychology: Learning, Memory, & Cognition, 21*, 1019–1036.

Srinivas, K. (1996). Contrast and illumination effects on explicit and implicit measures of memory. *Journal of Experimental Psychology: Learning, Memory, & Cognition, 22*, 1123–1135.

Tardif, T., & Craik, F.I.M. (1989). Reading a week later: Perceptual and conceptual factors. *Journal of Memory and Language, 28*, 107–125.

Toth, J.P., & Reingold, E.M. (1996). Beyond perception: Conceptual contributions to unconscious influences of memory. In G.D.M. Underwood (Ed.), *Implicit cognition* (pp. 41–84). New York: Oxford University Press.

Toth, J.P., Reingold, E.M., & Jacoby, L.L. (1994). Toward a redefinition of implicit memory: Process dissociations following elaborative processing and self-generation. *Journal of Experimental Psychology: Learning, Memory, and Cognition, 20*, 290–303.

Tulving, E. (1983). *Elements of episodic memory*. New York: Oxford University Press.

Tulving, E. (1985). Memory and consciousness. *Canadian Psychology, 26*, 1–12.

Tulving, E., & Schacter, D.L. (1990). Priming and human memory systems. *Science, 247*, 301–306.

Velichkovsky, B.M. (2002). Levels of processing: Validating the concept. In M. Naveh-Benjamin, M. Moscovitch, & H.L. Roediger (Eds.), *Perspectives on human memory and cognitive aging: Essays in honor of Fergus Craik*. New York: Psychology Press.

MEMORY, 2002, *10* (5/6), 381–388

Directed remembering:
Subliminal cues alter nonconscious memory strategies

Jason P. Mitchell

Harvard University, USA

C. Neil Macrae

Dartmouth College, UK

Jonathan W. Schooler

University of Pittsburgh, USA

Angela C. Rowe

University of Bristol, UK

Alan B. Milne

University of Aberdeen, UK

Much research on memory function has focused on changes in recognition performance brought about by differences in the processes engaged during encoding. In most of this work, participants either receive explicit instructions to remember particular items or they perform orienting (i.e., encoding) tasks that support different levels of memory performance. In daily life, however, the retention or dismissal of information often occurs without conscious intent, thereby suggesting an alternative, nonconscious route through which purposive remembering and forgetting can occur. Based on this line of reasoning, we speculated that recognition performance in a standard item-based forgetting paradigm may be moderated by subliminal cues that trigger the automatic activation of different mnemonic strategies. We report the results of two experiments that supported this prediction. In each experiment, the basic item-based forgetting effect was replicated, but via the subliminal presentation of "remember" and "forget" cues. In addition, cue-dependent differences in memory performance were traced to the operation of a covert rehearsal mechanism during encoding. We consider the implications of these findings for the nonconscious operation of memory processes in everyday life.

From cocktail parties to chemistry examinations to card games, failures of memory can have some troublesome consequences. An inability to remember the name of an acquaintance, the atomic weight of nitrogen, or the current trump suit may result in considerably more than mere frustration over the fragility of memory. Such lapses may promptly give rise to an embarrassing social interaction, an abysmal grade, or an irate bridge partner. It comes as little surprise, therefore, to learn that programmes promising to improve memory performance have existed since at least the Middle Ages (e.g., "memory theatres", see Schacter, 1996) and continue to the present

Requests for reprints should be sent to Jason P. Mitchell, Department of Psychology, Harvard University, William James Hall, 33 Kirkland Street, Cambridge, MA 02138, USA. Email: jmitchel@wjh.harvard.edu

This research was supported by a National Science Foundation graduate research fellowship to Jason P. Mitchell.

DOI:10.1080/09658210244000207

day in the form of self-help manuals and audio tapes (Greenwald, Spangenberg, Pratkanis, & Eskenazi, 1991; Higbee, 1977). Remembering, it would appear, is a skill worth having.

As it turns out, however, in charting the memorial operations that support effective daily functioning, remembering is only part of the story. Although interpersonal success clearly depends on the ability to retrieve information that is relevant to one's current goals and objectives, daily life also demands a mechanism through which unwanted, irrelevant, or inappropriate material can be screened out, ignored, or actively forgotten (see Anderson & Neely, 1996; Anderson & Spellman, 1995; Bjork, Bjork, & Anderson, 1998; Bjork, 1989; MacLeod, 1998). Just as an inability to encode information may prompt moments of embarrassment or confusion, indiscriminate or uncontrollable remembering can prove no less calamitous. Luria (1968) provided a now classic description of the mnemonist, S, whose nearly effortless memory for the most minute details of events severely hampered his everyday life. Similarly, Schacter (2001) relates the story of Donnie Moore, a baseball pitcher driven to despair and eventual suicide by the inescapable memory of a playoff game loss. Preventing the permanent etching of unwanted or inappropriate material in conscious memory is no less important than the ability to retain wanted and appropriate material, and both are basic requirements if the human mind is to function in an optimal manner (Freud, 1930/1989). Successful memory is defined by such selectivity: we must simultaneously remember that which should be remembered while forgetting (i.e., ignoring, discarding, or suppressing) that which should be forgotten.

So, how do we selectively remember and forget? Over the past three decades, one of the most useful answers to this question has been provided by the levels-of-processing (LOP) account, first introduced by Craik and Lockhart (1972) and subsequently expanded by Craik and Tulving (1975). Within the levels (or depth) of processing view, the mnemonic fate of information is determined by the amount of elaborative processing garnered by that material at encoding. All else being equal, information that attracts elaborative encoding operations tends to be better remembered than information afforded only relatively shallow, superficial processing. In work of this kind, elaborative processing is typically supported by encoding tasks in which participants are asked to integrate to-be-remembered items with existing semantic knowledge. This contrasts with shallow encoding tasks in which participants' attention is directed to perceptual features of the items (Craik & Tulving, 1975).

Admirably, the LOP account reflects our common experience of consciously choosing which information to discard or ignore and which information to commit to memory on a permanent basis. When attempting to retain a phone number for a temporary processing objective (e.g., ordering a pizza), we engage in rather shallow, rote rehearsal of the material (i.e., repeating the digits aloud). On the other hand, if the phone number is to be remembered into the future (e.g., the telephone number of one's new partner), we likely engage a different set of mnemonic strategies, perhaps considering how the number is similar to others we know or by thinking of the digits in some other system (such as golf scores or track & field times—see Schacter, 1996). Interestingly, however, everyday mnemonic operations rarely require such explicit intentions to remember or forget the past. Far more often, the processes underlying successful memory performance take place automatically and outside of consciousness. Although at times one may certainly make a conscious effort to remember or forget particular events or information, more often than not, these abilities do not require strategic deployment of encoding processes. For example, we may remember the details of a recent colloquium lecture we attended, despite the low probability that we consciously attempted to encode the information. At the same time, many such lectures have no doubt faded into obscurity in our minds— especially if the content was quite distant from our primary intellectual interests. Importantly, this information was likely discarded from memory in an effortless manner and did not require conscious inhibition of the material or the implementation of some counter-mnemonic; the unimportant material was simply forgotten. In both cases, we were likely to have been a quiet, attentive member of the audience, yet in one case information was easily remembered, whereas in the other it was readily forgotten.

What processes contribute to this automatic, nonconscious ability to remember or forget the past? The LOP account has proved useful for organising empirical observations that different memory performance is produced by encoding tasks that orient participants to different aspects of material. However, to what extent can this approach also incorporate the informal observation that such explicit orienting rarely occurs in everyday life, and yet successful, selective remembering nevertheless occurs? The present experiments provide evidence that LOP is indeed a useful framework for thinking about how memory processes are regulated (i) outside of conscious awareness, and (ii) without explicit manipulation of the processing orientation adopted by perceivers at encoding. In two experiments, we demonstrate that subliminally-rendered cues can successfully trigger shifts in the depth to which participants process stimulus items during an incidental encoding task.

These experiments dovetail with other recent investigations that suggest the power of subliminal cues to influence memory performance. In a recent investigation of implicit social cognition, Chartrand and Bargh (1996) demonstrated that the presentation of cues outside of conscious awareness can nevertheless prompt participants to adopt different mnemonic strategies. Indeed, subliminally-presented information was shown to influence not only participants' recall performance, but also the manner in which they represented material in memory. Participants read sentence fragments that described actions performed by a fictional person (e.g., "went skiing in Colorado", "had a party for some friends last week"). Prior to this phase of the experiment, however, a parafoveal priming technique (Bargh & Pietromonaco, 1982) was used to present some participants with subliminal cues that were related to impression-formation goals (e.g., *impression*, *judgement*, *personality*, *evaluate*). Critically, the subliminal presentation of these cues was sufficient to reproduce the pattern of memory performance that is observed when participants are given explicit impression-formation instructions, such as better memory for incongruent trait information (Hamilton, Katz, & Leirer, 1980). Thus, goal activation can seemingly be triggered automatically and can produce memorial effects identical to those elicited by conscious information-processing strategies (see also Bargh, 1997; Bargh & Chartrand, 1999; Bargh & Ferguson, 2000).

Extending work of this kind, we employed subliminal memory cues in a different experimental paradigm that has been shown to induce conscious changes in strategic encoding processes, namely, item-based directed forgetting (Basden & Basden, 1998; Bjork et al., 1998; Johnson, 1994; MacLeod, 1998). In the item-based method of directed forgetting, each stimulus is followed by a cue that signals whether the item should be remembered or forgotten. In this paradigm, participants adopt a rehearsal strategy (i.e., maintenance rehearsal) in which they minimally rehearse each item until the appearance of the cue (Basden & Basden, 1996). Then, depending on the nature of the cue (i.e., remember or forget), participants either initiate further processing of the item (for to-be-remembered items) or they suspend rehearsal altogether (for to-be-forgotten items). In other words, some items are processed more deeply or elaborately than others (Craik & Lockhart, 1972; Craik & Tulving, 1975), producing better recognition performance for items that were followed by "remember" (R) than by "forget" (F) cues (Basden & Basden, 1998; Johnson, 1994; MacLeod, 1998).[1]

In the two experiments reported here, we investigated whether the presentation of subliminal R and F cues would impact on people's subsequent memory performance. In a modified version of the item-based method of directed forgetting (Basden & Basden, 1998), participants were presented with a series of stimulus words (i.e., forenames) that were followed by subliminal R or F cues. Despite the subliminal nature of the cues, we anticipated that the standard differences in memory performance would emerge. That is, participants would show better recognition for items followed by R than F cues. As noted earlier, when previous research presented R and F cues supraliminally, differences in memory performance were directly linked to shifts in the encoding processes engaged by each type of cue. In the same way, we expected that subliminal cues to remember would likewise trigger deeper processing than subliminal cues to forget. Our second experiment tests this depth-of-processing prediction more directly.

Unlike previous research using the item-based directed forgetting method, participants in the present experiments were not forewarned about

---

[1] Of course, because the item-based method relies on differential rehearsal, memory differences between remember and forget items do not necessarily reflect intentional *forgetting, per se*. That is, within this paradigm, participants do not actively have to inhibit or suppress the retrieval of existing memories (Bjork, 1989; Johnson, 1994). Thus, directed *remembering* may be a better description of the effect that is elicited in work of this kind. Nevertheless, this approach is commonly used to investigate fundamental aspects of intentional forgetting, and we refer to the method as an item-based directed forgetting paradigm (Johnson, 1994; MacLeod, 1998).

an upcoming memory test. Because of the incidental nature of encoding in our experiments, participants were not likely motivated to explicitly commit the material to memory in the first place. Together with the subliminal presentation of the R and F cues, this incidental encoding task ensured that shifts in the depth to which stimuli were processed took place outside of conscious awareness.

EXPERIMENT 1

Experiment 1 examined whether subliminal cues to remember or forget material would impact memory performance. Participants incidentally encoded a series of forenames and, although no mention was made of a subsequent memory test, each item was followed by a subliminal R or F cue or a control cue that was unrelated to memory function. Following this incidental study phase, participants' memory for the items was assessed using a standard old/new recognition test.

Method

Participants and design.   A total of 12 students at the University of Bristol participated in the experiment. The experiment had a single factor (cue type: remember or forget or control) repeated-measures design.

Procedure and stimulus materials.   Stimulus presentation was controlled by an Apple Macintosh G3 computer. Participants sat in a darkened room with their head on a chin rest approximately 57 cm from the computer monitor. A pool of 120 common British forenames was assembled from Internet name compendia (e.g., www.babycentre.co.uk; www.namingbaby.co.uk) and divided into four lists of 30 names (15 female, 15 male). The average length and popularity of the forenames was equated across the lists. Counterbalancing ensured that each forename appeared equally often as a to-be-remembered (R), to-be-forgotten (F), control, or foil item. Stimuli were drawn in white on a black screen in Geneva 14-type font. In the first phase of the experiment, participants were introduced to a study on the effects of distraction on cognitive processing. No mention was made of an upcoming memory test. Each trial began with a forename presented in the centre of the screen for 1200 ms. Participants were instructed to read

each forename aloud into a microphone when the item appeared on the screen. The forename was then masked by a random string of 11 letters for 66 ms (e.g., vckzfqnjwpr). Immediately following the mask, the word "remember" or "forget" or "extract" (i.e., control cue) was presented for 34 ms and then replaced by a different random letter string. The second mask remained for 250 ms, a blank screen was presented for 1700 ms, and then the next trial began. Previous pilot testing confirmed that, at an exposure duration of 34 ms, participants were unable to identify the items.[2] Participants were presented with 60 forenames, with the stimulus items accompanied by an equal number of R, F, and control cues. On completion of the study phase, participants were given a surprise old/new recognition test. Participants were presented with the 60 original forenames randomly interspersed with 60 foils. Forenames were presented sequentially and participants indicated whether each item was "old" or "new" by pressing one of two appropriately labelled keys. Each item remained on the screen until the participant responded and the next item followed after a 1000 ms interval. Following the recognition memory test, participants were debriefed, thanked for their assistance, and dismissed.

Results and discussion

The hypothesis in Experiment 1 was that recognition performance would be better for forenames followed by subliminal R than F cues. To test this

---

[2] To confirm that R and F cues were indeed presented subliminally, a separate group of 17 participants completed a set of 60 trials identical to those described, without any mention of the subliminal cues. Following these trials, participants were asked whether they "noticed anything unusual in the experiment". Subsequently, these participants were alerted to the subliminal cues and asked to guess five times what these cues might have been. No participant spontaneously indicated awareness of the subliminal words or successfully guessed the identity of the cues. Finally, participants were shown a new series of six trials with the experimental parameters and, after each, were asked to indicate the identity of the subliminal cue. On the vast majority of these trials (71/102), participants declined to guess; however, of the 31 guesses, the cue was correctly identified only once (in this case, the word "forget"). Accordingly, these results confirm that the experimental parameters successfully rendered the vast majority of cues subliminal, even after participants were expressly alerted to the presence of the subliminal stimuli, and that participants naïve to the subliminal cues were highly unlikely to have spontaneously perceived any of the cues.

prediction, corrected recognition scores were calculated separately for R, F, and control items by subtracting the proportion of false alarms (.117) from the proportion of hits. The top panel of Table 1 presents participants' mean corrected recognition performance. A single factor (cue type: remember or forget or control) repeated measures analysis of variance (ANOVA) revealed an effect of cue type on recognition performance, $F(2, 22) = 3.69$, $p < .04$. Post-hoc tests confirmed that recognition performance was better following the presentation of R cues than either F or control cues (both $ps < .05$). No difference in recognition performance was observed following the presentation of F and control cues. These effects, then, supported our experimental prediction. Although participants were unable to detect the subliminal cues, recognition performance was better for R- than F-cued items.

EXPERIMENT 2

The results of Experiment 1 confirmed that subliminal R and F cues can produce results comparable to other studies using an item-based directed forgetting paradigm. Elsewhere, researchers have traced item-based forgetting effects to the operation of different rehearsal strategies during the encoding phase of the task (Basden & Basden, 1996; Basden, Basden, & Gargano, 1993). Specifically, the provision of explicit R and F cues prompts participants to selectively rehearse the to-be-remembered items and to suspend processing of the to-be-forgotten words (see Basden & Basden, 1998; Wetzel & Hunt, 1977; Woodward & Bjork, 1971). As a result of these processing differences (Craik & Lockhart, 1972; Craik & Tulving, 1975), recognition performance is better for items that are followed by R than F cues.

Does this selective rehearsal strategy also account for the results observed in Experiment 1? The fact that recognition performance was equivalent for items followed by both F and control cues and superior for items followed by R cues is suggestive of the operation of such a process. Accordingly, our assumption is that subliminal R and F cues may indeed moderate the extent of item rehearsal, albeit unconsciously and unintentionally. In particular, the superior memory performance that is observed for R over F items following the presentation of subliminal cues may be due to the additional (but covert) rehearsal that R items receive during the study phase of the task.

To test this prediction, in our second experiment we added a secondary task (i.e., articulatory suppression) that was intended to prevent further rehearsal following the presentation of the subliminal cues (Bjork & Geiselman, 1978). Half the participants performed the identical incidental encoding task as Experiment 1. However, the remaining participants performed an additional articulatory suppression task (Baddeley, 1986) in which they were instructed to repeat aloud the colour of the backward masking stimulus. As such, to the extent that superior memory for to-be-remembered material is driven by a process of covert (but elaborative) rehearsal, we anticipated that recognition performance for R and F items would be equivalent under conditions of articulatory suppression.

TABLE 1
Recognition performance by cue type (Expts 1 & 2)

	Cue Type		
	Remember	Forget	Control
Experiment 1	.754 (17.4)	.668 (15.7)	.675 (15.8)
Experiment 2			
no suppression	.615 (45.0)	.539 (40.4)	–
articulatory suppression	.454 (41.8)	.465 (42.4)	–

Values indicate corrected recognition scores, calculated as the proportion of hits (ratio of "old" responses to the total number of previously seen items) minus the proportion of false alarms for each condition. Values in parentheses indicate the raw number of hits per condition. Participants studied 20 items per condition in Experiment 1 and 60 items per condition in Experiment 2.

Method

Participants and design.   A total of 32 students at the University of Bristol were paid £3 ($4.50) for their participation in the experiment. The experiment had a 2 (cue type: remember or forget) × 2 (concurrent task: articulatory suppression or control) mixed design with repeated measures on the first factor.

Procedure and stimulus materials.   Experiment 2 was basically a replication of the previous experiment, but with some important modifications. First, the number of stimulus items was increased to 120 forenames. Second, as performance following the presentation of control and F-cued items was equivalent, only R and F cues were used in the current experiment. Stimulus presentation was controlled by an Apple Macintosh G3 computer running PsyScope software (Cohen, MacWhinney, Flatt, & Provost, 1993). The sequence of events comprising each trial was similar to Experiment 1, except that the inter-trial interval was increased to 2000 ms. Participants were again introduced to an experiment on the effects of distraction on cognitive performance and were randomly assigned to one of two experimental conditions. Half the participants were assigned to the no-suppression condition, in which they performed the identical name-reading task as in Experiment 1. The remaining participants were assigned to the articulatory-suppression condition, and also performed the name-reading task. In addition, however, the articulatory-suppression participants also repeated aloud the name of the colour of the second letter mask until the next trial commenced (Baddeley, 1986). The second mask was drawn in one of three colours (blue, green, or red). Thus, upon the presentation of a forename, participants in both conditions read the name aloud. Following the appearance of the second mask, however, participants in the articulatory-suppression condition also repeated the colour of the second mask as many times as possible until the next forename appeared on the screen. The only other change to the study phase of Experiment 2 was the addition of nine buffer trials at the beginning of the experiment to ensure that participants understood how to perform the articulatory-suppression task. The items comprising these buffer trials did not appear in the subsequent recognition test. Immediately following the study phase, memory was assessed using a standard old/new recognition task. On completion of this task, participants were debriefed, paid, thanked for their assistance, and dismissed.

Results and discussion

Recognition memory was again indexed by computing the corrected recognition scores for both R and F items. The bottom portion of Table 1 presents the treatment means. We anticipated that if the superiority of R over F items was due to the operation of a covert rehearsal mechanism, then only in the no-suppression condition would we observe better recognition memory for R- over F-cued items. No difference in recognition performance was expected to emerge under conditions of articulatory suppression. To test these predictions, the corrected recognition scores were submitted to a 2 (cue type: remember or forget) × 2 (concurrent task: articulatory suppression or control) mixed model ANOVA with repeated measures on the first factor. A significant effect of cue type emerged in this analysis, $F(1, 30) = 6.47$, $p < .02$, indicating that recognition performance was better for R- than F-cued items. As expected, however, this effect was qualified by a significant cue type × concurrent task interaction, $F(1, 30) = 11.87$, $p < .002$. Additional analyses confirmed that, in the no-suppression condition (proportion of false alarms = .135), recognition performance was better for R- than F-cued items, $t(31) = 4.72$, $p < .0003$. Importantly, no such effect emerged under conditions of articulatory suppression (proportion of false alarms = .242), $t(31) < 1$, *ns*. Thus, as expected, the observed recognition advantage for R- over F-cued items appeared to be a consequence of additional covert rehearsal engendered by the subliminal cues to remember (Basden & Basden, 1998), a mnemonic strategy that was triggered without participants' awareness or conscious intent. When the requirement to perform a concurrent working-memory task (i.e., articulatory suppression) eliminated differences in elaborative rehearsal of R and F items, recognition performance was equivalent for both types of items.

GENERAL DISCUSSION

A characteristic feature of memory is that it operates silently and effortlessly without the necessity of conscious control. Only occasionally do we purposely direct ourselves to remember or forget particular things. The more commonplace scenario is that relevant material somehow enters and remains in memory without one's conscious intervention, while irrelevant, outdated, or redundant information is discarded and forgotten. But what is the mechanism that moderates the memorability of encountered material? The current research identifies one such candidate process. Critical to the memorial fate of information may be situational cues that are present when the material is encountered, cues that signal the relative importance or value of the information. Following the implicit registration of these cues (Bargh, 1997; Bargh & Chartrand, 1999; Chartrand & Bargh, 1996), covert rehearsal mechanisms then serve to determine whether the information is likely to be remembered or forgotten (Craik & Lockhart, 1972; Craik & Tulving, 1975). Such triggering situational cues are undoubtedly a ubiquitous feature of everyday life (Bjork et al., 1998). A professor's subtle prosodic emphasis of a point in class, the institutional affiliation of a speaker at a scientific meeting, or the source credibility of a witness in court may all serve as cues that trigger covert rehearsal processes—processes that enhance the memorability of encountered information. Ultimately, such cues help to gate the expenditure of limited processing resources by directing covert rehearsal operations to the encoding of information that is salient, important, or potentially goal-relevant to perceivers (Bargh, 1997).

Throughout this article we have referred to covert rehearsal, but in what sense can rehearsal be considered to be covert? Recent neuroimaging investigations of incidental memory encoding by Wagner et al. (1998) and Brewer, Zhao, Desmond, Glover, and Gabrieli (1998) may help to illuminate this issue. In each of these studies, event-related fMRI was used to index neural activity while participants performed an incidental encoding task, such as word classification (Wagner et al., 1998) or picture categorisation (Brewer, et al., 1998). Participants' memories were later assessed on a surprise recognition test and items were conditionalised on the basis of whether they were correctly recognised as old (i.e., hits) or incorrectly classified as new items (i.e., misses). Critically, items that attracted greater neural activity in left inferior frontal cortex and the medial temporal lobe during incidental encoding had the greatest likelihood of being correctly recognised at test. Interestingly, the left inferior frontal areas identified in these studies have been associated with different rehearsal processes (see Cabeza & Nyberg, 2000; Smith & Jonides, 1997).

In such incidental encoding tasks, why is it that some items attract greater covert rehearsal than others? Item familiarity, frequency, self-relevance, and natural fluctuations in attention are all factors that are believed to contribute to the observed variance in neural activity and covert rehearsal across items. To this list, we suspect it is possible to add another factor—namely, situational cues that signal the mnemonic value of encountered information to perceivers, such as the subliminal R and F cues that were employed in the current investigation. Although speculative, the differences in recognition performance observed in the present studies may be attributable to modulation of the neural activity in brain regions associated with elaborative rehearsal, specifically left inferior frontal regions. Furthermore, because articulatory suppression likely engages the same mechanisms that underlie phonological rehearsal (Baddeley, 1986), we suspect that the subliminal cueing effect observed in these experiments probably results from the additional phonological rehearsal received by R-cued items. These possibilities await future empirical attention.

CONCLUSIONS

Through selective remembering and forgetting, perceivers can retain important, relevant, and appropriate information while discarding material that is unwanted, irrelevant, or trivial. Supporting this process are a variety of mechanisms, some with their foundations in consciousness, others with their origins in the silent workings of the unconscious mind. That memory operations can be triggered automatically has obvious benefits to perceivers as they go about their daily business. Rather than deliberating over what needs to be remembered or forgotten, memory control can be devolved to covert rehearsal mechanisms that are triggered following the nonconscious registration of critical situational cues (Bargh, 1997; Bargh & Chartrand, 1999). As a result of this processing strategy, perceivers can deploy consciousness and its limited resources to a range of other problems, such as planning, troubleshooting, and behavioural self-regulation. As demonstrated herein, despite its purposive quality, directed forgetting and remembering can indeed be implemented unintentionally.

REFERENCES

Anderson, M.C., & Neely, J.H. (1996). Interference and inhibition in memory retrieval. In E.L. Bjork & R.A. Bjork (Eds.), *Memory. Handbook of perception and cognition* (pp. 237–313). San Diego, CA: Academic Press, Inc.

Anderson, M.C., & Spellman, B.A. (1995). On the status of inhibitory mechanisms in cognition: Memory retrieval as a model case. *Psychological Review, 102*, 68–100.

Baddeley, A. (1986). *Working memory*. Oxford: Oxford University Press.

Bargh, J.A. (1997). The automaticity of everyday life. In R.S.J. Wyer (Eds.), *The automaticity of everyday life: Advances in social cognition* (pp. 103–137). Mahwah, NJ: Lawrence Erlbaum Associates Inc.

Bargh, J.A., & Chartrand, T.L. (1999). The unbearable automaticity of being. *American Psychologist, 54*, 462–479.

Bargh, J.A., & Ferguson, M.J. (2000). Beyond behaviorism: On the automaticity of higher mental processes. *Psychological Bulletin, 126*, 925–945.

Bargh, J.A., & Pietromonaco, P. (1982). Automatic information processing and social perception: The influence of trait information presented outside of conscious awareness on impression formation. *Journal of Personality and Social Psychology, 43*, 437–449.

Basden, B.H., & Basden, D.R. (1996). Directed forgetting: A further comparison of the list and item methods. *Memory, 4*, 633–653.

Basden, B.H., & Basden, D.R. (1998). Directed forgetting: A contrast of methods and interpretations. In J.M. Golding & C.M. MacLeod (Eds.), *Intentional forgetting: Interdisciplinary approaches* (pp. 139–172). Mahwah, NJ: Lawrence Erlbaum Associates Inc.

Basden, B.H., Basden, D.R., & Gargano, G.J. (1993). Directed forgetting in implicit and explicit memory tests: A comparison of methods. *Journal of Experimental Psychology: Learning, Memory, & Cognition, 19*, 603–616.

Bjork, E.L., Bjork, R.A., & Anderson, M.C. (1998). Varieties of goal-directed forgetting. In J.M. Golding & C.M. MacLeod (Eds.), *Intentional forgetting: Interdisciplinary approaches* (pp. 103–137). Mahwah, NJ: Lawrence Erlbaum Associates Inc.

Bjork, R.A. (1989). Retrieval inhibition as an adaptive mechanism in human memory. In H.L. Roediger & F.I.M. Craik (Eds.), *Varieties of memory and consciousness: Essays in honor of Endel Tulving* (pp. 309–330). Hillsdale, NJ: Lawrence Erlbaum Associates Inc.

Bjork, R.A., & Geiselman, R.E. (1978). Constituent processes in the differentiation of items in memory. *Journal of Experimental Psychology: Human Learning and Memory, 4*, 347–361.

Brewer, J.B., Zhao, Z., Desmond, J.E., Glover, G.H., & Gabrieli, J.D. (1998). Making memories: Brain activity that predicts how well visual experience will be remembered. *Science, 281*, 1185–1187.

Cabeza, R., & Nyberg, L. (2000). Imaging cognition II: An empirical review of 275 PET and fMRI studies. *Journal of Cognitive Neuroscience, 12*, 1–47.

Chartrand, T.L., & Bargh, J.A. (1996). Automatic activation of impression formation and memorization goals: Nonconscious goal priming reproduces effects of explicit task instructions. *Journal of Personality and Social Psychology, 71*, 464–478.

Cohen, J.D., MacWhinney, B., Flatt, M., & Provost, J. (1993). PsyScope: A new graphic interactive environment for designing psychology experiments. *Behavioral Research Methods, Instruments, and Computers, 25*, 257–271.

Craik, F.I.M., & Lockhart, R.S. (1972). Levels of processing: A framework for memory research. *Journal of Verbal Learning and Verbal Behavior, 11*, 671–684.

Craik, F.I.M., & Tulving, E. (1975). Depth of processing and the retention of words in episodic memory. *Journal of Experimental Psychology: General, 104*, 268–294.

Freud, S. (1989). *Civilization and its discontents* [James Strachey, Ed. & Trans.]. New York: W.W. Norton. [Original work published in 1930].

Greenwald, A.G., Spangenberg, E.R., Pratkanis, A.R., & Eskenazi, J. (1991). Double-blind tests of subliminal self-help audiotapes. *Psychological Science, 2*, 119–122.

Hamilton, D.L., Katz, L.B., & Leirer, V.O. (1980). Cognitive representation of personality impressions: Organizational process in first impression formation. *Journal of Personality and Social Psychology, 39*, 1050–1063.

Higbee, K.L. (1977). *Your memory: How it works and how to improve it*. Englewood Cliffs, NJ: Prentice-Hall.

Johnson, H. (1994). Processes of successful intentional forgetting. *Psychological Bulletin, 116*, 274–292.

Luria, A.R. (1968). *The mind of a mnemonist: A little book about a vast memory* [L. Solotaroff, Trans.]. New York: Basic Books.

MacLeod, C.M. (1998). Directed forgetting. In J.M. Golding & C.M. MacLeod (Eds.), *Intentional forgetting: Interdisciplinary approaches* (pp. 1–57). Hillsdale, NJ: Lawrence Erlbaum Associates Inc.

Schacter, D.L. (1996). *Searching for memory: The brain, the mind, and the past*. New York: Basic Books.

Schacter, D.L. (2001). *The seven sins of memory: How the mind forgets and remembers*. New York: Houghton Mifflin.

Smith, E.E., & Jonides, J. (1997). Working memory: A view from neuroimaging. *Cognitive Psychology, 33*, 5–42.

Wagner, A.D., Schacter, D.L., Rotte, M., Koutstaal, W., Maril, A., Dale, A.M., Rosen, B.R., & Buckner, R.L. (1998). Building memories: Remembering and forgetting of verbal experiences as predicted by brain activity. *Science, 281*, 1188–1191.

Wetzel, C.D., & Hunt, R.E. (1977). Cue delay and role of rehearsal in directed forgetting. *Journal of Experimental Psychology: Human Learning and Memory, 3*, 233–245.

Woodward, A.E., & Bjork, R.A. (1971). Forgetting and remembering in free recall: Intentional and unintentional. *Journal of Experimental Psychology, 89*, 109–116.

MEMORY, 2002, *10* (5/6), 389–395

The myth of the encoding–retrieval match

James S. Nairne

Purdue University, IN, USA

Modern memory researchers rely heavily on the encoding–retrieval match, defined as the similarity between coded retrieval cues and previously encoded engrams, to explain variability in retention. The encoding–retrieval match is assumed to be causally and monotonically related to retention, although other factors (such as cue overload) presumably operate in some circumstances. I argue here that the link between the encoding–retrieval match and retention, although generally positive, is essentially correlational rather than causal—much like the link between deep/elaborative processing and retention. Empirically, increasing the functional match between a cue and a target trace can improve, have no effect, or even decrease retention performance depending on the circumstance. We cannot make unequivocal predictions about retention by appealing to the encoding–retrieval match; instead, we should be focusing our attention on the extent to which retrieval cues provide diagnostic information about target occurrence.

As we mark the 30th anniversary of Craik and Lockhart's (1972) seminal article, its core mnemonic proposal, namely that memory performance is a positive function of the depth of initial processing, remains somewhat controversial. Although the proposal is generally true, and practically useful, the relationship between retention and depth is now widely suspected to be correlational rather than causal. Retrieval conditions can be arranged that favour shallow processing, reversing the standard deep-processing advantage (e.g., Morris, Bransford, & Franks, 1977), so we cannot make unequivocal predictions about retention by focusing on processing alone.

Today, with few exceptions, memory researchers rely instead on the principle of trace–cue compatibility. It is the encoding–retrieval match—the extent to which the conditions present at retrieval overlap with, or match, the conditions that existed during encoding (e.g., Tulving, 1983)—that is believed to control performance. From this perspective, deep processing may produce the best retention, on average, but only as an artifact of retrieval conditions. Deep processing simply leads to memory traces that are likely to be matched by the conditions of retrieval, especially traditional recall and recognition tests. At best, one might argue that deep processing affords more retrieval opportunities, or perhaps makes retrieval relatively more immune to changes in context (Lockhart & Craik, 1990). But once the encoding process is complete, the major determinant of performance is the encoding–retrieval match (Tulving, 1979, 1983).

This kind of analysis, particularly the assertion about the role of the encoding–retrieval match, is considered sacrosanct by many in the memory field today. But is it justified? In the present article, I take the position that the encoding–retrieval match, although practically useful, carries little true theoretical import—ironically, for essentially the same reason that many dismiss the core proposal of the levels-of-processing framework today (or consider it theoretically impotent).

Requests for reprints should be sent to James S. Nairne, Department of Psychological Sciences, PSYC 1364, Purdue University, West Lafayette, IN 47907-1364, USA. Email: nairne@psych.purdue.edu

Thanks are due to Gordon Brown, Gus Craik, Endel Tulving, and Roddy Roediger for helpful and entertaining comments on a previous version of this manuscript.

DOI:10.1080/09658210244000216

The link between the encoding–retrieval match and retention, although generally positive, is effectively correlational rather than causal. Increasing the functional similarity between a cue and a target trace can improve, have no effect, or even decrease retention performance depending on the circumstance. As a consequence, we cannot use the encoding–retrieval match to make unequivocal predictions about retention.

What matters instead, and what should receive the focus of our attention, is the extent to which retrieval cues provide diagnostic information about target occurrence (e.g., Eysenck, 1979; Jacoby & Craik, 1979). When we remember, we use the information at hand, in the form of retrieval cues, to make a decision about what occurred in the past. But the decision is unlikely to be based on a passive matching process, at least in the majority of retrieval contexts. Remembering is better characterised as an active process of discrimination: We use cues to pick and choose from among viable retrieval candidates. Increasing the encoding–retrieval match generally improves performance, but only because it increases the probability that distinctive features (features that uniquely predict a particular target occurrence) will come into play. Match, by itself, is not the operative factor behind retention and should not be stressed in our theoretical accounts.[1]

THE ROLE OF THE ENCODING–RETRIEVAL MATCH

The idea that reinstating original encoding conditions improves retention has a long history in psychology. McGeoch (1942), for example, used the match (or mismatch) between initial learning and test conditions to explain a number of retention phenomena; Estes (1955) used similar ideas to great advantage in his stimulus-sampling theory (see Crowder, 1976, for a review). We assume the same today, with the added caveat that it is the functional, rather than nominal, encoding–retrieval match that ultimately controls performance. We can match the nominal conditions between encoding and test (e.g., by using identical cues at study and test) but still not ensure a match

between the cue and relevant target trace, as coded (see Tulving, 1983). When discussing the role of the encoding–retrieval match, therefore, it is important to specify that it is the functional, rather than nominal, match that is of main interest.

With this in mind, we can entertain three positions on the role of the functional encoding–retrieval match: (1) match is sufficient to explain all memory phenomena; (2) match is causally and monotonically related to retention, but other factors are needed (e.g., cue overload); (3) no effective causal relationship exists between match and retention (although the two may be positively correlated). Advocates of the first two positions generally elevate match to the status of a "principle"; advocates of the last position, if there are any, contend that the typical monotonic relationship between match and retention is best viewed as an artifact and potentially reversible—just like the relationship between processing "depth" and retention.

Among these three alternatives, I suspect that most researchers would choose the second: The relation between match and retention is principled and positive, but other factors are needed to explain performance. In their tutorial review of retrieval processes, Roediger and Guynn (1996) propose two factors: (1) the similarity between the conditions of encoding and retrieval (the match) and (2) the principle of cue overload (or cue "distinctiveness"). Cue overload, a characteristic of retrieval cues, refers to whether a cue uniquely predicts, or is uniquely associated with, a given target memory. If a cue is associated to many things, or has been encoded as a part of many traces complexes, then it becomes harder for that cue to elicit any single target trace (e.g., Earhard, 1967; Watkins & Watkins, 1975).

If adopted, the cue overload principle is important because it suggests that we cannot explain retention by appealing simply to the match between study and test. Holding the functional match between an encoded target and cue constant, performance will vary depending on whether the cue matches other target events in memory. In the present context, it is interesting to note that Craik and colleagues have made somewhat similar claims about levels of processing and retention. Empirically, main effects of depth remain even when the conditions of encoding and retrieval are nominally equated (e.g., Craik, 1999; Fisher & Craik, 1977; Lockhart & Craik, 1990). This suggests that factors other than the

---

[1] The idea that the predictability (or distinctiveness) of a cue matters is, of course, not new (e.g., Moscovitch & Craik, 1976). At issue here is the question of whether the similarity (or match) between a cue and a target adds anything of mnemonic value over and above the predictive (or distinctive) ability of the cue.

encoding–retrieval match are needed to explain performance (i.e., processing depth). Unfortunately, however, in each of the relevant studies match was operationalised by using identical study and test cues which, in turn, does not ensure an equivalent functional cue–target match. One could still account for the main effect of depth by assuming that the encoding–retrieval match is greater for deep cues and targets than for the shallow ones (see Tulving, 1979).

The situation is markedly different for cue overload. Consider a typical instance in which the cue overload principle operates—the category size effect. When subjects are given categorised lists at study, and category cues at test, the likelihood of remembering any single instance from a category goes down as the number of category exemplars on the list goes up (e.g., Roediger, 1973). It is difficult to see how these data can be explained by appealing simply to trace–cue compatibility. One would need to assume that the functional match between a given exemplar and its category cue changes with the presentation of additional exemplars. One might "interpret" a cue differently at test if it has been encoded with many things, but this seems unlikely for a robust category cue. Moreover, it is reasonable to assume that the category size effect does not depend critically on the serial position of the presented exemplar—it is likely to be present for the last as well as the first exemplar in the list.

A similar analysis applies to the list length effect (Strong, 1912). Retention declines as the number of to-be-remembered items on a list increases, presumably because more retrieval candidates are subsumed under the functional retrieval cue "last list" (see Watkins & Watkins, 1975). The list length effect is robust for the first and remaining items on a list, which makes it extremely difficult to argue that the effect is caused by systematic changes in the interpretation of the cue as list presentation proceeds. Both the list length effect and the category size effect suggest instead that memory performance can be controlled by factors other than the similarity, or match, between encoding and retrieval.

DECOUPLING MATCH AND RETENTION

Of course, demonstrating that factors such as cue overload influence performance does not mean that the encoding–retrieval match is a "myth" or unimportant to memory performance. As noted, most researchers favour at least a two-factor account in which both match and cue overload (or distinctiveness) play important roles. One might argue, for example, that the relationship between match and retention is principled and direct, but that performance is inversely proportional to the amount of cue overload as well.

Once we accept such a two-factor view, however, for all practical purposes we lose the ability to generate unequivocal predictions about retention by appealing to the encoding–retrieval match. This can be easily shown through a thought experiment. Suppose we ask subjects to study and remember a list of target events: E_1, E_2, E_3, ... , E_N. Each event is assumed to consist of features or attributes (X_1, X_2, X_3, ... , X_N) and some of the features, we further assume, are represented in more than one target encoding (e.g., to take the simplest case, we might expect contextual features to be encoded as part of numerous target events). At test, we supply one or more of the features to serve as retrieval cues for recovery of a particular target event.

From the perspective of the encoding–retrieval match, we would expect performance to improve as the similarity between the retrieval environment (i.e., the constellation of retrieval cues) and the original encoding environment increases. In fact, performance should be best when we maximise the similarity, or overlap, between study and test. So, if event E_1 consists of the encoded features X_1, X_2, and X_3, then supplying the subject with all three of those features as cues should produce better performance than providing only two or one. Note that in this case we are talking about increasing the *functional* encoding–retrieval match across conditions—that is, we can assume (at least for our thought experiment) that the cues provided at test, as coded, exactly match the features in the original stored event.

On reflection, however, it is easy to see that the outcome of our thought experiment is very much in doubt. Assuming cue overload, the cue value of any feature will depend importantly on the extent to which it matches the target event to the exclusion of other events. Suppose that feature X_1 is unique to event E_1, but X_2 is present in E_1, E_2, E_3, and E_4. We could supply the subject with features X_1 and X_2 at test, thereby increasing the functional encoding–retrieval match (relative to a single cue condition), but performance will not necessarily improve. In fact, one might expect performance to decline in this case because the matching cue X_2 is consistent with other target traces. Increasing cue–target similarity in this case exacerbates the discrimination problem, potentially creating a nonmonotonic relationship between match and retention performance.

A simple model

We can express these ideas more formally by adopting a simple retrieval, or choice, rule of the type often found in categorisation and memory models (e.g., Nairne, 1990; 2001; Nosofsky, 1986). Under this formulation, the subject chooses an item to recall by comparing, or matching, the retrieval cue(s) to possible candidates in a long-term memory search set (see also Raaijmakers & Shiffrin, 1980). The probability that any particular event, E_1, will be chosen depends on how well the retrieval cue, X_1, matches E_1 to the exclusion of other possible recall candidates (e.g., $E_2, E_3, \ldots, E_N$):

$$P_r(E_1|X_1) = \frac{s(X_1, E_1)}{\Sigma s(X_1, E_i)} \qquad (1)$$

Here, $s(X_1, E_1)$ refers to the similarity of X_1 to E_1 which, in turn, is easily expressed in terms of the number of matching or mismatching features between the two terms (a distance measure). Shepard (1987) recommends relating distance (d) to similarity in the following manner:

$$s(X_1, E_1) = e^{-d(X_1, E_1)} \qquad (2)$$

This simple formulation, as described in Equation (1), captures most of the important components of the two-factor view of memory we have been considering. Memory is proportional to the match between the cue, X_1, and the target event, E_1, and inversely related to the number of items that are subsumed under the cue (cue overload). The value of the denominator is calculated by summing the similarities between the cue and each of the members of the search set. Consequently, as the size of the search set increases, the value of the denominator increases as well and the likelihood of recovering any single item declines (e.g., the category size effect and the list length effect).

In addition, as in our thought experiment, if we increase the similarity between the cue and the target, performance will increase or decrease depending on the circumstance. For example, suppose we increase the net cue–target similarity by adding a feature that "recruits" additional members into the set (perhaps by virtue of a

matched feature). Under these conditions, whatever increase we see in the numerator of Equation (1), by virtue of an increased match between cues and target, will be countered by a relatively larger increase in the denominator, leading to a net reduction in the probability of recall. Thus, in this version of the two-factor view, we cannot generate unequivocal predictions about retention by appealing to the status of the encoding–retrieval match.[2]

THE DISCRIMINABILITY OF CUES

According to our simple retrieval rule, cue–target match is a necessary but not a sufficient condition for correct retrieval. You need some degree of match—overlapping features—between the cue and a target candidate in order for the target to be selected and recalled. Yet it is not really the match *per se* that is critical—it is the *relative* match, or the extent to which a feature, X_1, uniquely specifies an event, E_1, to the exclusion of other possible recall candidates. In fact, knowing the overall value of the match (assuming the value is greater than zero) tells us nothing definitive about subsequent retention.

To see why, consider another thought experiment in which we ask subjects to read aloud lists of homophones presented visually on a screen (e.g., write, right, rite, rite, write, right). At test, we ask everyone to recall the homophone that occurred in the third serial position on the list. In one condition, subjects are given only the retrieval query, but in a second condition we give them an additional cue—the sound of the correct item ($ra^y t$). Notice in this second condition we have improved the functional cue–target match, by supplying a cue that was encoded as part of the original trace, but it is unlikely that performance will improve. The sound of the target is shared by all of the items on the list, so the retrieval cue provides no distinctive information about target occurrence. The subject cannot use the additional information, even though it matches the stored

---

[2] One might argue that these conclusions apply only to situations in which one must select a *specific* item to remember from among a set of possible output candidates. Yet most, if not all, episodic memory environments require just such a discrimination—we need to remember the items that occurred on the current memory list (as opposed to a previous list), or where we parked our car today, rather than yesterday or the day before.

trace, to help discriminate among the possible retrieval candidates.

We can show this mathematically by substituting Equation (2), our definition of similarity, into the ratio rule described by Equation (1). For simplicity, d_1 refers to the distance between X_1 and E_1 and d_i to the distance between X_1 and E_i. Algebraically, we can show that

$$\frac{e^{-d_1}}{\sum e^{-d_i}} = \frac{e^{-(d_1 - C)}}{\sum e^{-(d_i - C)}} \tag{3}$$

where C is a constant that increases the cue–target match (by decreasing the distance between the cue and the target). Thus, we can increase the cue–target match at will, and it will have no effect on retention, as long as the similarity between the cue and other possible retrieval candidates is increased by the same amount.

In some respects, the situation is analogous to the relationship between intensity and brightness perception. What mainly determines brightness perception is relative intensity information—how many photons are falling in the centre compared to the surround (although absolute intensity may be important in some circumstances). Intensity and brightness are decoupled in phenomena such as brightness constancy, in which perceived brightness remains constant even though the overall intensity information increases (or decreases). It is even possible to increase absolute intensity and have a spot seem darker (a non-monotonic relationship between intensity and brightness perception). Our perceptual systems tend to throw away absolute information—e.g., overall changes in intensity—in favour of relative comparisons. Similarly, for retrieval, it is not the absolute cue–target match that is critical, but rather the diagnostic (or relative) value of the match.

Ceteris Paribus

From the standpoint of building a general theory of memory, therefore, the notion that match is causally and monotonically related to retention becomes quite suspect. Asserting that the relationship between match and retention is principled and direct, although perhaps qualified by cue overload, implies that retention will improve whenever we increase the cue–target match but hold the amount of cue overload constant. Put more generally, the monotonic relationship between match and retention holds, but only when all other factors remain constant. Yet our thought experiment—and Equation (3)—shows that increasing the overall match will not necessarily translate into a performance gain, even when the amount of cue overload remains constant. Instead, the link between match and retention is effectively correlational rather than causal. Increasing the functional similarity between a cue and a target trace may generally increase retention performance—because it increases the probability that diagnostic features will come into play—but it can easily have no effect or even decrease retention performance depending on the circumstance. Our retrieval system devalues absolute cue–target similarity in favour of the relative, diagnostic value of the cue.[3]

The relationship between time and forgetting serves as another useful analogy. Most memory researchers agree that time is correlated with forgetting—and some modicum of time is needed to demonstrate forgetting—but few would argue today that the passage of time causes forgetting. Instead, it is the events that happen in time that lead to forgetting. As time passes, there are simply more opportunities for forgetting-related activities to occur (e.g., interference). Furthermore, once you accept that interference is the main causal source of forgetting, it no longer seems fruitful to argue that both time + interference are important, or to give them equal weight in a theory, even though you could see the influence of both. It is more appropriate to say that interference is the critical factor and time is important only because it gives interference the opportunity to occur (interference can only happen in time).

It is in this sense that the encoding–retrieval match becomes a "myth", at least with respect to its role in controlling retention. It is misleading to propose two-factor accounts that give equal weight to the encoding–retrieval match and cue overload when it is the diagnostic value of a cue that truly matters. Like the passage of time, the overall match *per se* doesn't predict anything about retention—memory might improve, stay the same, or get worse. When the relevant diagnostic cues are present, however, you will always increase the chances that the right memory will

---

[3] It is of interest to note that a somewhat comparable conclusion has been reached by those studying judgements of similarity, which seem to be context-dependent. Thus, adding a common feature to two scenes does not necessarily increase their perceived similarity and, in some cases, may decrease it (e.g., Goldstone, 1996).

occur. It is the predictability of cues—that is, how well the cues specify a particular target item to the exclusion of others—that should receive the brunt of our theoretical attention.

CONCLUSIONS AND REFLECTIONS

Modern memory researchers tend to worship almost exclusively at the altar of trace–cue compatibility. The claim that memory improves to the extent that test conditions match those present during original encoding is widespread, to the point that some researchers have elevated the link between the encoding–retrieval match and retention to "one of the most important principles ever articulated about memory" (Toth & Hunt, 1999). Current textbooks and review chapters commonly assert that "maximizing the similarity ... between a study and a test occasion benefits retention" (Roediger & Guynn, 1996, p. 204) or that "successful retrieval depends on the similarity of encoding and retrieval operations" (Brown & Craik, 2000, p. 99).

In principle, of course, we could conceptualise the concept of an encoding–retrieval match in many ways, but it is almost always described in terms of feature overlap, or the similarity, between the cue and an encoded target (or engram). The encoding specificity principle—the idea that retrieval cues must be a part of the original encoding to be effective—follows directly from this perspective. If retention is a function of matching features between a cue and a target, then retrieval cues will be effective if and only if they are part of the original encoding event (Thomson & Tulving, 1970). Retrieval cues that are not part of the original encoding cannot "match" the trace complex at test and, as a result, cannot lead to its retrieval.

It is worth noting that there is nothing in the formulations discussed here that invalidates the principle of encoding specificity. One could still accept that retrieval cues are effective if and only if they match the target trace, but recognise that the main controller of performance is the diagnostic rather than the absolute cue–target match. In fact, the simple retrieval model introduced earlier assumes that the encoding specificity principle must be true (the functional similarity between a cue and target must be greater than zero). However, asserting that cues, as coded, must match previously encoded traces does not mean that manipulating the number of over-

lapping features, or maximising the similarity between a cue and a target, is the best route to successful retention.

It is also possible that there are situations in which the match between a cue and a target trace is both necessary and sufficient to predict mnemonic performance. Certain types of recognition judgements, for instance, might be based on a global measure of familiarity that increases or decreases directly with the cue–target match (e.g., Gillund & Shiffrin, 1984; Hintzman, 1988). Moreover, one could accept the kind of ratio-based retrieval rule offered earlier—that is, as a way of discriminating a target from among a set of possible alternatives—but still assume that the absolute level of cue–target match is important (see Raaijmakers & Shiffrin, 1980). Empirically, however, our thought experiments suggest that absolute levels of cue–target similarity are likely to be discarded, in much the same way that absolute intensity is typically discarded in the perception of brightness.

Finally, on a practical level, it still seems reasonable to champion the value of the encoding–retrieval match as a vehicle for improving retention. In most situations, maximising the similarity between encoding and retrieval conditions is likely to lead to the best performance. But the exceptions are important, and should matter to us as memory theorists. In the case of levels of processing, deep or elaborative encoding still typically produces the best retention, but the exceptions—those instances in which shallow processing prevails (e.g., Morris et al., 1977)—have placed important constraints on how we think about the role of deep processing. Deep processing is an excellent encoding vehicle, but only because it leads to elaborate memory traces that are likely to be tapped by a range of different retrieval cues. Similarly, when we think about the encoding–retrieval match, it is not the match *per se* that is of main theoretical value; instead, it is the diagnostic value of the retrieval environment that matters most.

REFERENCES

Brown, S.C., & Craik, F.I.M. (2000). Encoding and retrieval of information. In E. Tulving & F.I.M. Craik (Eds.), *The Oxford handbook of memory* (pp. 93–107). New York: Oxford University Press.

Craik, F.I.M. (1999). Levels of encoding and retrieval. In B.H. Challis & B.M. Velichkovsky (Eds.), *Stratification in cognition and consciousness* (pp. 97–104).

Philadelphia, PA: John Benjamins Publishing Company.

Craik, F.I.M., & Lockhart, R.S. (1972). Levels of processing: A framework for memory research. *Journal of Verbal Learning and Verbal Behavior, 11*, 671–684.

Crowder, R.G. (1976). *Principles of learning and memory*. Hillsdale, NJ: Lawrence Erlbaum Associates Inc.

Earhard, M. (1967). Cued recall and free recall as a function of the number of items per cue. *Journal of Verbal Learning and Verbal Behavior, 6*, 257–263.

Estes, W.K. (1955). Statistical theory of spontaneous recovery and regression. *Psychological Review, 62*, 145–154.

Eysenck, M.W. (1979). Depth, elaboration, and distinctiveness. In L.S. Cermak & F.I.M. Craik (Eds.), *Levels of processing in human memory* (pp. 89–118). Hillsdale, NJ: Lawrence Erlbaum Associates Inc.

Fisher, R.P., & Craik, F.I.M. (1977). Interaction between encoding and retrieval operations in cued-recall. *Journal of Experimental Psychology: Human Learning and Memory, 3*, 701–711.

Gillund, G., & Shiffrin, R.M. (1984). A retrieval model for both recognition and recall. *Psychological Review, 91*, 1–67.

Goldstone, R.L. (1996). Alignment-based non-monotonicities in similarity. *Journal of Experimental Psychology: Learning, Memory, and Cognition, 22*, 988–1001.

Hintzman, D.L. (1988). Judgments of frequency and recognition memory in a multiple-trace memory model. *Psychological Review, 95*, 528–551.

Jacoby, L.L., & Craik, F.I.M. (1979). Effects of elaboration of processing at encoding and retrieval: Trace distinctiveness and recovery of initial context. In L.S. Cermak & F.I.M. Craik (Eds.), *Levels of processing in human memory* (pp. 1–21). Hillsdale, NJ: Lawrence Erlbaum Associates Inc.

Lockhart, R.S., & Craik, F.I.M. (1990). Levels of processing: A retrospective commentary on a framework for memory research. *Canadian Journal of Psychology, 44*, 87–112.

McGeoch, J.A. (1942). *The psychology of human learning*. New York: Longsman, Green.

Morris, C.D., Bransford, J.D., & Franks, J.J. (1977). Levels of processing versus transfer appropriate processing. *Journal of Verbal Learning and Verbal Behavior, 16*, 519–533.

Moscovitch, M., & Craik, F.I.M. (1976). Depth of processing, retrieval cues, and uniqueness of encoding as factors in recall. *Journal of Verbal Learning and Verbal Behavior, 15*, 447–458.

Nairne, J.S. (1990). A feature model of immediate memory. *Memory & Cognition, 18*, 251–269.

Nairne, J.S. (2001). A functional analysis of primary memory. In H.L. Roediger, J.S. Nairne, I. Neath, & A.M. Surprenant (Eds.), *The nature of remembering: Essays in honor of Robert G. Crowder* (pp. 282–296). Washington, DC: American Psychological Association.

Nosofsky, R.M. (1986). Attention, similarity, and the identification–categorization relationship. *Journal of Experimental Psychology: General, 115*, 39–57.

Raaijmakers, J.G.W., & Shiffrin, R.M. (1980). Search of associative memory. *Psychological Review, 95*, 93–134.

Roediger, H.L.III. (1973). Inhibition in recall from cueing with recall targets. *Journal of Verbal Learning and Verbal Behavior, 12*, 644–657.

Roediger, H.L.III, & Guynn, M.J. (1996). Retrieval processes. In E.L. Bjork & R.A. Bjork (Eds.), *Memory* (pp. 197–236). New York: Academic Press.

Shepard, R.N. (1987). Toward a universal law of generalization for psychological science. *Science, 237*, 1317–1323.

Strong, E.K. Jr. (1912). The effect of length of series upon recognition memory. *Psychological Review, 19*, 447–462.

Thomson, D.M., & Tulving, E. (1970). Associative encoding and retrieval: Weak and strong cues. *Journal of Experimental Psychology, 86*, 255–262.

Toth, J.P., & Hunt, R.R. (1999). Not one versus many, but zero versus any: Structure and function in the context of the multiple memory systems debate. In J.K. Foster & M. Jelicic (Eds.), *Memory: Systems, process, or function? Debates in psychology* (pp. 232–272). New York: Oxford University Press.

Tulving, E. (1979). Relation between encoding specificity and levels of processing. In L.S. Cermak & F.I.M. Craik (Eds.), *Levels of processing in human memory* (pp. 405–428). Hillsdale, NJ: Lawrence Erlbaum Inc.

Tulving, E. (1983). *Elements of episodic memory*. New York: Oxford University Press.

Watkins, O.C., & Watkins, M.J. (1975). Buildup of proactive inhibition as a cue-overload effect. *Journal of Experimental Psychology: Human Learning and Memory, 104*, 442–452.

MEMORY, 2002, *10* (5/6), 397–403

Levels of processing, transfer-appropriate processing, and the concept of robust encoding

Robert S. Lockhart

University of Toronto, Canada

The theoretical status of levels of processing and its relation to the general principle of transfer-appropriate processing is discussed. One possible description of this relationship is that levels of processing has its effect by influencing the likelihood that the processing will prove to be transfer-appropriate. This transfer account of the levels effect is discussed in terms of the concept of robust encoding (Lockhart & Craik, 1990). Available evidence provides little support for any simple form of this concept, but a modified version is suggested as a possibility.

At the age of 30, levels of processing would seem to be still very much alive. However, recent years, have seen it undergo an apparent change of status. Once a focal subject in the introduction and general discussion of experimental reports, it is now more often to be found in the method section: levels of processing has become an experimental manipulation, a paradigm. To some, this shift in status from conceptual to methodological may seem to make being alive at 30 a dubious achievement, but a consideration of the original ideas (Craik & Lockhart, 1972) justifies a more positive view. It must be remembered that levels of processing was presented, not as a theory of memory, but as a framework for memory research. The claim was that our understanding of memory would be greatly enhanced by research that examined the consequences for remembering of qualitatively different forms of processing.

Recent research using the "levels paradigm" can be thought of as doing precisely this. Exploring the "levels effect" has done much to clarify our understanding of the relations among memory systems and their distinctive roles in traditional memory tasks. The experiments reported by Challis, Velichkovsky and Craik (1996) provide a good example. More specifically, the presence or absence of levels effects has become a benchmark for the distinction between implicit and explicit memory (e.g., Roediger, Weldon, Stadler, & Riegler, 1992). Similarly, manipulating levels of processing has substantially added to our understanding of the difference between remembering and knowing as distinct components of recognition (Gardiner, 1988; Rajaram, 1993).

IS LEVELS OF PROCESSING A TAUTOLOGY?

These examples of the pragmatic success of the levels-of-processing framework is a partial answer to those critics who interpreted it as a theory, the truth or falsity of which might be decided by a suitable *experimentum crucis*. The answer is only partial, however, in that it sidesteps the basic concerns that motivated the criticism in the first place. This is the claim that the concepts underlying levels of processing are untestable and unfalsifiable.

The accusation of being "circular" or tautological has been one of the most persistent criticisms

Requests for reprints should be sent to Robert S. Lockhart, Department of Psychology, University of Toronto, Toronto, Ontario, Canada M5S 3G3. Email: lockhart@psych.utoronto.ca

I thank F.I.M. Craik for helpful comments on an earlier version of this paper.

http://www.tandf.co.uk/journals/pp/09658211.html

DOI:10.1080/09658210244000225

of levels of processing. The claim is that because the concept of depth lacks an independent definition, levels of processing involves a tautology in which the putative cause (deep processing) is nothing more than a restatement of the effect (better remembering). By their very nature tautologies are unfalsifiable, thus rendering the concept of depth devoid of empirical substance (Nelson, 1977). This criticism has been discussed briefly in a number of places (e.g., Lockhart & Craik, 1978, 1990), and most of the points made there will not be repeated here. However, apart from attempting to put the circularity argument finally to rest, there are aspects of this issue that warrant further attention because they lead to a number of other matters. The most important of these is the relation between levels of processing and the closely related concepts of transfer-appropriate processing (Morris, Bransford, & Franks, 1977) and the encoding specificity principle (Tulving & Thomson, 1973).

In standing accused of tautology, levels of processing is in distinguished company. Darwinian natural selection has frequently been similarly criticised and defended (see, for example, Gould, 1977; Stamos, 1996) and it is instructive to compare the two cases. With natural selection, the focus of criticism is usually the concept of adaptation, and in particular Herbert Spencer's phrase "the survival of the fittest", a phrase that Darwin adopted in later editions of the *Origin of Species* where it was added to the heading to Chapter 4. The circularity argument is that there is no independent definition of fitness: the fittest are defined in terms of those that survive. Fitness is thus a cause that is nothing more than a restatement of its effect. Evolution by natural selection is therefore a tautology.

It is instructive to pursue this parallel between levels of processing and natural selection. Concepts such as "fitness" (or any other description of adaptability) and "depth of processing" (or any other description of the memory trace) have an important feature in common. Neither is capable of fully predicting its relevant outcome—survival and retrievability respectively. At best they can speak probabilistically: certain characteristics of the organism might increase the likelihood of survival, and certain features of a memory trace may make retrieval more probable. It is this inability to predict deterministically that gives both concepts their post hoc quality, thus making them vulnerable to the accusation of circularity. Outside of the laboratory, a full account of a particular instance of survival or retrieval is possible only after the event. The reason for this state of affairs is basically the same in both cases: Adaptability and retrievability are concepts that are intrinsically relational. Survival is not fully predictable on the basis of some a priori definition of fitness, or any other property of the organism, because survival is a relationship between such properties and environment conditions. Analogously, retrievability is not fully predicted by some a priori definition of depth of processing, or any other property of the memory trace (such as strength or distinctiveness) because retrievability is a relationship between such properties and conditions under which retrieval is required.

This post hoc quality is not damaging to the scientific status of either, and it should not be confused with circularity or a tautology. The important point is that mechanisms of survival can be studied and subjected to experimental evaluation. Moreover, some degree of predictability is possible to the extent that future environmental conditions can be specified, or controlled in the laboratory. Similarly, mechanisms of memory retrieval can be studied and subject to experimental evaluation and predictions made contingent on specified retrieval conditions. The scientific integrity of natural selection or levels of processing is not compromised by the inability to specify in advance the conditions in which they will operate.

TRANSFER-APPROPRIATE PROCESSING

The relational property between the memory trace and the conditions of retrieval is, of course, the fundamental claim underlying the concepts of transfer-appropriate processing (Morris et al., 1977) and the encoding specificity principle (Tulving & Thomson, 1973). The evidence supporting the general validity of these conceptual twins is overwhelming. Notice, however, that transfer-appropriate processing is vulnerable to the same inappropriate accusation of circularity as levels of processing, and for exactly the same reason: it, too, possesses a certain post-hoc quality and lacks a precise definition. Under circumstances in which retrieval conditions cannot be specified in advance, processing can be identified as "transfer-appropriate" only after retrieval has occurred. Its defence is the same as that made for levels of processing in the preceding paragraph. Moreover, a lack of precision in defining concepts such as levels of processing or transfer-appropriate processing is not as great a weakness as is often claimed. Many important scientific ideas begin as vague concepts and their clarification is the goal of research, not its starting point.

Granted the general validity of transfer-appropriate processing and the encoding specificity principle, the question that then arises is whether these concepts render levels of processing irrelevant or redundant. Is transfer-appropriate processing, when suitably elaborated, sufficient, or is there still a place for concepts such as levels of processing which claim that some forms of processing are more likely than others to afford subsequent retrieval, and, if so, in what sense can such a claim be justified? Moreover, even if this claim is granted, fundamental questions remained unanswered. Roediger and Gallo (2001) put the matter succinctly when they point out that after 30 years of research, we do not know why or how we get the typical levels-of-processing effect.

In addressing this question it is helpful to push the analogy with natural selection one step further. A possible line of argument runs as follows. Certain species are fitter than others in the limited sense that the species could survive under a wider range of future environmental conditions, or survive under conditions that are the most likely to obtain in the future. According to this view, a rodent such as the rabbit might be described as fitter than a marsupial such as the koala. The rabbit has qualities (such as fecundity and dietary flexibility) that would support survival across a wide range of environments whereas the koala has worked itself into an extraordinarily narrow ecological niche. It is possible, of course, to specify environments in which the koala would survive and the rabbit become extinct; but the former are highly specific, intolerant of even slight variation, and unlikely to arise in practice. In betting on survival in an uncertain future environment, smart money will take the rabbit.

The claim, then, is that the typical levels-of-processing effect reflects the greater "survival" value of deep processing for those retrieval conditions most likely to occur. Again, it is possible to arrange retrieval conditions such that shallow processing outperforms deep processing, a point demonstrated by Morris et al. (1977) when they showed that for rhyme-recognition, rhyme encoding yielded superior performance to semantic encoding. Granted the theoretical importance of this result in establishing the validity of the principle of transfer-appropriate processing, the result obtains only under highly specific retrieval conditions of rhyme recognition. It is reasonable to predict that with almost any other retrieval task (such as "standard" recognition) the usual superiority of semantic processing would be observed. In betting on retrieval in an uncertain future retrieval environment, smart money will take deep processing.

ACCOUNTING FOR THE MATCHED-TRANSFER LEVELS EFFECT

However, even if we grant that typical retrieval environments are more likely to favour deep processing, this appeal to the demographics of memory sidesteps more fundamental questions about the relationship between levels of processing and transfer-appropriate processing. In this matter, the typical levels effect, such as the superiority in free recall of a semantic over a non-semantic orienting task, is not the most critical evidence favouring the generally beneficial effects of deep processing. Rather, it is the well-documented finding (e.g., Fisher & Craik, 1977; Morris et al., 1977) that even under conditions aimed at maximising transfer-appropriateness, shallow encoding yields poorer performance than deep encoding. Rhyme recognition following rhyme encoding is poorer than standard recognition following semantic encoding. Because the following discussion will make continued reference to this particular finding it is convenient to label it. It will be referred to as the *matched-transfer* levels effect. More recently, Marmurek (1995) has shown that this effect cannot be attributed to differences in the difficulty of retrieval tasks, thereby clarifying the rather careless use of the term "main effect" by Lockhart and Craik (1990).

Conceptually, it is possible to distinguish two potential sources of the matched-transfer levels effect. The first source consists of characteristics of the memory trace itself, qualities that could be specified independently of any particular retrieval environment. Such qualities might be, for example, distinctiveness, resistance to interference, or even something as traditional as strength. We will refer to this account as the *trace* explanation of the matched-transfer levels effect. On the basis of their experimental findings Moscovitch and Craik (1976) and Fisher and Craik (1977) argued for such an explanation, emphasising the role of trace-distinctiveness.

The second possible influence on the matched-transfer levels effect is transfer-appropriate processing itself. Such a possibility may seem unlikely, given the claim that transfer-appropriateness has been matched. However, despite the nominal equating of the level of transfer-appropriate processing for the two encoding conditions, it is conceivable that semantic processing in conjunction with semantic cueing nevertheless represents a greater degree of transfer appropriateness than the corresponding match for shallower processing such as rhyme. Assuming that processing is never fully transfer-appropriate—that the retrieval environment never achieves a perfect recapitulation of encoding processes—shallow processing may be more vulnerable to a mismatch produced by small variations in the retrieval environment. It presents, as it were, a smaller target for retrieval processing and, to pursue the metaphor, is thus vulnerable to the slightest misdirection. We will refer to this account as the *transfer* explanation of the matched-transfer levels effect. This view does not deny the general advantage of deep processing, but claims levels of processing is a phenomenon that can be subsumed under transfer-appropriate processing; transfer-appropriate processing is the mechanism through which it operates. Levels of processing is simply an indirect way of influencing the degree to which processing is transfer-appropriate.

The transfer and trace accounts of the matched-transfer levels effect are not, of course, mutually exclusive. It is possible that both are operative either additively or interactively. The evidence for the trace account as a contributing factor is quite strong (e.g., Fisher & Craik, 1977; Marmurek, 1995). The contribution of the transfer factor, if any, is less clear and therefore warrants further attention.

THE CONCEPT OF ROBUST ENCODING

According to the transfer account, for an unspecified future retrieval context, levels of processing has its effect by influencing the likelihood that the processing will prove to be transfer-appropriate. Using the language of the encoding specificity principle, another way of expressing this claim is to say that deep processing expands the domain of elements that can interact ecphorically with the retrieval environment. Lockhart and Craik (1990) introduced the term *robust encoding* to capture this concept. Schacter (1996, p.63) expresses a similar idea when he suggests that a major reason why a semantic orienting task typically works better than a non-semantic one might be because the semantic processing yields a trace that is accessible to a broader range of retrieval cues. A robust trace, then, is one more likely to survive variations in the subsequent retrieval context because it presents a broader target to subsequent retrieval processing.

Encoding variability

The term "robust encoding" is in need of clarification, not to mention supporting evidence. Note first that the general idea is by no means new. For example, it will no doubt seem familiar to those who have followed the fortunes of the concept of encoding variability. This idea predates levels of processing (e.g., Madigan, 1969; Martin, 1968; Melton, 1970), and continues to have some currency (e.g., Soraci et al., 1999). Thus one interpretation of robust encoding is that it represents a special form of encoding variability in which deep processing (such as semantic elaboration) has its effect by laying down a greater range of potential retrieval routes. General support for the beneficial effects of encoding variability would therefore seem essential to the plausibility of the robust encoding concept. Two lines of experimental evidence are relevant. First, if robust encoding is a form of encoding variability, then experimentally eliminating encoding variability from processing should eliminate any benefit that deep processing might impart to subsequent retrieval. Second, the experimental enhancement of encoding variability should benefit retrieval. We will briefly consider each of these points before a consideration of more direct evidence on the concept of robust encoding.

The concept of maintenance (or type 1) rehearsal as described by Craik and Lockhart (1972) can be thought of as a form of processing designed to eliminate, or at least minimise, the kind of encoding variability envisaged in the concept of robust encoding. Experimental support for the claim that maintenance rehearsal yields no additional benefit to retrieval would therefore seem essential to the plausibility of robust encoding. On the other hand, although such evidence is necessary, it provides only weak positive support in that it also supports (and is demanded by) virtually any interpretation of the levels-of-processing effect.

The evidence relating to the effects of maintenance rehearsal has been thoroughly reviewed by Greene (1987). The data offer support for the general conclusion that in so far as maintenance rehearsal facilitates retrieval its effects are largely limited to recognition memory. The evidence is quite strong, especially when one takes into account the fact that pure maintenance processing is an ideal that actual experimental conditions can only approximate. Poor approximations to the ideal may well account for the occasional finding that maintenance rehearsal facilitates free recall. Greene attributes the effect of maintenance rehearsal on recognition memory to "self-coding". Naveh-Benjamin and Jonides (1984) discuss a similar explanation in terms of intra-item integration. A more specific version of this interpretation, making use of dual-process theories of recognition, is that maintenance rehearsal has its effects via the non-recollective component of recognition. Such an account meshes nicely with the finding that this non-recollective component is unaffected by level of processing (Gardiner, 1988; Rajaram, 1993) leading to the conclusion that, although maintenance rehearsal may facilitate some aspects of retrieval, its effects are qualitatively distinct from those of levels of processing. Thus the data would seem to leave intact (and provide weak support for) the initial claim that the experimental elimination of encoding variability from processing should remove any benefit that deep processing might impart to subsequent retrieval.

However, the evidence for the effects of increased encoding variability is anything but clear-cut. Despite some success in accounting for the spacing effect in free recall (Glenberg, 1979; Madigan, 1969) and the effect on final recall of different forms of initial retrieval (McDaniel & Masson, 1985) direct evidence is mixed. Postman and Knecht (1983), for example, performed a direct test by comparing the recall of words repeated within the same sentence with words repeated in different sentences. They found no support for the encoding variability hypothesis. McDaniel and Masson (1985) suggest that this failure may be the consequence of an experimental manipulation that produced insufficient variation in encoding. This may be a valid explanation of the Postman and Knecht results, but if

so, it does little to help the interpretation of robust encoding as a form of encoding variability. It is surely implausible to claim that the typical semantic orienting task such as judging synonymity yields greater encoding variability than the manipulation used by Postman and Knecht (1983). Moreover, it is possible to make the opposite claim and argue that enhanced encoding variation of the type used by Postman and Knecht adds no further benefit because the semantic analysis achieved in a single presentation is sufficient to produce maximum effects of encoding variability, at least of the kind envisaged by the concept of robust encoding. It would seem that encoding variability is a slippery concept.

A thorough review of the experimental findings surrounding encoding variability shows an intricate pattern of interactions that makes it difficult to speak in general terms about the effects of encoding variability. Experiments reported by McDaniel and Masson (1985), or Soraci et al. (1999) provide a good illustration of this point. Such complexity should not surprise anyone who takes seriously the underlying encoding specificity principle or transfer-appropriate processing. According to these principles, encoding variability is not intrinsically or universally beneficial, but should be effective only in so far as the variability encompasses elements that are recapitulated at retrieval. The effect of variability not so recapitulated would at best be neutral or, by exerting some form of interference or lessening discriminability, the effect could quite possibly be negative. The relevant question with respect to the concept of robust encoding is this: Does deep processing result in form of encoding variability (robust encoding) that is more likely to transfer appropriately to the retrieval conditions typical of free recall and the recollective component of recognition? We turn now to a consideration of experiments that attempt to manipulate directly the relationship between levels of processing and variations in the conditions of retrieval.

Direct tests of robust encoding

A straightforward interpretation of robust encoding leads to a simple prediction. Variations in the retrieval environment should have a smaller effect for items that have been deeply processed. Results reported by Hannon and Craik (2001) support this prediction. They argue that deeper processing makes successful recognition less dependent on the reinstatement of the original encoding context. However, most of the evidence relevant to the prediction contradicts it. Marmurek (1995) points this out with respect to the data from Morris et al. (1977) as well as his own data, and experiments by Fisher and Craik (1977) and Moscovitch and Craik (1976) show exactly the same result. When the retrieval environment is varied by providing either semantic or non-semantic retrieval cues, the effect of this cue variation is much greater for items that were deeply processed. Such results indicate that the concept of robust encoding is either badly mistaken or in need of some very serious refinement. Evidence, as it stands, would seem to favour some version of the trace account, but clearly the issue needs more research.

Refinement of the concept of robust encoding may well be possible, but it is beyond the scope of this paper to attempt such a task. However, a few points can be made. First, there is no reason to suppose that the conjectured robustness resulting from deep encoding should extend beyond the semantic domain. It seems more appropriate to consider it a range of semantic elaboration that can be taken advantage of by semantic cueing. If this is true, then the robustness associated with deep encoding should not enhance transfer-appropriateness in relation to a non-semantic cue. It is to be expected, therefore, that despite semantic encoding, retrieval will be poor under conditions of non-semantic cueing, the result obtained by Morris et al. (1977) and Fisher and Craik (1977). Given the relatively high level of performance of semantic cueing following semantic encoding, a large difference between the two cueing conditions is inevitable and, it could be argued, irrelevant to any plausible realisation of robust encoding. Defenders of robust encoding might further point out that the low level of performance for rhyme encoding, even when the task is rhyme recognition, allows little room for downward variation for other sub-optimal cueing conditions. In brief, such experiments constitute too blunt an instrument to provide a critical test.

CONCLUSION

The challenge facing the concept of robust encoding (or any other transfer-based concept) as an account of the matched-transfer levels effect is to show that there exist more sharply focused cueing conditions that can elevate performance for non-semantic encoding. That challenge seems formidable. A more promising alternative is to qualify the sharp distinction made between trace- and transfer-based accounts. Whereas this distinction can be drawn at a conceptual level, empirically the two may be largely inseparable. That is to say, the features of the memory trace envisaged by trace accounts of deep processing may be precisely those that, at the same time, impart the robustness envisaged by transfer accounts. If this is so, then no refinement of cueing conditions alone will elevate performance for non-semantic encoding to that of semantic encoding paired with semantic cueing. The only way in which to increase transfer-appropriateness would be tantamount to introducing greater depth of processing. This interactive interpretation of the relationship between the trace and transfer accounts is entirely compatible with that given by Fisher and Craik (1977) in their general discussion.

These speculations clearly need to be spelled out in ways that make them amenable to experimental investigation. However, the questions raised by concepts such as robust encoding are central to any thorough understanding of human memory. The fundamental issues remain what they have been for 30 years: the nature of the interactive relationship between encoding and retrieval processes. Broad concepts such as levels of processing and transfer-appropriate processing have generated a large body of research that has greatly increased our understanding, although much work remains to be done.

REFERENCES

Challis, B.H., Velichkovsky, B.M., & Craik, F.I.M. (1996). Levels-of-processing effects on a variety of memory tasks: New findings and theoretical implications. *Consciousness & Cognition: An International Journal, 5,* 142–164.

Craik, F.I.M., & Lockhart, R.S. (1972). Levels of processing: A framework for memory research. *Journal of Verbal Learning and Verbal Behavior, 11,* 671–684.

Fisher, R.P., & Craik, F.I.M. (1977). Interaction between encoding and retrieval operations in cued recall. *Journal of Experimental Psychology: Human Learning and Memory, 3,* 701–711.

Gardiner, J.M. (1988). Functional aspects of recollective experience. *Memory & Cognition, 16,* 309–313.

Glenberg, A.M. (1979). Component-levels theory of the effects of spacing of repetitions on recall and recognition. *Memory & Cognition, 7,* 95–112.

Gould, S.J. (1977). Darwin's untimely burial. In *Ever Since Darwin* (pp. 39–45). New York: Norton.

Greene, R.L. (1987). Effects of maintenance rehearsal on human memory. *Psychological Bulletin*, *102*, 403–413.

Hannon, B., & Craik, F.I.M (2001). Encoding specificity revisited: The role of semantics. *Canadian Journal of Experimental Psychology*, *55*, 231–243.

Lockhart, R.S., & Craik, F.I.M. (1978). Levels of processing: A reply to Eysenck. *British Journal of Psychology, 69*, 171–175.

Lockhart, R.S., & Craik, F.I.M. (1990). Levels of processing: A retrospective analysis of a framework for memory research. *Canadian Journal of Psychology*, *44*, 87–112.

Madigan, S.A. (1969). Intraserial repetition and coding processes in free recall. *Journal of Verbal Learning and Verbal Behavior*, *8*, 828–835.

Marmurek, H.H. (1995). Encoding, retrieval, main effects and interactions: were Lockhart and Craik (1990) on the level? *Canadian Journal of Experimental Psychology*, *49*, 174–192.

Martin, E. (1968). Stimulus meaningfulness and paired-associate transfer: An encoding variability hypothesis *Psychological Review*, *75*, 421–441.

McDaniel, M.A., & Masson, M.E.J. (1985). Altering memory representations through retrieval. *Journal of Experimental Psychology: Human Learning and Memory*, *11*, 371–385.

Melton, A.W. (1970) The situation with respect to the spacing of repetitions and memory. *Journal of Verbal Learning & Verbal Behavior*, *9*, 596–606.

Morris, C.D., Bransford, J.D., & Franks, J.J. (1977). Levels of processing versus transfer-appropriate processing. *Journal of Verbal Learning and Verbal Behavior*, *16*, 519–533.

Moscovitch, M., & Craik, F.I.M. (1976). Depth of processing, retrieval cues, and uniqueness of encoding as factors in recall. *Journal of Verbal Learning and Verbal Behavior*, *15*, 447–458.

Naveh-Benjamin, M., & Jonides, J. (1984). Maintenance rehearsal: A two-component analysis. *Journal of Experimental Psychology: Human Learning and Memory*, *10*, 369–385.

Nelson, T.O. (1977). Repetition and levels of processing. *Journal of Verbal Learning & Verbal Behavior*, *16*, 151–171.

Postman, L., & Knecht, K. (1983). Encoding variability and retention. *Journal of Verbal Learning & Verbal Behavior*, *22*, 133–152.

Rajaram, S. (1993). Remembering and knowing: Two means of access to the personal past. *Memory & Cognition*, *21*, 89–102.

Roediger, H.L.III, & Gallo, D.A. (2001). Levels of processing: Some unanswered questions. In M. Naveh-Benjamin, M. Moscovitch, & H.L. Roediger III (Eds.), *Perspectives on human memory and cognitive aging: Essays in honour of Fergus Craik* (pp. 28–47). Philadelphia, PA: Psychology Press.

Roediger, H.L.III, Weldon, M.S., Stadler, M.L., & Riegler, G.L. (1992). Direct comparison of two implicit memory tests: Word fragment and word stem completion. *Journal of Experimental Psychology: Learning, Memory, and Cognition*, *18*, 1251–1269.

Schacter, D.L. (1996). *Searching for memory*. New York: Basic Books.

Soraci, S.A., Carlin, M.T., Chechile, R.A., Franks, J.J., Wills, T., & Watanabe, T. (1999). Encoding variability and cuing in generative processing. *Journal of Memory & Language*, *41*, 541–559.

Stamos, J. (1996). Popper, falsifiability, and evolutionary biology. *Biology and Philosophy*, *11*, 161–191.

Tulving, E., & Thomson, D.M. (1973). Encoding specificity and retrieval processes in episodic memory. *Psychological Review*, *80*, 359–380.

MEMORY, 2002, 10 (5/6), 405–419

Heterarchy of cognition: The depths and the highs of a framework for memory research

Boris M. Velichkovsky

Dresden University of Technology, Germany

To celebrate the levels-of-processing approach, I describe a multilevel evolutionary architecture for human behaviour and cognition. New experimental data on human eye movements are presented that demonstrate a possibility of splitting visual perceptual activity at least on two hierarchical but closely interrelated levels of processing. Furthermore, data from behavioural studies of human memory and neuroimaging testify that within the domain of cognition proper two higher levels can be differentiated. I call them "conceptual structures" and "metacognitive coordinations" and provide evidence that the latter may residue in the phylogenetically new structures of prefrontal and particularly right prefrontal cortices. From this point of few, the most natural framework for an analysis of the levels-of-processing effects on human memory is to consider them as interactions within the main gradients of evolution and development of the corresponding neurophysiological mechanisms. Finally, several new, still unanswered questions for the future research are formulated.

The purpose of the article is to give a prospective outlook on research within the levels-of-processing approach. Nevertheless, let me start with a deeply retrospective remark. The notions of layers, strata, and levels have their roots in geology, particularly mining. In a psychological context, the notion of depth (as "depths of soul") was first used by the founder of the Romantic movement and a former student of the Mining Academy in Freiberg, Novalis (Friedrich Hardenberg) in the late 18th century. In the same cultural context of Romanticism, one finds for the first time a passionate emphasis on goal-directed activity. As Novalis wrote: "Activity is the only true reality. The notion of identity should include the notion of activity, since what I am, I am owing to my activity. Furthermore, activity should be considered in its relationships, not in isolation. It is always a relationship to the object and to my own state" (Novalis, 1926, 403).

The geological metaphor of stratification influenced, through early palaeontologists' work, biological and evolutionary thinking. John Houghling-Jackson, Peter Weiss, and Paul MacLean started the search for evolutionary levels in organisation of brain and behaviour, while Nikolai Bernstein (1947) applied the ideas in his pioneering studies on construction of movements. The romantic notions of activity and levels in particular influenced developmental psychology, where starting with Pierre Janet and Lev Vygotsky the differentiation of lower and higher—acculturated or cultural-historical—psychological functions has become a standard (for a recent analysis, see Tomasello, 1999).

Requests for reprints should be sent to Boris M. Velichkovsky, Applied Cognitive Research/Psychology III, Dresden University of Technology, D-01062 Dresden, Germany. Email: velich@psychologie.tu-dresden.de

Thanks are due to Anna B. Leonova, Bruce Bridgeman, Fergus I.M. Craik, Jaan Panskepp, and Norbert Bischof for discussion of the article and the laboratory team—Alexandra Rothert, Bastian Pannasch, Darius Maniotas, Hannes Marx, Jens Helmert, Markus Joos, Pieter Unema and Sascha Dornhoefer—for help and enthusiasm. Our research is supported by a grant from German Science Foundation (Deutsche Forschungsgemeinschaft: VE 192/8). Eye-tracking experiments, described in the article, were supported by BMW AG, Munich (Project "Hazard Cognition").

DOI:10.1080/09658210244000234

The experimental psychology of memory was shaped by a completely different set of metaphors, from that of "*la statue anime*" to the later von Neumann computer. In cognitive psychology all activities, or forms of processing, were for a long time strictly contingent on the corresponding memory stores, which were really omnipresent—to an extent that is hardly conceivable today. Indeed, who else remembers "iconic memory", the hypothetical container of visual sensory processes? In their manifesto, Craik and Lockhart (1972) basically proposed reversing the relationship of storage and processing by considering memory as a by-product of human activities. These activities may evolve at different levels aimed at processing of shallow, or physical, features of the material or being directed to analysis of deeper, semantic information (Craik & Tulving, 1975; Lockhart & Craik, 1990). It is the idea of different levels of processing that will be primarily addressed in this article.

THEORIES AND MODELS: THE MULTILEVEL HYPOTHESIS

To facilitate further analysis, I will try to place the framework for memory research into a more explicit evolutionary context. This enforces a reversal of terminology. The "shallow" sensory processing, common to the wide variety of biological species, will correspond to a low-level processing, and the "deep" (semantic or, e.g., phonological) processing, will correspond rather to the group of higher-level activities. Presuming that there is such a "vertical dimension" of mental functioning, what could its granularity and distinct characteristics of levels be? This is not a trivial question as until now different approaches operating with the notions "level of processing" and "hierarchical organisation" have simply ignored each other (see Cohen, 2000).

It is clear that dichotomies are too unspecific: authors as different as only Wundt, Vygotsky, and Jerry Fodor could be, used two-levels theories. There is, of course, an old tradition of three-levels theories—in developmental research (Karl Buehler), human factors engineering (Jens Rasmussen), and, especially, neuroscience. However, some disagreement here implies that more levels may be at work: if Houghling-Jackson and Luria identified the highest control instances of behaviour with the frontal lobes, the upper level of MacLean's "triune" conception was the whole of

the neocortex (everything above the so-called "reptilian brain", which included basal ganglia and the limbic system). The founders of modern biomechanics and a protagonist of ecological psychology, Bernstein (1947), described four levels, from A to D, involved in realisation of human movements. I adapted his views some time ago, which led to a working model with as many as six different levels of organisation. The first group (from A to D) is primarily built up by the sensorimotor mechanisms. The second group (from E to F) consists of mechanisms of higher symbolic coordination. Here is the list of these levels in bottom-up order (after Velichkovsky, 1990, 1994).

Level A: *Paleokinetic Regulations*. Bernstein also called it the "rubro-spinal" level, having in mind the structures of spinal cord and brain stem (up to midbrain) involved in regulation of the muscles' tonus, and paleovestibular reflexes, as well as basic defensive and startle responses. The awareness of functioning is reduced here to Henry Head's (1920) protopathic sensitivity, which is so hedonistic, diffuse, and lacking any precise local signs (spatial coordinates) that even the term sensation seems to be too intellectual in this case.

Level B: *Synergies*. Due to evolution of new neurological mechanisms—the "thalamo-pallidar system" after Bernstein—the broad sensory integration and regulation of the organism's movements as a whole become possible, transforming it into a "locomotory machine". The specialisations of this level are movements involving large groups of muscles of different body parts, e.g., rhythmic and cyclic patterns of motion underlying all forms of locomotion. Possibilities of awareness are limited to proprio- and tangoreceptoric sensations within the body's frame of reference.

Level C: *Spatial Field*. The next round of evolution adds exteroception to the repertoire of sensory corrections. This opens outer 3D space and makes possible one-time goal/place-directed movements as well as topographically contingent behaviour in the near environment. The control instances of the level are phylogenetically new parts of basal ganglia (striatum) and stimulotopically organised cortical areas, especially in posterior parietal cortex. The corresponding subjective experience is that of a stable voluminous surrounding filled with localised but only globally sketched objects.

Level D: *Object Actions*. A new spiral of evolution leads to the building of a variety of secondary areas of neocortex with parietal, premotor, and partially temporal regions as the main instances. This permits detailed form perception and object-adjusted manipulations. Individualised objects affording some but not other actions come to the focus of attention. Formation and tuning of sophisticated higher-order sensorimotor and perceptual skills is supported by a memory of the procedural type. Phenomenal experience is the perceptual image (as described by Gestalt school—Koffka, 1935).

Level E: *Conceptual Structures*. Supramodal associative cortices of temporal and frontal structures, particularly on the left side, provide the highest integration of various modalities supporting the ability to categorise objects and events as members of generic classes. Development of language and human culture fosters this ability and virtually leads to formation of the powerful declarative-procedural mechanisms of symbolic representation of the world, which is widely (but not quite correctly) known as semantic memory. Common consciousness is the mode of awareness at this level.

Level F: *Metacognitive Coordinations*. Changes in conceptual structures result not only from accretion of factual experience but also from experimentation with ontological (truth-value) parameters of knowledge. This "personal view of the world" and its counterpart, "theory of mind", are supported by those parts of the neocortex that show largest growth in anthropogenesis, notably by the prefrontal and, especially, right prefrontal regions. This level is behind personal and interpersonal reference, reflective consciousness, and productive imagination. It provides resources of dealing with novel situations and tasks without (known) solution.

Perhaps an example may help to illustrate the levels at work in everyday circumstances. Try to imagine that you are giving a talk when, suddenly, something crashes to the side and slightly behind you. For a split second (with latency of only 90–100 ms—Pannasch, Dornhoefer, Unema, & Velichkovsky, 2001), all your activities will be stopped and even your gaze "freezes" in its actual location. This is a level A performance, which is so robust across species that butterflies use it to immobilise their predators by abruptly displaying wing patterns (Schlenoff, 1985). Next, a typical synergy, i.e., level B movement starts to evolve— the rotation of the body towards the side of the event with increasing speed in the upper limbs and the head. Then, high-amplitude saccades towards

the place of the accident are initiated. Sometimes, stretching the arm can assist these level C movements. After that, perceptual identification (D), semantic categorisation (E), and metacognitive evaluation (F) follow in a rapid succession. First of all, this is attentive processing mediated by relatively short-amplitude saccades within the object's borders (in other situations, the analysis could be supported by finer hand movements adjusted to the object's form and texture—see Jannerod, 1981). With identification and binding, the object's properties (e.g., as black, flat, rectangular), its further categorisation as a technical artefact and a computer, as well as the self-referential apprehension "My notebook!" are possible. This is where the more systematic problem solving begins with further emotionally loaded queries: "Can I finish the lecture?" or "Who could recover the files?".

Several aspects of this illustrative example need qualification. First of all, nothing prescribes that the sequence of events should always go from A to F. In fact, any of the levels may assume a leading role, depending on the task at hand. Therefore, rigorously speaking, this is a heterarchy, not a hierarchy (Turvey, Shaw, & Mace, 1978). Most of the levels are simultaneously at work providing their specific competences and resources—either as *leading* or as *background* coordinations—to the task solution (Bernstein, 1947; Velichkovsky, 2001). The linear depiction of events also ignores strong top-down loops in evolution such as enabling "reptilian brain" to take part in playing the piano or, on a larger scale, propelling the development of human language and communication (see Deacon, 1996). Although levels are semiautonomous entities, they are not modules in the sense of a random mosaic of the orthodox modularity approach (Fodor, 1983). There can be an abundance of domain-specific effects in such types of architecture. What makes a difference to the modular theories is that these contributions are not all equivalent, being embedded in a kind of global *gradient* of evolutionary mechanisms (Goldberg, 1991), so that *systematic asymmetries* in relations of local, domain-specific effects should be expected (Velichkovsky, 1982, 1994).

Second, I shifted the emotional reactions to higher levels in the description of the imaginary accident. This is an issue that has recently been energetically disputed. As a matter of fact, multilevel models have become increasingly popular in investigation of emotion and affective states. Heckhausen (1985, p. 5) outlined the architecture in the following way:

> At the lowest level, we find automatic reactions of the autonomic nervous system, the endocrine and immune systems ... Then follow basic drives, which counterbalance the body's household. Above these we find acquired needs, which are derived from the primary drives, but have become independent. Then there are all those primary affects such as happiness, grief, fear, anger, surprise, and disgust that colourate our experience ... And only then, on the very top, do we find the higher, i.e. the social and cultural motives from which most of our wishes spring, provided that the lower systems do not happen to be busy in repairing homeostatic crises in the organism.

Although the placement of grief among primary affects is an obvious mistake, this approach deserves further elaboration. The modern versions of hierarchical theories of emotions operate with two (Öhman, 1992) or three levels (Scherer, 2001), emphasising differences between automatic (inborn as well as learned) and reflective (or "conceptual") mechanisms. The real disagreement, however, is in the treatment of the relation between emotions and cognitive appraisal. Can a low-level cognitive processing, such as our level C spatial localisation, activate emotional responses even if it is too global to lead to object identification? This is the opinion behind the presumption of a fast subcortical pathway from early stages of visual processing to the amygdala-hippocampal region (LeDoux, 1996). A preattentive processing of emotional events in humans would have serious consequences for perception and memory (Robinson, 1998). In the next part of the article, I will address the question of operational distinction of different forms of low-level processing and their cognitive and behavioural implications.

LEVELS "BELOW" PERCEPTUAL (FORM-ORIENTED) PROCESSING

Shortly after the beginning of the success story of Craik and Lockhart's (1972) framework for memory research, fellow-colleagues discovered what was called "a circularity in the definition of levels": while it was memory performance that provided the initial impetus to differentiate levels of processing, the results of further memory tests were used to evaluate the validity of these distinctions. Let me note that the same circularity is not less typical for complementary conceptualisations, such as transfer-appropriate processing and the encoding specificity principle (e.g., Tulving, 1983). It reflects the unfortunate encapsulation of cognitive memory research, which was for a long time isolated from the rest of behavioural and brain sciences.

Two main independent sources of evidence for levels of processing have been established in the last few years. The first is consistent with the general shift towards cognitive neuroscience and will be considered later in the article. The second is relatively less known, at least in memory research. Instead of, or in addition to, still extremely cumbersome brain imaging, high-resolution eye tracking can be applied for a microanalysis of the on-going exploratory behaviour at encoding and retrieval (Reingold, 2002; Velichkovsky, 1999). Only such an analysis explicates what the subject does with the individual items conveying clear-cut differences in parameters of visual fixations for the typical levels-of-processing encodings and their variation. The analysis can also be applied to the memory tasks themselves, for example by demonstrating that recognition is also a perceptual and not only a conceptually driven test as has often been assumed.

The typical studies of the last 30 years used encoding manipulations that can be identified with attentive processes aimed at figurative or semantic features of the material. They therefore mainly involved levels D and E. In the following, I will briefly describe a recent investigation where processing at a lower level—Spatial Field, or C—was also taken into account (Velichkovsky, Rothert, Kopf, Dornhoefer, & Joos, in press). In this investigation, subjects (all experienced drivers) must drive through a virtual town following traffic rules while their eye movements and behaviour are continuously registered. Of particular interest were subjects' perception of and responses to emotional, hazardous events, such as an abrupt change from green to red of a traffic-light or a pedestrian jumping out on the road in front of the car (Figure 1 A, B).

To differentiate several levels in perception of the realistic dynamic environments, one can benefit from Trevarthen's (1968) early distinction between ambient and focal visual processing. It is consistent with our general multilevel model in separating processes of level C, on the one hand, from those of level D and higher mechanisms, on the other. In order to find criteria for ambient and focal processing modes, it is useful to consider the

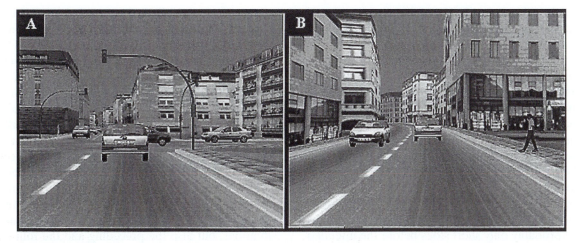

Figure 1. A. An immediate hazard—traffic light switches to red when the car is close to the crossing; B. A potential hazard—a pedestrian facing the road.

relationships between duration of visual fixations and amplitude of related saccades. Figure 2A shows the typically skewed distribution of fixation durations. One should note that in the road-traffic situations, visual fixations include a smooth pursuit component and, as a rule, are longer than fixations in reading or in exploration of static scenes. As can easily be seen from Figure 2B, some of the fixations are preceded and followed by saccades that are larger than the radius of the parafoveal area (c. 4°). This means that these saccades cannot be oriented by any detailed— "focal"—visual representation of objects. Inter-

estingly, corresponding fixations also have a relatively short duration, from 100 to about 300 ms. Due to these and other properties (e.g., insensitivity to the cognitive tasks—Dornhoefer, Pannasch, Velichkovsky, & Unema, 2000), the fixations from this segment of durations can be considered as manifestations of the low-level, ambient processing mode, i.e., level C in the terms of our multilevel model.

In contrast, the fixations with duration above 300 ms are typically preceded and also followed by relatively short-range saccades. These fixations are therefore located mostly within the same

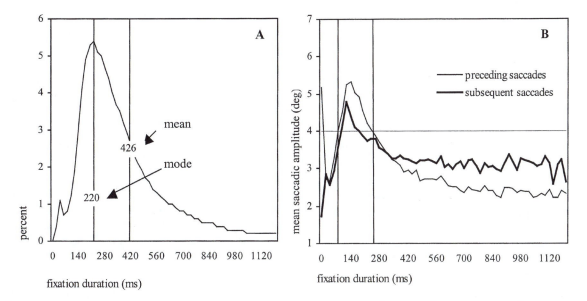

Figure 2. A. Distribution of fixation durations in the simulated driving experiments (based on 187, 324 fixations); **B.** Distributions of the amplitudes of preceding and following saccades dependent on fixation durations.

parafoveal area that facilitates detailed perceptual analysis and continuous focal attention. In addition, the group of fixations seems to be highly sensitive to the explicit cognitive tasks (Dornhoefer et al., 2000). This is why the segment of longer fixations can be considered as related to attentive processing, at least of the type that is necessary for an identification of objects and events. The last comment is on the possible role of the rather small group of very short (less than 90 ms), or express fixations. They often result from the particularly long saccades but the subsequent saccades are extremely small, of almost microsaccadic range. Thus, the express fixations are probably only short stops before the intended position of a long-distance saccade is finally achieved through a fine corrective movement.

After this basic introduction to the diagnostics of visual processing, the main results of the experiment can be presented. Figure 3 demonstrates the temporal range of visual fixations immediately before, at, and after a potential hazard suddenly transforms into an acutely dangerous situation (here the green traffic-light at a crossing becomes a red one). To find the base line data, we evaluated the parameters of visual fixation durations within the driving intervals, which included various dynamic changes but where no hazardous events took place. In the resulting distribution, thresholds values of 5, 50, and 95 percentiles of the fixation durations were estimated.

In Figure 3A, the results of all the cases of adequate braking responses on the part of the subjects are presented. The exploding fixation duration at the moment of the critical event is only one of the relevant aspects of these data. The second aspect is that several preceding fixations are approximately 400 ms long, which testifies to the attentive, focal processing mode of the evolving situation. A rather different pattern of results can be seen in Figure 3B. This shows data of the few cases (N = 12, less than 2% of all immediate hazards) where subjects overlooked the danger and drive through the crossing on red (even if they mostly directly fixated the traffic light). Not only is a comparable prolongation of fixation at the critical moment lacking in these unfortunate situations, but also the preceding and the following fixations are significantly lower ($p < .05$) than during the hazardous episodes that end with adequate braking reaction. Moreover, with their duration of about 200 ms these inattentive fixations are all from the ambient, or level C processing mode.

A tentative conclusion from these data is that visual events with an immediate affective valence have to be attentively processed, at least at the level D of our multilevel ladder. Otherwise, they do not give rise to the appropriate appraisal and behavioural reactions. Thus, emotional processes in humans may indeed be related to and partially controlled by the higher symbolic coordinations (Holodynsky & Friedlmeier, in press). The conclusion is supported by other recent research, raising doubts about the presumed preattentive access to the amygdalo-hippocampal region

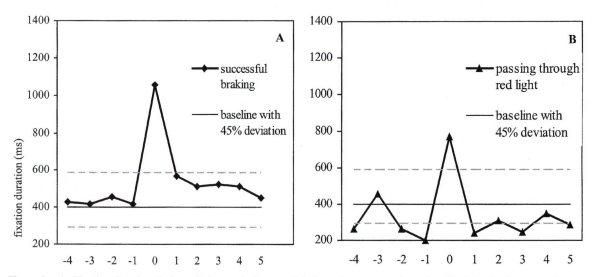

Figure 3. **A.** Fixation durations before, during, and after a switch from the green to the red traffic light, in the cases of correct responses ("0" corresponds to the fixation during the critical event). **B.** Same parameters in the cases where hazards were "overlooked".

(Robinson, 1998; Scherer, 2001). Level C processing, necessary to build up and update the spatial skeleton of the scene, cannot in itself be sufficient for perceptual, affective, or mnemonic description of individualised objects and events (see also Creem & Proffitt, 1999).

One could make the traces of ambient and focal processing literally visible by applying a gaze-contingent filtering of visual scenes known as the method of "attentional landscapes" (see Velichkovsky, Pomplun, & Rieser, 1996b). For instance, in perception of complex pictures such as Jan Steen's painting shown in Figure 4A, similar patterns of fixation durations and saccadic amplitudes as in the dynamic road-traffic scenarios can be found. However, one difference is generally shorter fixations, so that the ambient mode corresponds to durations from 90 to about 150 ms. If the spatial distribution of these and longer fixations over the picture is computed separately and applied as a filter, one gets the representations shown in Figure 4B and C. (The subject's task in this case consisted in evaluation of social relations of the actors in the scene.) These representations can be called respectively, *ambient* and, *focal views* of the picture. Obviously the focal view, but not the ambient one, can easily be recognised as a representation of the initial picture. It is important that the surface covered by the ambient (low-level) fixations is not only larger than that of their focal counterparts, but remains relatively constant under different encoding instructions. On the contrary, spatial distribution of the focal fixations is sensitive to the instruction, i.e., it is task-dependent (Dornhoefer et al., 2000). In other words, the method of "attentional filtering" seems to provide a reconstruction of the specific perspectives that different levels have on the same situation.

Thus, data on eye movements provide strong evidence on some additional, earlier forms of processing, preceding that of form-oriented (level D), or "physical", encoding from the classical levels-of-processing studies. Although the type of low-level processing may be relatively uninteresting from the point of view of memory research (as being a typical example of the visual scanning activities evolving in "eternal present tense"—see Horowitz & Wolfe, 1998), the question is open whether it can demonstrate any kind of perceptual priming effects. Inspection of Figure 4B shows that with its emphasis on diffuse masses, simple landmarks, and borders, level C processing cannot produce the priming effects that are known from the form-oriented perceptual tasks. Should we once compare both level C and level D with respect to their influence on the implicit (perceptual) memory tests, this could well lead to a discovery of a strong "LOP-effect"—where today only a meta-analysis of dozens of experiments is able to show a marginally significant trend (Challis & Brodbeck, 1992).

The fascination of the current eye-tracking experiments is that in fact the whole range of evolutionary mechanisms can be investigated with their help—from the paleokinetic regulations of level A (as demonstrated in the elementary startle and orienting reactions mediated by midbrain structures—Pannasch et al., 2001) to the level F metacognitive coordinations (represented by the joint attention effects connected with the taking into account of other person's gaze direction and deictic components of communication—see e.g., Velichkovsky, 1995). My next goal is to analyse this later form of processing, above that of traditional semantic encoding, in the context of contemporary studies of memory tasks.

FORMS OF PROCESSING "ABOVE" SEMANTIC CATEGORISATION

Self-referential encoding is a challenge for levels-of-processing research, as it can have an even larger memory effect than semantic encoding (e.g., Bower & Gilligan, 1979; Miall, 1986). Is it a genuinely new level or only an elaboration of semantic processing? The growing evidence for the role of metacognition lends itself to integration with the concept of levels, particularly with respect to this controversial issue (see Lockhart & Craik, 1990; Velichkovsky, 1994). The major data on the specifics of the highest level of cognitive organisation come from the developmental studies that demonstrate, around the age of 4 years, the emergence of theory of mind as well as reflective thinking and increasingly sophisticated forms of communication (Bischof-Köhler, 2000; Perner, 2000). The question can also be answered by contrasting neurophysiological mechanisms behind semantic and self-referential encoding.

In line with many similar proposals, I would argue that memory processes have different "functional anatomy". In particular, the *leading* level of all the direct (explicit) tests—whether they are called "perceptual" or "conceptual" ones—is usually the same as level F. It is not surprising therefore that one mostly finds a right

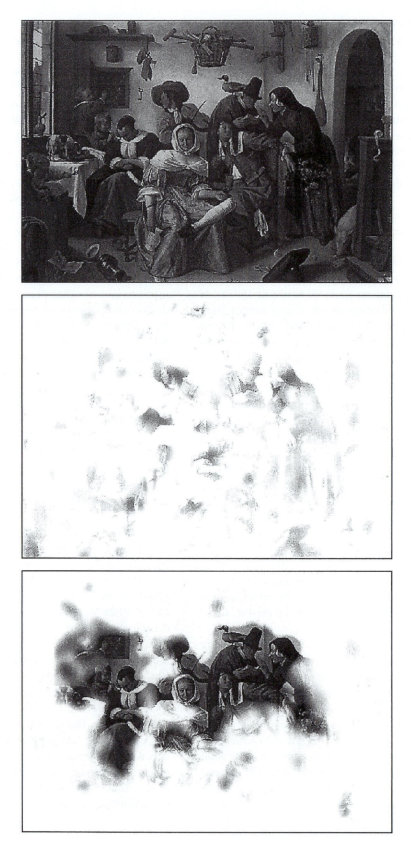

Figure 4. "The twisted world" by Jan Steen (1663): A. copy of the original; B. ambient view; C. focal view (after Velichkovsky, 2001, see text for details).

prefrontal activation (the "retrieval volition" component—e.g., Gardiner, Richardson-Klavehn, Ramponi, & Brooks, 2001) with this group of memory tasks. They are, however, different in their *background* coordinations, so that, for instance, recognition and free recall—both claimed to be conceptual explicit tests—differ, first, in their use of level E facilities and, second, in the involvement of the perceptual levels D and C with recognition only and not with free recall (see also Reingold, 2002). As to indirect (implicit) memory tests, their levels composition is defined by the content of the non-memory "carrier" tasks—the leading levels of these tasks are often D or E. Thus, the list of levels involved in implicit memory tasks is usually shorter and the projection of their mechanisms on the vertical dimension of mental processing is *narrower* than in the case of explicit tasks.

Blaxton (1989) investigated for the first time a large group of memory tests under the same experimental conditions. One aspect of her study, the difference in behaviour of perceptual implicit tests and conceptual implicit tests, has been confirmed in several later experiments (e.g., Tulving & Schacter, 1990). On a larger scale, Challis, Velichkovsky, and Craik (1996) analysed the effects of five different encoding conditions (plus baseline condition) of visually presented lists of words on 13 memory tests. The tests were selected according to major theoretical views, such as perceptual versus conceptual and implicit versus explicit. Due to the still unique dimensions of the study, I will contrast its results from the perspective of our multilevel model and modular approaches (see Velichkovsky, 1999, 2001).

With the large matrix of conditions, several predictions are possible. From the modular position, one would expect several clusters of interaction between encoding and retrieval in memory performance. That is, performance would be relatively high when encoding and retrieval processing "matched" (or are "appropriate"), and equally low elsewhere. From the multilevel view, one would expect the clusters of interaction to be asymmetric through the creation of something like *a gradient* from weak, to strong and perhaps even stronger memory effects.

Our data, shown in Figure 5, were quite compelling in relation to these predictions. To see the trends, one need only re-order incidental encoding conditions in the sequence of perceptual (counting of letters deviating in form), phonological (counting of syllables), semantic (categoris-

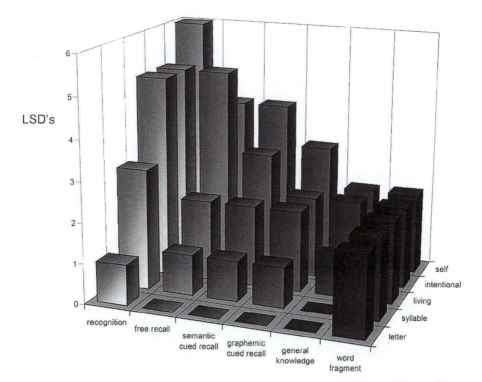

Figure 5. The number of statistically significant deviations from baseline (Least Significance Differences) in six memory tasks dependent on five encoding conditions (after Challis et al., 1996).

ing as living thing), and metacognitive (evaluation of personal significance) processing. In addition, explicit and implicit memory tests have to be considered separately. In the group of four explicit memory tasks (which were recognition, free recall, semantically cued and graphemically cued recall) resulting interactions demonstrate a systematic, gradient-like growth—the perfect level-of-processing effect—across at least most of the higher-order encoding conditions.

Thus, when memory tests are explicit, performance functions are of the monotonic growth type, but in implicit tests they are rather of a flat or a step-like type. Indeed, priming functions in this last group of tests, which were word fragment completion and general knowledge tests, look different: they are much flatter, or there seems to be no level-of-processing effect at all. However, some regularity can be discovered with respect to the point in the row of encoding conditions where variation in encoding starts to influence memory performance. In the general knowledge test, this starting point is semantic encoding. In the word fragment completion test, priming is present in all encoding conditions—one can argue that the crucial influence is already present here at the stage of perceptual encoding (our level D), and it is included in all further, higher-level encodings as well.

It is quite remarkable that in all but one case, the incidental self-referential processing leads to better memory performance than even the intentional encoding. The only one deviation is found in free recall. It can be attributed to the fact that the intentional instruction often invokes encoding strategies of particular benefit for a free-recall task (see Brown, 1979).

This pattern of results supports the idea of multiple levels. A dichotomous interpretation of the same data would be that incidental encoding conditions provide a variable amount of semantic information, which increases from perceptual to metacognitive conditions (Craik & Tulving, 1975; Roediger & Gallo, 2001). However it is not immediately clear why syllable encoding should involve more semantic activity than counting letters, or why judgement of personal significance should recruit more semantic associations than semantic categorisation itself. An attribution of the levels-of-processing effects to semantic processing alone (i.e., to contributions of level E) is dubious in light of other aspects of the data. For instance, free recall and recognition benefit from study conditions in different ways. Whereas it

might be argued that free recall utilises semantic information to a greater degree, empirically it is recognition that shows a stronger increase in performance as a function of the encoding manipulations. As I argued earlier, recognition has a more extended projection to the multilevel ladder: from C to F—in contrast to E and F in the case of free recall. It can only be level D that additionally enhances the recognition function *across all the encoding conditions*. In fact, recognition performance already deviates from baseline after perceptual (form-oriented) encoding, although this study condition involves little if any semantic processing.

There is another important aspect of the data. In all explicit tests in Figure 5, one can see approximately the same rate of growth in memory performance, i.e., if the levels-of-processing effect is visible later in the chain of encoding conditions, then effects of metacognitive encoding are also lower. This testifies to an integration of contributions from several levels—an idea that has been supported by further analysis (Velichkovsky, 2001). Why are there no signs of such integration in implicit tasks? As these tasks address narrow mechanisms (for instance, only level D or level E), there may simply be no basis for the integration.

Thus, the integration among the levels seems to be dependent on the type of task. A feature of explicit memory tests is usually a high degree of "vertical integration", so that evidence from several levels of processing is accumulated. There are no signs of this integration in implicit tests where responsibility is taken over—without much interference "from above"—by narrowly tuned mechanisms, sometimes at a rather low segment of the multilevel evolutionary ladder. In view of such flexibility, the notion of "heterarchy", as I said earlier, may be more appropriate for describing the underlying functional architecture.

DISCRETE LEVELS OR CONTINUOUS GRADIENTS?

One of the crucial questions for memory theory is, of course, why memory changes with the encoding manipulations (Tulving, 2001). In response to this question, there have been a number of attempts to find mechanisms and independent measures (or correlates) of levels of processing in neurophysiological data. Particularly convincing are studies of memory encoding and retrieval using methods of neuroimaging. There are two recent lines of evidence, compatible with the broad levels-of-processing view. First of all, the data on the storage of semantic categories showed, in a surprisingly clear form, that their cortical locations are immediately adjacent (perhaps with a slight shift in the anterior direction) to the mechanisms of corresponding sensorimotor and perceptual processing (see Schachter, Wagner, & Buckner, 2000, for a review). Second, recent data have demonstrated a high degree of consistency in the activation of the brain's structures under the influence of levels-of-processing instructions.

In one of the earliest studies, Blaxton and her colleagues (Blaxton et al., 1996) conducted a positron emission tomography (PET-scan) analysis of regional cerebral blood flow in several memory tests. Larger changes were found between perceptual and conceptual tasks. Memory effects for perceptual fragment completion tests (both implicit and explicit) were localised in posterior regions including occipital cortex with some right-side asymmetry. In contrast, the conceptual tests of semantic cued recall and word association revealed metabolic changes in the medial and superior temporal cortex, as well as in the left frontal cortex. Of course, these neuroanatmical differences have been found with respect to localisation of retrieval processes, so it can be interesting to compare them with results of encoding studies.

Gabrieli et al. (1996) used functional magnetic resonance imaging (fMRI) for a comparison of perceptual and semantic encoding of visually presented words. They discovered a greater activation of left inferior prefrontal cortex for semantic encoding. This makes it possible that the level I have called "conceptual structures" (or level E) could have connections with the left frontal regions and perhaps with the temporal lobes of the cortex. Gardiner et al. (2001) report right prefrontal and parietal activation in a combined EEG and MEG study of a word-stem completion task. This suggests the involvement of two levels: F as the leading level (due to the relatively unusual character of the task) and D (with its rich repertoire of pattern-recognition procedures) as the major background structure.

We investigated encoding with a method known as evoked coherences analysis of EEG (Velichkovsky, Klemm, Dettmar, & Volke, 1996a). In this method, coherence of neural activity in a particular region and incoherence between some region and the rest of the cortex can testify to its involvement in intensive infor-

mation processing. In a series of experiments, we investigated free recall of visually and acoustically presented words in dependence on three encoding conditions: perceptual, semantic, and metacognitive (self-referential). In the perceptual (form-oriented) encoding of visually presented words, the major coherences were localised in the occipital and right occipito-temporal areas. In semantic encoding, they expanded to the more anteriorly located regions, including bilateral temporal and left frontal areas. Remarkably, in our third condition—self-referential encoding—even more anteriorly located regions within frontal and *right prefrontal* lobes were involved.

Although the database of the EEG analysis is different from PET-scan or fMRI, the loci of coherence in perceptual and semantic orienting tasks have been found in approximately the same regions where Gabrieli et al. (1996) found them and where Blaxton et al. (1996) discovered changes for the corresponding memory tests. Similar data have been reported in other PET-scan investigations of neuroanatomical correlates of levels-of-processing effects (e.g., Kapur et al., 1994).

Of importance, in my opinion, are not only these neuroanatomical changes *per se*, but their direction. The posterior–anterior gradient, which is seen in most neuroimaging studies of levels-of-processing effects, corresponds to the main direction of evolutionary growth of the cortex (e.g., Deacon, 1996) as it is visualised in Figure 6. In other words, a purely functional interpretation of the levels-of-processing effects does not go far enough and should be revisited, perhaps, along with a simple principle: The "higher" (or "deeper", in the initial formulation of Craik and Lockhart) is a particular "level of processing", the more massive is an involvement of *phylogenetically recent* brain mechanisms in the task's solution. This correspondence of genetic, functional, and structural parameters is of course only a heuristic rule—our knowledge of brain functional evolution is too fragmentary. However, the rule may work in several other cases.

Until now, I have mainly discussed the posterior–anterior gradient. There are other lines of brain evolutionary development, for instance, one reflecting differences between subcortical and cortical mechanisms (for such analysis of motor control, see Bernstein, 1947/90, 1996). One of the peculiarities of human cortex is a relatively strongly developed right prefrontal lobe (Galaburda, LeMay, Kempter, & Geschwindt, 1978;

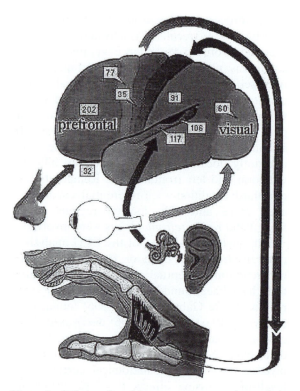

Figure 6. Relative size of human cortex areas (percent) in comparison to that of higher primates, illustrating the posterior–anterior gradient of evolution (after Deacon, 1996).

Holloway & De la Coste-Lareymondie, 1982). Of particular interest is the trend from the predominantly left anterior localisation in semantic encoding to an involvement of right prefrontal cortex in self-referential encoding (Velichkovsky, 1999; Velichkovsky et al., 1996a). The shift from left to right (especially to BA 9, 10, and 45) has been confirmed in a recent PET study of self-referential encoding (Craik et al., 1999) contrasting with the attribution of episodic encoding to the left frontal lobe (Tulving, 1998). The role of these structures in autobiographical and episodic remembering is well established (Cimino, Verfaillie, Bowers, & Heilman, 1991; Gardiner et al., 2001; Tulving et al., 1994).

However, the role is not limited to higher forms of memory. In a later study, Christoff and Gabrieli (2000) came to the conclusion that activations in right frontopolar cortex are not specific to episodic memory retrieval, but may instead be related to the especially demanding cognitive operations. Under these meta-operations, the structuring of the tasks and the building up of new goals can play an important role (Braver & Bongiolatti, 2002). The same regions seem to be involved in dealing with novel tasks, pragmatics of speech commu-

nication, understanding of fresh metaphors, irony, and humour, as well as in self-awareness and in the aspects of reflective social behaviour known as manifestation of the "theory of mind" (Bihle, Brownell, Powelson, Gardner, 1986; Goldberg & Podell, 1995; Shammi & Stuss, 1999; Wheeler, Stuss, & Tulving, 1997). The structures are also of importance for "the higher, i.e. the social and cultural motives from which most of our wishes spring" (Heckhausen, 1985, p. 5). As I noticed on several occasions (Velichkovsky, 1990, 1994), this list goes beyond the span of memory phenomena demarcating the "metacognitive coordinations", or level F in the multilevel classification presented at the beginning of this article.

CONCLUSIONS AND AN OUTLOOK

Current investigations in fields as different as human factors engineering, verbal learning, and neurophysiology of emotions demonstrate the viability of the search for different hierarchically organised levels of cognitive organisation. What is the reason for the rare stability of the levels-of-processing effects on memory performance?

The data are consistent with the emerging view that memory performance depends on a synchronisation of neural activities in the hippocampus and its environment (Fell et al., 2001). Now, it is only one step to acknowledge that this neuroanatomical environment also includes temporal and frontal cortices with the amygdala as the major "amplifie" (Mishkin, Suzuki, Gardian, & Vargha-Khadem, 1999). Given this, a number of questions arise. Is it the cumulative influence of all the synchronous activities—from temporal, frontal, and prefrontal cortices—converging on the amygdalo-hippocampal region that causes the strongest levels-of-processing effects in explicit memory tasks? Is that not the known asymmetry in the connection of left and particularly right prefrontal cortices with the amygdalo-hippocampal complex (see, e.g., Kawasaki et al., 2001; Murphy & Lawrence, 2001), which could explain differences in the "higher-level", semantic vs metacognitive encoding effects on memory? Furthermore, the amygdalo-hippocampal activation can lead (directly or via basal ganglia and substantia nigra) to an inhibition of the eye-movement centres in the midbrain that would exactly produce the observed prolongation of visual fixations in dependence on the level of processing (Velichkovsky, 1999).

These and other sensible questions may remain unanswered for a while, perhaps until the next anniversary of Craik and Lockhart's romantic appeal to consider activity first in the investigation of human memory.

REFERENCES

Bernstein, N.A. (1947). *O postrojenii dvizhenij [On the construction of movements]*. Moscow: Medgiz. [Reprinted in N.A. Bernstein, *Physiologija aktivnosti (Physiology of activity)*. Moscow: Nauka, 1990.]

Bernstein, N.A. (1996). *Dexterity and its development*. Mahwah, NJ: Lawrence Erlbaum Associates Inc.

Bihle, A.M., Brownell, H.H., Powelson, J.A., & Gardner, H. (1986). Comprehension of humorous and nonhumorous materials by left and right brain damaged patients. *Brain and Cognition, 5*, 399–411.

Bischof-Köhler, D. (2000). *Kinder auf der Zeitreise [Children on the trip through time]*. Bern: Hans Huber.

Blaxton, T.A. (1989). Investigating dissociations among memory measures. *Journal of Experimental Psychology: Learning, Memory, and Cognition, 15*, 657–668.

Blaxton, T.A., Bookheimer, S.Y., Zefiro, Th.A., Figlozzi, C.M., Gaillard, W.D., & Theodore, W.H. (1996). Functional mapping of human memory using PET: Comparisons of conceptual and perceptual tests. *Canadian Journal of Experimental Psychology, 50(1)*, 42–56.

Bower, H., & Gilligan, S.G. (1979). Remembering information related to one's self. *Journal of Research in Personality, 13*, 420–432.

Braver, T.S. & Bongiolatti, S.R. (2002). *The role of frontopolar prefrontal cortex in subgoal processing*. Manuscript submitted for publication.

Brown, A.L. (1979). Theories of memory and the problem of development. In L.A. Cermak & F.I.M. Craik (Eds.), *Levels of processing in human memory* (pp. 225–258). Hillsdale, NJ: Lawrence Erlbaum Associates Inc.

Challis, B.H., & Brodbeck, D.R. (1992). Level of processing affects priming in word fragment completion. *Journal of Experimental Psychology: Learning, Memory and Cognition, 18*, 595–607.

Challis, B.H., Velichkovsky, B.M., & Craik, F.I.M. (1996). Levels-of-processing effects on a variety of memory tasks: New findings and theoretical implications. *Consciousness & Cognition, 5(1/2)*, 142–164.

Christoff, K., & Gabrieli, J.D.E. (2000). The frontopolar cortex and human cognition: Evidence for a rostrocaudal hierarchical organization within the human prefrontal cortex. *Psychobiology, 28(2)*, 168–186.

Cimino, C.R., Verfaillie, M., Bowers, D., & Heilmann, K.M. (1991). Autobiographical memory: Influence of right hemisphere damage on emotionality and specificity. *Brain and Cognition, 15*, 106–118.

Cohen, G. (2000). Hierarchical models in cognition: Do they have psychological reality? *European Journal of Cognitive Psychology, 12(1)*, 1–36.

Craik, F.I.M., & Lockhart, R. (1972). Levels of processing: A framework for memory research. *Journal of Verbal Learning and Verbal Behavior, 11*, 671–684.

Craik, F.I.M., Moroz, T.M., Moscovitch, M., Stuss, D.T., Winokur, G., Tulving, E., & Kapur, S. (1999). In search of the self: A positron emisson tomography study. *Psychological Science, 10(1)*, 26–34.

Craik, F.I.M., & Tulving, E. (1975). Depth of processing and the retention of words in episodic memory. *Journal of Experimental Psychology: General, 104*, 268–294.

Creem, S., & Proffitt, D.R. (1999). Separate memories for visual guidance and explicit awareness. In B.H. Challis & B.M. Velichkovsky (Eds.), *Stratification in cognition and consciousness*. (pp. 73–94) Amsterdam/Philadelphia: John Benjamins.

Deacon, T.W. (1996). Prefrontal cortex and symbolic learning: Why a brain capable of language evolved only once. In B.M. Velichkovsky & D.M. Rumbaugh (Eds.), *Communicating meaning: The evolution and development of language* (pp. 103–138). Mahwah, NJ: Lawrence Erlbaum Associates Inc.

Dornhoefer, S., Pannasch, S., Velichkovsky, B.M., & Unema, P. (2000). "Attential landscapes" and phasic changes of fixation duration in picture perception. *Perception, 29*, 11–12, Suppl.

Fell, J., Klaver, P., Lehnertz, K., Grunwald, T., Schaller, C., Elger, C.E., & Fernández, G. (2001). Human memory formation is accompanied by rhinal-hippocampal coupling and decoupling. *Nature Neuroscience, 4(12)*, 1259–1264.

Fodor, J.A. (1983). *The modularity of mind*. Cambridge, MA: MIT Press.

Gabrieli, J.D.E., Desmond, J.E., Demb, J.B., Wagner, A.D., Stone, M.V., Vaidya, C.J., & Glover, G.H. (1996). Functional magnetic resonance imaging of semantic memory processes in the frontal lobes. *Psychological Science, 7*, 278–283.

Galaburda, A.M., LeMay, M., Kempter, T.L., & Geschwindt, N. (1978). Right–left asymmetries in the brain. *Science, 199*, 852–856.

Gardiner, J.M., Richardson-Klavehn, A., Ramponi, C., & Brooks, B.M. (2001). Involuntary levels-of-processing effects in perceptual and conceptual priming. In M. Naveh-Benjamin, M. Moscovitch, & H.L. Roediger (Eds.), *Perspectives on human memory and cognitive aging: Essays in honor of Fergus Craik* (pp. 71–83). New York: Psychology Press.

Goldberg, E. (1991). Higher cortical functions in humans: The gradiental approach. In E. Goldberg (Ed.), *Contemporary neuropsychology and legacy of Luria* (pp. 229–275). Hillsdale, NJ: Lawrence Erlbaum Associates Inc.

Goldberg, E., & Podell, K. (1995). Lateralization in the frontal lobes. In H.H. Jasper, S. Riggio, & P.S. Goldman-Rakic (Eds.), *Epilepsy and the functional anatomy of the frontal lobe* (pp. 85–96). New York: Raven Press.

Head, H. (1920). *Studies in neurology*. Oxford: Oxford University Press.

Heckhausen, H. (1985). *Wünschen-Wählen-Wollen*. Vortrag gehalten bei der Eröffnung des Max-Planck-Instituts für psychologische Forschung, Munich.

Holloway, R.L. & De la Coste-Lareymondie, M. (1982). Brain endocast asymmetry in pongids and hominids. *American Journal of Physical Anthropology*, *58*, 108–116.

Holodynski, M. & Friedlmeier, W. (in press). *Emotional development in the sociocultural perspective*. Dordrecht/Boston: Kluwer Academic Publishers.

Horowitz, T.S., & Wolfe, J.M. (1998). Visual search has no memory. *Nature*, 357, 575–577.

Jannerod, M. (1981). Intersegmental coordination during reaching at natural visual objects. In J. Long & A. Baddeley (Eds.), *Attention and performance IX* (pp. 153–172). Hillsdale, NJ: Lawrence Erlbaum Associates Inc.

Koffka, K. (1935). *Principles of Gestalt psychology*. New York: Harcourt, Brace & World.

Kapur, S., Craik, F.I.M., Tulving, E., Wilson, A.A., Houle, S., & Brown, G.M. (1994). Neuroanatomical correlates of encoding in episodic memory: Levels of processing effect. *Proceedings of the National Academy of Sciences, USA*, *91*, 2008–2011.

Kawasaki, H., Buchanan, T.W., Oya, H., Howard M., III., Kaufman, O., Damasio, H., Granner, M., & Adolphs, R. (2001). *Human prefrontal cortex and amygdala show correlated single-unit responses to emotional pictures*. Paper presented to the Annual Meeting of the Cognitive Neuroscience Society.

LeDoux, J.E. (1996). *The emotional brain*. New York: Simon & Schuster.

Lockhart, R., & Craik, F.I.M. (1990). Levels of processing: A retrospective commentary on a framework for memory research. *Canadian Journal of Psychology*, *44*, 87–112.

Miall, D.S. (1986). Emotion and the self: The context of remembering. *British Journal of Psychology*, 77, 389–397.

Mishkin, M., Suzuki, W.A., Gardian, D.G., & Vargha-Khadem, F. (1999). Hierarchical organization of cognitive memory. In N. Burgess, K.J. Jeffrey, & J. O'Keefe (Eds.), *The hippocampal and parietal foundations of spatial cognition* (pp. 290–303). New York: Oxford University Press.

Murphy, F.C., & Lawrence, A.D. (2001). *A role for frontal asymmetry in positive and negative emotions: A view from functional neuroimaging*. Paper presented to the Annual Meeting of the Cognitive Neuroscience Society.

Novalis (1926). *Fragmente*. Dresden: Wolfgang Jess Verlag.

Öhman, A. (1992). Orienting and attention. In B.A. Campbell & H. Heine (Eds.), *Attention and information processing in infants and adults*. (pp. 263–295) Hillsdale, NJ: Lawrence Erlbaum Associates Inc.

Pannasch, S., Dornhoefer, S., Unema, P. & Velichkovsky, B.M. (2001). The omnipresent prolongation of visual fixations: Saccades are inhibited by changes in situation or subject's activity. *Vision Research*, *41*(25–26), 3345–3351.

Perner, J. (2000). Memory and theory of mind. In E. Tulving & F.I.M. Craik (Eds.), *The Oxford handbook of memory* (pp. 297–314). New York/Oxford: Oxford University Press.

Reingold, E. (2002). On the perceptual specificity of memory representations. *Memory*, *10*, 000–000.

Robinson, M.D. (1998). Running from William James' bear. A review of preattentive mechanisms and their contributions to emotional experience. *Cognition and Emotion*, *12*, 667–696.

Roediger, H.L., & Gallo, D. (2001). Levels of processing: Unanswered questions. In M. Naveh-Benjamin, M. Moscovitch, & H.L. Roediger (Eds.), *Perspectives on human memory and cognitive aging: Essays in honor of Fergus Craik* (pp. 28–47). New York: Psychology Press.

Schachter, D.L., Wagner, A.D., & Buckner, R.L. (2000). Memory systems of 1999. In E. Tulving & F.I.M. Craik (Eds.), *The Oxford handbook of memory* (pp. 627–643). New York/Oxford: Oxford University Press.

Scherer, K.R. (2001). Appraisal considered as a process of multilevel sequential checking. In K.R. Scherer, A. Schorr, & T. Johnston (Eds.), *Appraisal processes in emotion*. New York/Oxford: Oxford University Press.

Schlenoff, D.H. (1985). The startle responses of blue jays to *Catocala* (Lepidoptera: Noctuidae) prey models. *Animal Behavior*, *33*, 1057–1067.

Shammi, P., & Stuss, D.T. (1999). Humor appreciation: A role for the right frontal lobe. *Brain*, *122*, 657–666.

Tomasello, M. (1999). *The cultural origins of human cognition*. Cambridge, MA: Harvard University Press.

Trevarthen, C. (1968). Two visual systems in primates. *Psychologische Forschung*, *31*, 321–337.

Tulving, E. (1983). *Elements of episodic memory*. New York: Oxford University Press.

Tulving, E. (1998). Brain/mind correlates of human memory. In M. Sabourin, F.I.M. Craik, & M. Robert (Eds.), *Advances in psychological sciences, Vol.2*. Hove, UK: Psychology Press.

Tulving, E. (2001). Does memory encoding exist? In M. Naveh-Benjamin, M. Moscovitch, & H.L. Roediger (Eds.), *Perspectives on human memory and cognitive aging: Essays in honor of Fergus Craik* (pp. 6–27). New York: Psychology Press.

Tulving, E., Kapur, S., Craik, F.I.M., Moscovitch, M., & Houle, S. (1994). Hemispheric encoding/retrieval asymmetry in episodic memory. *Proceedings of the National Academy of Sciences, USA*, *91*, 2016–2020.

Tulving, E., & Schacter, D.L. (1990). Priming and human memory systems. *Science*, *247*, 301–305.

Turvey, M.T., Shaw, R.E., & Mace, W. (1978). Issues in the theory of action. In J. Requin (Ed.), *Attention and performance VII* (pp. 189–207). Hillsdale, NJ: Lawrence Erlbaum Associates Inc.

Velichkovsky, B.M. (1982). Visual cognition and its spatial-temporal context. In F. Klix, J. Hoffmann, & E. van der Meer (Eds.), *Cognitive research in psychology* (pp. 63–79). Amsterdam: North Holland.

Velichkovsky, B.M. (1990). The vertical dimension of mental functioning. *Psychological Research*, *52*, 282–289.

Velichkovsky, B.M. (1994). The levels endeavour in psychology and cognitive science. In P. Bertelson, P. Eelen, & G. d'Ydewalle (Eds.), *International perspectives in psychological sciences: Leading themes* (pp. 143–158). Howe, UK: Lawrence Erlbaum Associates Ltd.

Velichkovsky, B.M. (1995). Communicating attention: Gaze position transfer in cooperative problem solving. *Pragmatics and Cognition*, *3*(2), 199–222.

Velichkovsky, B.M. (1999). From levels of processing to stratification of cognition. In B.H. Challis & B.M. Velichkovsky (Eds.), *Stratification in cognition and consciousness* (pp. 203–226). Amsterdam/Philadelphia: John Benjamins.

Velichkovsky, B.M. (2001). Levels of processing: Validating the concept. In M. Naveh-Benjamin, M. Moscovitch, & H.L. Roediger (Eds.), *Perspectives on human memory and cognitive aging: Essays in honor of Fergus Craik* (pp. 48–70). New York: Psychology Press.

Velichkovsky, B.M., Klemm, T., Dettmar P., & Volke, H.-J. (1996a). Evoked coherence of EEG II: Communication of brain areas and depth of processing. *Zeitschrift für EEG-EMG, 27*, 111–119.

Velichkovsky, B.M., Pomplun, M., & Rieser, H. (1996b). Attention and communication. In W.H. Zangemeister, S. Stiel & C. Freksa (Eds.), *Visual attention and cognition* (pp. 125–154). Amsterdam/New York: Elsevier.

Velichkovsky, B.M., Rothert, A., Kopf, M., Dornhoefer, S., & Joos, M. (in press). Towards an express-diagnostics for level of processing and hazard perception. *Transportation Research, Part F.*

Wheeler, M.A., Stuss, D.T., & Tulving, E. (1997). Toward a theory of episodic memory: The frontal lobes and autonoetic consciousness. *Psychological Bulletin, 121*, 331–354.

Subject Index

Activity-based approach, 320–321, 405
Acts, 320
Ageing
 consolidation, 310
 name memory, 312
Ambient view, 411
Ambient visual processing, 408–411
Amnesia, 310
Amygdalo-hippocampal region, 408, 410–411,
 416
Associationism, 333, 334
Attention
 analysis depth, 309
 divided, 310
 focal, 410
 selective, 305, 339
Attentional filtering, 411
Attentional landscapes, 411
Autobiographical memory, 313
Automatic retrieval, 349–364

Background coordinations, 407
Belongingness, 334

Categorisation, 335
Category size effect, 391
Circularity, 340, 397–398, 408
Cognition, processing approaches, 319–332
Components-of-processing, 327
Comprehension, 306
Conceptual structures, 407
Congruity, 307
Consciousness, 320, 407
 retrieval, 361
Consolidation, 310, 315
Control, 311, 314
Controlled retrieval, 350, 362
Coordinate structures, 336

Coordination, 314, 407
Covert rehearsal, 385, 386, 387
Cues
 discriminability, 392–394
 memory trace, 307
 overload, 390, 391
 semantic, 402

Deep processing, 336–337
 retrieval environment, 401–402
Dementia, semantic, 376
Depth
 index, 308–309, 315
 qualitative processing, 307
Differentiation, 306–307
Directed forgetting, 383
Directed remembering, 381–388
Discriminability, 392–394
Dissociations, 322, 324–325, 326–327, 366–367
Distinctiveness, 306–307, 312, 315, 335
Divided attention, 310
Domains of processing, 311

Elaboration, 306–307, 311, 335, 336
Electroencephalography (EEG), 415
Emotional processing, 407–408, 410
Encoding, 306–307
 enriched, 306, 311
 frontal cortex, 328, 347, 387, 415
 potential retrieval, 307
 prefrontal cortex, 315, 347, 415
 robustness, 400–402
 self-referential, 411, 414, 415, 416
 temporal cortex, 328, 347, 387
 variability, 400–401
Encoding-appropriateness, 335
Encoding-retrieval interactions, 309–310, 315,
 328, 345–348, 389–395

Encoding specificity principle, 309, 394, 398, 399
Enrichment, 306, 311
Environment
    deep processing, 401–402
    top down influence, 315
Episodic buffer, 308
Episodic memory, continuum with semantic
        memory, 313
Event-related fMRI, 327–328, 347, 387
Evoked coherence analysis, 415
Evoked potentials, depth index, 309
Evolutionary cortical growth, 415
Express fixations, 410
Eye movements
    depth index, 309
    gaze contingent window paradigm, 368–369
    hazard perception, 408–411

Familiarity, 350, 362
Fitness, 398
Focal attention, 410
Focal view, 411
Focal visual processing, 408–411
Forgetting
    benefits, 382
    directed, 383
    temporal aspects, 393
Free recall, 413, 414, 415
Frontal cortex, 416
    encoding, 328, 347, 387, 415
    rehearsal, 387
    retrieval, 415
Frontopolar cortex, 416
Functional magnetic resonance imaging (fMRI),
        309, 328, 345–348, 415
    event-related, 327–328, 347, 387
Fusiform gyri, 347

Gaze contingent window, 368–369
Generate–recognise strategy, 351, 354, 360
Generation effects, 368
Genetics, 314–315
Geological metaphor, 405

Hardenberg, Friedrich, 405
Hazard perception, eye movements, 408–411

Heart rate, depth index, 309
Heterarchy, 311, 405–419
Hierarchical processing, 311
Hippocampus, 408, 410–411, 416
Hyperspecific priming, 327

Implicit memory, 413
Incidental reactivation, 346
Information processing, 342
Integrative processes, 336
Interconnectedness, 335
Interference, 393
Interpretation, 314

James, William, 320

Knowing, 313
Knowledge, means-dependent, 366

Leading coordinations, 407
Levels, reality of, 310–312
Levels of analysis, 305
Levels of control, 311
Levels of representation, 312–314
List length effect, 391
Long-term memory, 307–308

Magnetic resonance imaging, see Functional
        magnetic resonance imaging
Magnetoencephalography (MEG), 309, 415
Maintenance rehearsal, 400–401
Matched-transfer levels effect, 399–400, 402
Meanings, 334, 335, 337, 366
Memory trace, 342
    matched-transfer levels effect, 399–400, 402
    retrieval cue, 307
Mental acts, 320
Metacognition, 411
Metacognitive coordinations, 407
Mirror neurons, 328
Models and theories, 341
Moore, Donnie, 382
Multilevel hypothesis, 406–408

Name memory, 312
Natural selection, 340, 398

Neuroimaging, 309, 327–328, 345–348, 387, 414–416
Nonconscious memory, 381–388
Novalis, 405

Object actions, 406–407
Occipital cortex, 415
Occipito-temporal areas, 415
Old age, *see* Ageing
Organisation theory, 333–338
Orienting tasks, 319, 339, 340

Paleokinetic regulations, 406
Parahippocampal activity, 347
Parietal cortex, 328, 415
'Pearl-in-the-oyster' theory, 366, 377
Perception, 306
Perceptual fluency, 367
Perceptual identification, 367–368
Perceptual implicit tests, 368
Perceptual priming, 368
    modality-specific, 361–362
Perceptual processing, 336
    recognition memory, 368–377
Perceptual specificity, 365–379
'Personal view of the world', 407
Picture–word effect, 368
Positron emission tomography (PET)
    depth index, 309
    encoding–retrieval overlap, 345–348
    retrieval, 415
    self-referential encoding, 416
Power-to-complexity ratio, 341
Prefrontal cortex
    brain evolution, 415–416
    encoding, 315, 347, 415
    retrieval, 313–314, 315, 413
Primary memory, 308
Proceduralism, 321–324, 327–329, 366–367
Process-dissociation procedure, 349–364
Processing
    pure, 307
    specificity, 325–327
Processing time, as depth index, 308–309
Proordinate structures, 336
Protopathic sensitivity, 406

Reading, 322–324, 367
Recognition, 368–377, 413, 414
Recollection, 350
Reconstructive retrieval, 307
Regulation, 314
Rehearsal, 339
    covert, 385, 386, 387
    maintenance, 400–401
Remembering
    directed, 381–388
    and knowing, 313
    as processing, 306
    retrieval processes, 315
Repetition, 341
Representation, levels of, 312–314
Response deadline procedure, 362
Retrievability, 398
Retrieval, 306
    automatic, 349–364
    consciousness, 361
    controlled, 350, 362
    encoding-retrieval interactions, 309–310, 315, 328, 345–348, 389–395
    environment, 401–402
    frontal cortex, 415
    as interactions, 315
    potential, 307
    prefrontal cortex, 313–314, 315, 413
    reconstructive, 307
    temporal cortex, 415
Retrieval cues
    discriminability, 392–394
    memory trace, 307
    overload, 390, 391
Rhyme-related encoding, 309
Robust encoding, 400–402
Romanticism, 405
Rubro-spinal level, 406

S (mnemonist), 382
Savings, 322
Selective attention, 305, 339
Self-coding, 401
Self-referential encoding, 411, 414, 415, 416
Semantic cueing, 402
Semantic dementia, 376

Semantic encoding, 309, 415
Semantic memory, 407
  continuum with episodic memory, 313
Semantic primacy, 365, 366, 368, 376
Shallow processing, 337
Short-term memory, 307–308
Signal detection, 305
Situational cues, 387
Spatial field, 406
Specificity
  perceptual, 365–379
  of processing, 325–327
  of transfer, 366–367
Stem completion, 368
Stream of consciousness, 320
Structure, 320, 334, 335, 336
Subliminal cues, 381–388
Subordinate structures, 336
Superaddition, 341
Synergies, 406

Temporal cortex, 416
  encoding, 328, 347, 387
  retrieval, 415
Thalamo-pallidar system, 406
Theories and models, 341
Theory of mind, 407
Time
  as depth index, 308–309
  and forgetting, 393
Transfer
  matched-transfer levels effect, 400, 402
  specificity, 366–367
Transfer-appropriate processing, 309, 324–325,
    367, 398–399
  matched-transfer levels effect, 400
Transformed texts, 322–324, 367

Visual processing, ambient and focal, 408–411